SpringerBriefs in Criminology

SpringerBriefs in Criminology present concise summaries of cutting edge research across the fields of Criminology and Criminal Justice. It publishes small but impactful volumes of between 50-125 pages, with a clearly defined focus. The series covers a broad range of Criminology research from experimental design and methods, to brief reports and regional studies, to policy-related applications.

The scope of the series spans the whole field of Criminology and Criminal Justice, with an aim to be on the leading edge and continue to advance research. The series will be international and cross-disciplinary, including a broad array of topics, including juvenile delinquency, policing, crime prevention, terrorism research, crime and place, quantitative methods, experimental research in criminology, research design and analysis, forensic science, crime prevention, victimology, criminal justice systems, psychology of law, and explanations for criminal behavior.

SpringerBriefs in Criminology will be of interest to a broad range of researchers and practitioners working in Criminology and Criminal Justice Research and in related academic fields such as Sociology, Psychology, Public Health, Economics and Political Science.

Vania Ceccato • Jonatan Abraham

Crime and Safety in the Rural

Lessons from research

Vania Ceccato
Department of Urban Planning
and Environment
KTH Royal Institute of Technology
Stockholm, Sweden

Jonatan Abraham
Department of Urban Planning
and Environment
KTH Royal Institute of Technology
Stockholm, Sweden

This book is an open access publication.

ISSN 2192-8533   ISSN 2192-8541   (electronic)
SpringerBriefs in Criminology
ISBN 978-3-030-98289-8   ISBN 978-3-030-98290-4   (eBook)
https://doi.org/10.1007/978-3-030-98290-4

© The Author(s) 2022
Open Access This book is licensed under the terms of the Creative Commons Attribution 4.0 International License (http://creativecommons.org/licenses/by/4.0/), which permits use, sharing, adaptation, distribution and reproduction in any medium or format, as long as you give appropriate credit to the original author(s) and the source, provide a link to the Creative Commons license and indicate if changes were made.
The images or other third party material in this book are included in the book's Creative Commons license, unless indicated otherwise in a credit line to the material. If material is not included in the book's Creative Commons license and your intended use is not permitted by statutory regulation or exceeds the permitted use, you will need to obtain permission directly from the copyright holder.
The use of general descriptive names, registered names, trademarks, service marks, etc. in this publication does not imply, even in the absence of a specific statement, that such names are exempt from the relevant protective laws and regulations and therefore free for general use.
The publisher, the authors and the editors are safe to assume that the advice and information in this book are believed to be true and accurate at the date of publication. Neither the publisher nor the authors or the editors give a warranty, expressed or implied, with respect to the material contained herein or for any errors or omissions that may have been made. The publisher remains neutral with regard to jurisdictional claims in published maps and institutional affiliations.

This Springer imprint is published by the registered company Springer Nature Switzerland AG
The registered company address is: Gewerbestrasse 11, 6330 Cham, Switzerland

This book is dedicated to all those working to make rural environments safe and sustainable.

Foreword

The discourse on urbanization is departing from the traditional and outdated dichotomy of urban and rural divide to one that understands the continuum between urban and rural. Crime does not exist in territorial compartments given that urban and rural spaces are inextricably linked economically, socially and environmentally and cannot be adequately dealt with in isolation from one another. Recognizing this urban-rural continuum also highlights how partnerships, collaboration and unity in crime prevention action can yield dividends for all people, regardless of age, gender or whether they live in urban or rural areas.

Based on this recognition, the UN systemwide Guidelines on Safer Cities and Human Settlements underscores the importance of the principle of co-production of safety and security for all, across divides, taking into account all forms of human settlements.

It is a great pleasure to be associated with this publication spearheaded by the Department of Urban Planning and Environment at KTH Royal Institute of Technology, Stockholm, Sweden, in promoting calls for new theoretical frameworks that can provide a better understanding of crime and safety in rural conditions, just as in urban conditions. The book provides a comprehensive overview of relevant topics that can serve both as a catalyst for new research in this area and as a reference for practitioners concerned with the conditions of people and places on the rural-urban continuum. I am convinced that *Crime and Safety in the Rural: Lessons from Research* is essential reading material for all those who are interested in rural criminology. I am also confident that it will serve as a valuable reference source for international, as well as local, training activities, for both the UN-Habitat Safer Cities Programme and partners in the Global Network on Safer Cities (GNSC) as we advance on the implementation of the 2030 Agenda for Sustainable Development and the New Urban Agenda.

Juma Assiago
Specialist/Coordinator, Safer Cities Programme,
UN-Habitat
Oxford, UK

Acknowledgments

We thank all the participants in the colloquium "Safety, resilience and community: Challenges and opportunities beyond the city" organized by the Safeplaces Network in Stockholm, Sweden, on September 29, 2020. The fruitful discussions in the sessions helped catalyze this book project. Thanks to all my colleagues, and in particular, Richard Yarwood, Susanne Stenbacka, Susanne Strand, Joseph Donnermeyer, Karina Landman, and Rob Mawby for their contribution to the colloquium. Thanks also all our colleagues from municipalities and other regional and national public authorities for taking part in the conference as well as the Rural Sweden (*Hela Sverige ska leva*) which is a national civil society organization for rural development in Sweden. Last but not least, thanks to the support of Juma Assiago, who is coordinator of the UN-Habitat Safer Cities Programme and whose work is devoted to the importance of ensuring safety for all across the rural-urban continuum as part of the 2030 Agenda for Sustainable Development.

Following the colloquium "Safety, resilience and community," Ceccato organized three special issues focused on crime and safety in rural conditions. Thanks to all editorial teams, in particular Gorazd Mesko, for the article "Special Issue: Crime, Fear of Crime and Environmental Harm in Rural Areas" in the journal *International Criminology*, and Richard Yarwood, for the focus session of the journal *Professional Geographer*: "The geographies of crime and policing in the global countryside." Thanks also to Scott Thomas Jacques and the *International Criminal Justice Review* for welcoming the idea of the special issue "Crime and safety in rural contexts: Innovative methods." Thanks to all speakers in the conference who turned their presentations into articles.

During the systematic literature review for this book, we also received support from several colleagues who sent information and materials that were not available online. Thanks goes to Ralph Weisheit, Walter DeKeseredy, Joseph Donnermeyer, Kreseda Smith, Alistair Harkness, and other colleagues at the International Society for the Study of Rural Crime (ISSRC). We would also like to thank our colleagues in the Department of Urban Planning and Environment at KTH Royal Institute of Technology, Stockholm, Sweden, for all the support throughout these years. We are also grateful for all the knowledge shared by our colleagues Peter Lundqvist, Eva

Göransson, and Catharina Alwall Svennefelt from the Swedish University of Agricultural Sciences and Anders Drottja and Håkan Johansson from the Federation of Swedish Farmers – LRF during the project "Criticism, crime and threats against Swedish animal production" regarding farmers' victimization and animal rights activism between 2019 and 2021.

We wrote this book while receiving funding for two research projects devoted to Swedish rural areas, namely FORMAS – Forskningsrådet för miljö, areella näringar och samhällsbyggande (Swedish Research Council for Sustainable Development, grant number 2016-01424) and the Swedish Farmers' Foundation for Agricultural Research, project number/grant number 2028.4.1-609. Thanks for making this research possible.

We would also like to thank our publisher, Springer, for believing in this effort. We particularly wish to acknowledge Anna Goodlett for her stewardship of the project, and also Srividya Subramanian, Mario Gabriele, and Lavanya Devgun, as well as our colleague Dr. Jana Sochor for proofreading this manuscript.

Lastly and importantly, a big thank you goes to our families for all their love, support, and patience as we put together this book. Vania wishes to thank Anders in particular, and she dedicates the book to her family on both sides of the Atlantic, especially Anders, Filip, Amanda, and *in memorian* of Luiza and Lydio. Jonatan would like to both thank and dedicate this book to Rosanna, Sara, Elizabeth, and Abraham.

Stockholm, Sweden   Vania Ceccato
November 20, 2021   Jonatan Abraham

Endorsements

This valuable little book presents the results of a literature survey of ten key issues in rural crime. These are not only well chosen but are succinctly presented. Thus, *Crime and Safety in the Rural: Lessons from Research* serves as a comprehensive introduction to rural crime for those who come fresh to this important but often neglected field as well as presenting new insights to those more familiar with the topics covered. A particular strength of the book is its recognition of the contributions possible from a diverse interdisciplinary community, which has not previously engaged with the field.

Ronald V. Clarke, University Professor in the School of Criminal Justice at Rutgers University, Newark, USA

In this compact but extensive survey of issues and resources, the authors address the myths and realities of rural places, rural crime, and rural justice while skillfully avoiding clichés. Including materials from around the globe, *Crime and Safety in the Rural: Lessons from Research* is certain to encourage research in this understudied area.

Ralph Weisheit, Distinguished Professor of Criminal Justice, Department of Criminal Justice Sciences, Illinois State University, USA

The book provides a comprehensive overview of relevant topics that can serve both as a catalyst for new research in this area and as a reference for practitioners concerned with the conditions of people and places on the rural-urban continuum. I am confident that *Crime and Safety in the Rural: Lessons from Research* will serve as a valuable reference source for international, as well as local, training activities, for both the UN-Habitat Safer Cities Programme and partners in the Global Network on Safer Cities (GNSC) as we advance on the implementation of the *2030 Agenda for Sustainable Development* and the New Urban Agenda.

Juma Assiago, MSc (Oxford), Coordinator, UN-Habitat Safer Cities Programme

Contents

1	Crime and Safety in Rural Areas	1
2	Reasons Why Crime and Safety in Rural Areas Matter	9
3	Current Knowledge on Crime and Safety in Rural Areas	29
4	Crime, Offenders, and Victims	41
5	Safety Perceptions in Rural Areas	77
6	Police and Criminal Justice	85
7	Crime Prevention and Safety Interventions	93
8	Emergent Topics in Research in Rural Areas	101
9	Implications for Practice	113
10	Conclusions and Recommendations	117
Index		121

List of Figures

Fig. 2.1	UN-Sustainable Development Goals (SDG), 2030	21
Fig. 3.1	Research on rural crime and safety 1980–2020 collected in Scopus, JSTOR, and ScienceDirect (N = 410), where each publication was assigned a maximum of two themes	30
Fig. 3.2	(a) Reviewed publications on rural crime and safety 1980-2020 by university affiliation (first author) (b) Reviewed publications on rural crime and safety 1980-2020 by study area	34
Fig. 3.3	Methods utilized in the reviewed publications on rural crime and safety 1980–2020 (N = 410). Studies were assigned one or more methods	36
Fig. 4.1	Index of violent and property victimization in the United States, 1993 = 100; 1993–2019	43
Fig. 4.2	Index of total violent and property crime in Sweden 2004 = 100, 2004–2020	45
Fig. 4.3	Median of rates of homicide in Brazil; police-registered data, 2007–2017. Rate per 100,000 inhabitants per municipality	46

List of Tables

Table 4.1 Self-reported victimization of assault and burglary 2016–2020 type of residence, share victimized people/households, respectively 44

About the Authors

Vania Ceccato is a professor in the Department of Urban Planning and Environment, School of Architecture and the Built Environment, KTH Royal Institute of Technology, Stockholm, Sweden. Geographical information systems (GIS) and spatial statistical methods underlie her research, which includes the geography of crime and fear in urban and rural environments. The intersectionality of safety is an essential approach in her research and teaching. Ceccato wrote the open access book *Rural Crime and Community Safety*, and she is the coordinator of the Safeplaces network, a partner of the UN-Habitat Safer Cities program. She is also a British Society of Criminology International Ambassador and a member of the International Society for the Study of Rural Crime (ISSRC).

Jonatan Abraham is a PhD candidate in the Department of Urban Planning and Environment, School of Architecture and the Built Environment, KTH Royal Institute of Technology, Stockholm, Sweden. His research interests cover the intersections of social sustainability issues, such as crime and safety, with aspects of the built environment. His previous research has focused on crime and fear in rural and farm environments using statistical analysis and geographical information systems (GIS).

Chapter 1
Crime and Safety in Rural Areas

Crime is not simply an urban phenomenon. Yet, until recently, criminology and other related sciences have neglected the nature and levels of crime outside urban areas (Donnermeyer 2016). There exists a multitude of reasons why scholars, policy and decision-makers as well as individuals in general should care about crime and safety in rural areas.

First, some acts of crime in rural areas may only be possible when embedded in those particular situational contexts, which, if not considered, may hamper crime prevention; environmental and wildlife crimes are typical examples. Second, low crime rates in rural areas are often taken as an indication that rural crime and safety are not worthy of attention (Yarwood 2001), which obviously disregards the impact of crime on local residents. A reason for this lack of attention is perhaps the widespread belief in a dichotomy between urban and rural; the former being criminogenic, and the latter being problem-free, idyllic, healthy, and friendly (Ceccato 2016). Therefore in this book we distance ourselves from these assumptions to unravel facets of the rural as both safe and criminogenic, a hybrid place (Woods 2007) worthy to be examined in its own right.

We contest the idea of rural areas as homogenous entities. We instead adopt the notion of a *rural-urban continuum* that captures the nuances of environments of varied nature, spanning from remote and desolate spaces to accessible and connected environments of the urban fringe. Areas on the rural-urban continuum may be in constant transformation given local and global influences, which imposes challenges for policing and long-term social sustainability. In this book, we examine these challenges via four decades of English-language research on crime and safety in rural areas, including the most recent theoretical developments and examples from studies of the Global South.

The reader can identify emergent calls for new theoretical frameworks that provide a better understanding of crime and safety in rural conditions and the variety of safety needs of rural residents. Furthermore, there exists a wide range of experiences with crime prevention of significance for rural contexts which is worthy of recognition, and of importance to other disciplines. Therefore, this book can also be

© The Author(s) 2022
V. Ceccato, J. Abraham, *Crime and Safety in the Rural*, SpringerBriefs in Criminology, https://doi.org/10.1007/978-3-030-98290-4_1

inspirational to those from other disciplines such as geography, and rural and sustainability studies, just to name a few.

Finally, this book discusses the need for new evidence on crime and safety in rural areas, which is aligned with the 2030 Sustainable Development Goals (UN 2015). By doing so, this book provides a comprehensive overview of relevant topics that can serve both as a catalyst for new research in this area and as a reference for practitioners concerned with the conditions of people and places on the rural-urban continuum. Most importantly, the book offers a quick introduction to issues of crime and safety in the rural for undergraduate and graduate students, in particular from criminology, geography and rural studies.

Aims and Scope

This book, best understood as an extended essay, examines the evidence of crime in rural contexts, feelings of perceived safety or lack thereof, rural policing with examples of crime prevention practices. The aim of this book is to demonstrate the importance of crime and safety in areas on the rural-urban continuum in general, and from a social sustainability perspective in particular. This aim is achieved by first outlining 20 reasons as to why crime and safety matter, which also serves to delineate the field of research and illustrate its complexity, with many interdisciplinary ramifications. Then, by reviewing the international literature, the book reports four decades of English-language studies within the field and, finally, presents a research agenda which takes into consideration emergent areas of research, implications for practice, and the UN 2030 Agenda for Sustainable Development. Expanding our knowledge on rural crime and safety is not only an important step for the future of criminology, but a prerequisite for ever obtaining a truly sustainable society.

The Rural-Urban Continuum and Other Concepts

In this section, we introduce a set of basic concepts used throughout the book. In rural criminology, the term *rural* is often applied to the opposite of *urban* on a binary scale. The *rural-urban continuum* constitutes a more appropriate, continuous scale that acknowledges that rural localities can differ in their criminogenic conditions based on their locations and contexts. There are rural areas that are located close to large towns that are different from those areas located close to small towns, or in isolated spots, or in vast, remote locations far from any type of urban reference. According to Dewey (1960), differences along the rural-urban scale derive from the fact that variations in population size and density induce variations in a number of factors such as anonymity, division of labor, informally and formally prescribed relationships, and symbols of status which are independent of personal acquaintance. All these factors can significantly affect the criminogenic and safety conditions of such areas. The concept of the rural-urban continuum is used here to stress the notion that there are no sharp demarcations in the degree or quantity of rural/urban differences (Planning Tank 2017). Rather there are flows of people, activities, and goods in space where crime takes place; some visible and tangible, others fluid and non-space dependent. We hold that in a globalized, interconnected world, these places may be rural in some respects and urban in others. In this book, we make use of the "rural-urban continuum" concept as well as accept the legacy of many decades of research in this area by allowing the use of interchangeable terms such as rural areas, countryside (as in the United Kingdom), sparsely populated areas, non-metropolitan areas, remote rural, accessible rural, vast areas, urban fringe, rural environments, outback, and the bush (as in Australia).

Urban fringe is an area of transition from urban use (city) to rural land use (countryside) and may be neglected as it falls in between the administrative limits of the urban area. Although many researchers consider the urban fringe area as a synonym of rural-urban continuum,[1] we do not; our definition of rural-urban continuum encompasses locations beyond the urban fringe which are not limited to tangible spaces or limited geographical boundaries.

Crime is an action or omission which constitutes an offense and is punishable by law. However, in this book *crime* is loosely used as a synonym of criminality, victimization, or criminogenic conditions of a particular place, while *safety* is applied here as a general term to indicate people's safety perceptions, and sometimes, more specifically, low levels of fear of crime. However, note that in Chaps. 3, 4, 5, 6, and 7 the use of these terms follows the unique reference of each study reported in the systematic literature review.

Rural crime includes here acts of crime that may only be possible when embedded in particular situational contexts that are found in areas on the rural-urban continuum, for instance, theft of cattle (Fleisher 2002) and crime against nature and/or wildlife (Lowe et al. 1996).

Crime in the rural refers here to all types of offences that take place in rural contexts, for instance, drug-related crimes (Weisheit and Brownstein 2016), residential burglary (Wilhelmsson and Ceccato 2015), or street crime (Glosser 2016; Sampson 1983).

While there is no official definition of *farm crime*, Donnermeyer et al. (2011) suggest two categories of farm crime: *ordinary crime*, which includes general theft of livestock, machinery and equipment, vandalism, dumping of waste, damage from trespassing and hunting; and *extraordinary crime*, which includes activities such as organized drug production. Ceccato (2015a) notes that the definition can encompass different things in different parts of the world, as violent farm crime in a European context may involve crime against nature and wildlife, whereas in Africa and South America there have been cases of lethal violence against farmers. Although farm crime has increased over a longer time (Jones 2012; Sugden 1999), it has largely been neglected by criminologists (Jones 2010).

Security is a term associated with the risk of becoming a crime victim, measured by a variety of metrics and crime statistics, while *safety* refers to people's safety

---

[1] The evolution of the term "urban fringe" goes back to von Thünen (1826) in which the city is surrounded by a system of concentric belts of land use. For short review of the history of rural-urban fringe development as a concept, see Lotus Arise (2021).

perceptions through the lens of fear and anxiety. In many cases, sociospatial characteristics influence whether a particular place has high levels of crime and violence. Demographic, social, and economic fragmentation feed insecurity but also affect people's safety perceptions (UN-Habitat 2019).

Crime prevention involves measures and strategies that disrupt the mechanisms that enable criminal events (Ekblom 1994). Those who work with situational crime prevention, for example, aim to reduce the opportunities for crime by making crime more risky or less rewarding, for example, through installation of alarms, locks, and CCTV (Clarke 1997). Advocates of social crime prevention are offender-oriented, addressing social factors that influence criminal behavior, or preventing relapses into crime, for example, through early intervention with youth programs (Ekblom 1994; Mullane 2015). Moreover, Brantingham and Faust (1976) define three categories of crime prevention: *primary prevention*, which concerns identifying and altering conditions that provide opportunities for crime in social and urban environments; *secondary prevention* which involves the early detection of offenders and intervention in their lives; and *tertiary prevention* which focuses on reducing offender relapses into crime.

Policing in this book is a broad concept that involves not just the police but also public and private actors regulating themselves and each other, working toward governing safety (Ceccato 2015b; Mawby and Yarwood 2011a). This can take place through formal policing partnerships such as neighborhood watch programs, or through informal control by demonstrating and enforcing social moral codes and values (Mawby and Yarwood 2011b).

Fear of crime has historically been referred to as the individual's perceived probability, or risk, of becoming a crime victim (Brantingham et al. 1986). Ferraro (1995), however, argues that fear of crime is rather the emotional response expressed in relation to potential victimization, anxiety about crime in general, or symbols of crime. In this book, we refer to a more inverse concept, namely, the *perception of safety*, where a low perception of safety indicates a high fear of crime and vice versa.

Gender-based violence is defined by the Council of Europe (2019, p. 18) as "any type of harm that is perpetrated against a person or group of people because of their factual or perceived sex, gender, sexual orientation and/or gender identity." This harm can take shape physically, verbally, psychologically and emotionally, sexually, or even socioeconomically. The term has often been used interchangeably with "violence against women" due to women being disproportionately affected, but this has been criticized as it may neglect men and/or individuals of non-binary gender identities as victims of gendered violence (Council of Europe 2019; DeKeseredy and Schwartz 2011).

Gendered violence may also relate to people of other expressions of gender and sexual orientation, such as those within the LGBTQ+ community. Additionally, intersections with other social identifiers, for example, age, class, race, and ability, are also important when addressing gender-based violence (see, e.g., Meer and Combrinck 2015; Sokoloff and Dupont 2005; Straka and Montminy 2006).

Globalization "is thought to be the widening, deepening and quickening of worldwide interconnectedness in all aspects of contemporary social life, from the cultural to the criminal, the financial to the spiritual." In other words, globalization involves spatiotemporal processes of change which underpin a transformation in the organization of human affairs by linking together and expanding human activity across regions and continents (Held et al. 2000, pp. 2–15).

The *Global South* encompasses Africa, Latin America and the Caribbean, Pacific Islands, and the developing countries in Asia, including the Middle East, while the term *Global North* is used as a synonym for developed countries, often Western Europe and North America. There is an ongoing controversy about the adequacy of these terms regarding geographical boundaries or regional entities, see, for example, Hollington et al. (2015).

A simple definition of *sustainable development* refers to the process of "protecting and conserving the planet's natural environment and promoting social equity and a degree of economic equality within and between nations" (Blewitt (2012, p. 13). The process is materialized by the interplay of the environmental, the economic, and the social dimensions of sustainability.

Social sustainability is the least defined core concept of sustainability but can be characterized as "specifying and managing both positive and negative impacts of systems, processes, organizations, and activities on people and social life" (Balaman 2019, p. 86). This concerns topics such as health and social equity, human rights, labor rights, working conditions, community development and well-being, community resilience, and social responsibility and justice (Balaman 2019). Crime is a clear obstacle for socially sustainable development, and in turn socially unsustainable development is a large cause of crime (Sengupta and Mukherjee 2018).

Sustainable Development Goals (SDGs) 2030 – The United Nations (n.d.) established The 2030 Agenda for Sustainable Development in 2015, which "provides a shared blueprint for peace and prosperity for people and the planet, now and into the future." The blueprint consists of 17 Sustainable Development Goals to be reached by 2030 and intends to tackle global challenges, including hunger and poverty, health and education, as well as climate change and preservation of oceans and forests. Part of the end goal is to create peaceful, just, and inclusive societies, free from both violence and fear.

Chapter Synopsis

This book is composed of ten chapters. Following this introductory chapter, which presents the subject area, basic concepts, and chapter synopsis, Chap. 2 motivates why we should care about crime and safety in rural areas. We present 20 reasons, from common misconceptions of crime in rural areas to illustrations of how globalization and climate change link to crime and safety in areas on the rural-urban continuum, as well as how all these are associated with rural development and sustainability. Chapter 3 reports the growing body of literature on crime and safety in rural areas via a systematic literature review of four decades of publications, from 1980 to 2020. The chapter focuses on English-language literature (in Scopus, JSTOR, and ScienceDirect) using articles, books, and book chapters to identify several research themes. Then, in Chaps. 4, 5, 6, and 7, we draw attention to a specific selection of the research on crime and safety in areas on the rural-urban continuum. The topics include concepts and theories in rural criminology, endemic offending and criminal mobilities, situational conditions of crime and fear, safety perceptions, queer and the rural, technology, offending and crime prevention, climate change and crime, organized crime, as well as safety as a dimension of sustainability and as a public health issue. Chapter 8 presents the most central questions of these topics as a research agenda. Chapter 9 first summarizes the overarching findings of this book and then discusses implications for practice, while Chap. 10 concludes by linking future research to the 2030 Sustainable Development Goals.

References

Balaman, Ş. Y. (2019). Chapter 4 - Sustainability Issues in Biomass-Based Production Chains. In Ş. Y. Balaman (Ed.), *Decision-Making for Biomass-Based Production Chains* (pp. 77-112). Academic Press. https://doi.org/10.1016/B978-0-12-814278-3.00004-2

Blewitt, J. (2012). *Understanding sustainable development*. Routledge.

Brantingham, P. J., & Faust, F. L. (1976). A Conceptual Model of Crime Prevention. *Crime and Delinquency, 22*(3), 284-296.

Brantingham, R. J., Brantingham, P. L., & Butcher, D. (1986). Perceived and actual crime risks. In F. M. Figlio, S. Hakim, & G. Fengert (Eds.), *Metropolitan Crime Patterns*. Criminal Justice Press.

Ceccato, V. (2015a). Farm crimes and environmental wildlife offenses. In *Rural Crime and Community Safety* (pp. 165-193). Routledge.

Ceccato, V. (2015b). Police, rural policing, and community safety. In *Rural Crime and Community Safety* (pp. 259-290). Routledge.

Ceccato, V. (2016). *Rural crime and community safety* (p. 424). Routledge.

Clarke, R. V. (1997). Introduction. In R. V. Clarke (Ed.), *Situational crime prevention: successful case studies* (2nd ed., pp. 1-43).

Council of Europe. (2019). Gender identity, gender-based violence and human rights. In A. Pandea, D. Grzemny, E. Keen, & R. Gomes (Eds.), *Gender Matters* (2nd ed.). Council of Europe.

DeKeseredy, W. S., & Schwartz, M. D. (2011). Theoretical and definitional issues in violence against women. In C. M. Renzetti, J. L. Edleson, & R. K. Bergen (Eds.), *Sourcebook on violence against women* (pp. 3-22).

Dewey, R. (1960). The rural-urban continuum: Real but relatively unimportant. *American Journal of Sociology, 66*(1), 60-66.

Donnermeyer, J. F. (2016). *The Routledge international handbook of rural criminology*. Routledge.

Donnermeyer, J. F., Barclay, E., & Mears, D. P. (2011). Policing agricultural crime. In R. I. Mawby & R. Yarwood (Eds.), *Rural policing and policing the rural: A constable countryside* (pp. 193-204). Ashgate.

Ekblom, P. (1994). Proximal Circumstances: A Mechanism-BasedClassification of Crime Prevention. In R. Clarke (Ed.), *Situational Crime Prevention Studies*. Monsey.

Ferraro, K. F. (1995). *Fear of crime: interpreting victimization risk*. SUNY Press.

Fleisher, M. L. (2002). 'War is good for thieving!' The symbiosis of crime and warfare among the Kuria of Tanzania. *Africa, 72*(1), 131-149. https://doi.org/10.3366/afr.2002.72.1.131

Glosser, A. M. (2016). Homies of the corn. In J. F. Donnemeyer (Ed.), *The Routledge International Handbok of Rural Criminology* (pp. 85-91). Routledge.

Held, D., McGrew, A., Goldblatt, D., & Perraton, J. (2000). Global transformations: Politics, economics and culture. In *Politics at the Edge* (pp. 14-28). Springer.

References

Hollington, A., Tappe, O., Salverda, T., & Schwarz, T. (2015). *Introduction: Concepts of the Global South*. https://web.archive.org/web/20160904205139/http://gssc.uni-koeln.de/node/451

Jones, J. (2010). The neglected problem of farm crime: An exploratory study. *Safer Communities, 9*(1), 36-44. https://doi.org/10.5042/sc.2010.0013

Jones, J. (2012). Looking beyond the 'rural idyll': Some recent trends in rural crime: Jane Jones describes recent trends in the theft of livestock and agricultural machinery in the countryside. *Criminal Justice Matters, 89*(1), 8-9. https://doi.org/10.1080/09627251.2012.721964

Lotus Arise. (2021, 2021-07-27). *Rural-Urban Fringe – UPSC (Settlement Geography)*. Retrieved November 5 from https://lotusarise.com/rural-urban-fringe-geography-upsc/

Lowe, P., Ward, N., Seymour, S., & Clark, J. (1996). Farm pollution as environmental crime. *Science as Culture, 5*(4), 588-612. https://doi.org/10.1080/09505439609526448

Mawby, R., & Yarwood, R. (2011a). *Rural policing and policing the rural: a constable countryside?* Ashgate. https://https://doi.org/10.4324/9781315607191

Mawby, R., & Yarwood, R. (Eds.). (2011b). *Rural policing and policing the rural: a constable countryside?* Ashgate.

Meer, T., & Combrinck, H. (2015). Invisible intersections: Understanding the complex stigmatisation of women with intellectual disabilities in their vulnerability to gender-based violence. *Agenda, 29*(2), 14-23.

Mullane, T. (2015). *NSW Police Force Crime Prevention Strategy 2015-2017*.

Planning Tank. (2017, 2017-01-05). *Rural-urban continuum and causes of rural-urban continuum*. Retrieved November 5 from https://planningtank.com/settlement-geography/rural-urban-continuum

Sampson, R. J. (1983). Structural Density and Criminal Victimization. *Criminology, 21*(2), 276-293. https://doi.org/10.1111/j.1745-9125.1983.tb00262.x

Sengupta, R., & Mukherjee, S. (2018, 2018/12/01). Crime, Deprivation and Social Sustainability—Evidence across States in India. *Indian Journal of Human Development, 12*(3), 354-377. https://doi.org/10.1177/0973703018811173

Sokoloff, N. J., & Dupont, I. (2005). Domestic violence at the intersections of race, class, and gender: Challenges and contributions to understanding violence against marginalized women in diverse communities. *Violence against women, 11*(1), 38-64.

Straka, S. M., & Montminy, L. (2006). Responding to the needs of older women experiencing domestic violence. *Violence against women, 12*(3), 251-267.

Sugden, G. (1999). Farm crime: Out of sight, out of mind: A study of crime on farms in the county of Rutland, England. *Crime Prevention and Community Safety, 1*(3), 29-36. https://doi.org/10.1057/palgrave.cpcs.8140023

UN-Habitat. (2019, 2020/02/12). *Safer Cities Programme*. UN-Habitat. https://unhabitat.org/safer-cities

UN – United Nations. (2015, 2022/05/22). *Transforming our World: The 2030 Agenda for Sustainable Development*. https://www.unfpa.org/resources/transforming-our-world-2030-agenda-sustainable-development

United Nations. (n.d., 2022/05/22). *The 17 Goals*. https://sdgs.un.org/goals.

von Thünen, J. H. (1826). *Der isolirte Staat in Beziehung auf Landwirthschaft und Nationalökonomie* (Vol. 1). GB Leopold.

Weisheit, R. A., & Brownstein, H. (2016). Drug production in the rural context. In J. F. Donnermeyer (Ed.), *The Routledge International Handbook Of Rural Criminology* (pp. 235-241). Routledge.

Wilhelmsson, M., & Ceccato, V. (2015, 2015/06/01/). Does burglary affect property prices in a nonmetropolitan municipality? *Journal of Rural Studies, 39*, 210-218. https://doi.org/10.1016/j.jrurstud.2015.03.014

Woods, M. (2007, 2007/08/01). Engaging the global countryside: globalization, hybridity and the reconstitution of rural place. *Progress in Human Geography, 31*(4), 485-507. https://doi.org/10.1177/0309132507079503

Yarwood, R. (2001). Crime and Policing in the British Countryside: Some Agendas for Contemporary Geographical Research. *Sociologia Ruralis, 41*(2), 201-219. https://doi.org/10.1111/1467-9523.00178

Open Access This chapter is licensed under the terms of the Creative Commons Attribution 4.0 International License (http://creativecommons.org/licenses/by/4.0/), which permits use, sharing, adaptation, distribution and reproduction in any medium or format, as long as you give appropriate credit to the original author(s) and the source, provide a link to the Creative Commons license and indicate if changes were made.

The images or other third party material in this chapter are included in the chapter's Creative Commons license, unless indicated otherwise in a credit line to the material. If material is not included in the chapter's Creative Commons license and your intended use is not permitted by statutory regulation or exceeds the permitted use, you will need to obtain permission directly from the copyright holder.

Chapter 2
Reasons Why Crime and Safety in Rural Areas Matter

Safety is a human right. For an individual to feel free from risk (and fear) of danger is a fundamental necessity regardless of where one lives, whether in the countryside or in megacities. Yet, safety has too often been associated with rural environments, and unsafety with urban environments. Images of "the rural" consisting of simple, harmonious, cohesive, and homogeneous communities are placed in contrast to "the urban" as complex, unbalanced, fragmented, and heterogeneous (Doyle 1981; Lockie and Bourke 2001; Squire 1993; Wangüemert 2001).

Now more than ever, the dynamics of rural and urban areas show strong interlinkages (e.g., Sethi and Puppim de Oliveira 2015). While urban areas may provide employment opportunities, development of technology and information systems, almost all societally critical resources are imported from the rural such as water and other raw materials. These interlinkages are also expressed by the way criminality takes place in cities and villages, connected in cyberspace and/or places far away (e.g., Harding 2020), and by the way societies are dealing with these increasing safety challenges (e.g., Donnermeyer 2018; Hodgkinson and Harkness 2020).

Because research and policy have been dominated by "the urban agenda" (Koch and Ahmad 2018) and have therefore failed to recognize these broader societal challenges, we call for in-depth knowledge about crime and safety conditions on the rural-urban continuum. We argue that better knowledge about these rural-urban interlinkages is crucial to moving closer to the 2030s sustainability goals.

What follows is a consideration of 20 reasons of why crime and safety in areas on the rural-urban continuum matter. This list of reasons builds on the original ten-item list published in the book *Rural Crime and Community Safety* (Ceccato 2016) and aligns with other international publications to illustrate the urgency of the subject matter for criminology and society in general. Given the terminological legacy of this field of research, the term "rural areas" will be used here as a synonym of areas on the rural-urban continuum.

Twenty Reasons why Crime and Safety in Rural Areas Matter
Reason 1 – The "rural" is a heterogeneous and complex place.
Reason 2 – Misconceptions of "idyllic" rural areas are problematic.
Reason 3 – Rural areas are under constant transformation.
Reason 4 – Low crime rates in rural areas do not mean "no problems".
Reason 5 – Crime is influenced by the very nature of rural areas.
Reason 6 – Safety perceptions in rural areas are unequal.
Reason 7 – Violence characterizes rural contexts in the Global South.
Reason 8 – The commodification of security is affecting rural areas.
Reason 9 – Drug production, dealing, and use threaten rural areas.
Reason 10 – The theoretical legacy is urban-centric and Global North-dominated.
Reason 11 – Rural-urban linkages are neglected issues in governance.
Reason 12 – Rural safety is a public health issue.
Reason 13 – Crime underreporting in rural areas is a problem.
Reason 14 – Policing and crime prevention models neglect rural challenges.
Reason 15 – Technology can become an asset in situational rural crime prevention.
Reason 16 – Gendered and intersectional perspectives on rural safety are critical.
Reason 17 – There is a need for including trans and nonbinary experiences of safety in rural contexts.
Reason 18 – Climate change is impacting crime on the rural-urban continuum.
Reason 19 – Animal welfare is central to rural sustainability.
Reason 20 – Crime and safety are intertwined dimensions of sustainable rural development.

Reason 1 – The "rural" is a heterogeneous and complex place
Rural areas are heterogeneous entities, and thus the search for a singular definition of the rural is illusory (Halfacree 1993). Despite the fact that 32 percent of the European population lives in towns and suburbs and 29 percent in rural areas (Eurostat 2020), the idea of the "rural" as a homogeneous environment is commonly fueled by mediated, streamlined images of what the "rural" is expected to be. Jansson (2013) argues that the challenge is not to recognize that the urban and rural are different, but rather to identify "forgotten places" that may fall in between these two binary categories. These "forgotten places" are close to suburbs, small towns, and other in-between spaces with their own identities that may not be rural or urban. Taking distance from simplistic views of the rural, we call for the need to untangle possible facets of rural areas as both safe and criminogenic – hybrid places with "assemblages of human and non-human entities, knitted-together intersections of networks and flows that are never wholly fixed or contained at the local scale, and whose constant shape-shifting eludes a singular representation of place" (Woods 2005; Woods 2007, p. 499).

Rural areas as hybrid environments can be better defined as areas on a *rural-urban continuum*, that is, a scale that stretches from remote and desolated spaces to accessible and connected environments of the urban fringe. Therefore, instead of designating an area as rural (non-urban), we adopt the term *rural-urban continuum* to analytically capture possible interlinkages of socioeconomic, cultural, and technological dynamics that are criminologically relevant to impact crime levels and safety conditions in a particular place. Some of these places can be considered "the real forgotten places," but with today's information and communication technology (ICT), they may be "rural" in some respects and "urban" in others. Crime and safety levels reflect therefore the hybrid nature of areas on the rural-urban continuum.

Reason 2 – Misconceptions of "idyllic" rural areas are problematic
Crime is not just an "urban problem." Yet, interpretations of rural space which draw upon the "rural idyll" assume crime in the rural context to be either exceptional or a lagged effect of urbanization, but never endemic to rural culture or rural communities (Donnermeyer and DeKeseredy 2008). The "rural idyll" (e.g., Bell 1997; Short 1991) is considered to be a socially constructed and commonly shared idealized image, or stereotype, of life in villages, which are often depicted as quiet places, harmonious, cohesive, and homogeneous communities surrounded by a hinterland of farms and ranches with little or no conflict (Lockie and Bourke 2001; Squire 1993; Wangüemert 2001), and where the world is unaffected by global changes (Bell 1997, 2006; Short 2006; Short 1991). Although stemming from imperial England at the turn of the nineteenth century, the myth of the rural idyll is still very much alive and can be found everywhere on the globe, from England to Argentina, from Sweden to Australia. While the rural idyll imagines rural space as an object of desire because it is not urban, rural space may also be represented as an object of dread because it is not urban (Bell 1997; Scott and Biron 2010). As suggested by Donnermeyer et al. (2013), the rural idyll myth works to exaggerate rural "strangeness" and "otherness" in so doing works to broaden the assumed gap which separates rural and urban life.

We suggest that people's perceptions of rural areas as "idyllic" are not only important in defining rurality, but they may also be responsible for misconceptions of rural areas as static, innocuous places, incapable of generating critical conditions for crime. This can be particularly problematic because it, first, rejects the existence of agency in rural areas and denies people's daily practices in local cultures with a variety of actors, interests, and actions interlinked in complex ways (Giddens 1991). Second, it overlooks the local and global socioeconomic and technological interlinkages found in areas on the rural-urban continuum which, currently, are better references for redefining the complexities of rurality in a globalized world (Castells 1996, 2015) and are, we argue, essential to the process of pursuing social sustainability in rural contexts.

Reason 3 – Rural areas are under constant transformation
It is increasingly recognized that rural areas are global, hybrid places that are shaped by forces far beyond their local realities (Shortall and Warner 2012; Woods 2011). In some cases, the restructuring process has forced rural communities to move away from traditional economies toward more diversified, local employment bases (Krannich et al. 2011). Crime is part of the transformation occurring at different

paces and scales around the rural world (Ceccato 2013), both in and beyond rural communities.

Globalized networks of crime profoundly impact rural places and people. Recent examples include human trafficking, slavery, drugs, hate crime against animal production, violence against women and minorities, international theft, "county drug lines" and environmental crimes (NPCC 2018; Yarwood 2021), and demand new ways of tackling crime and ensure people's safety. These transformations are not specific to the Global North and show global ramifications relevant to explain crime dynamics in areas on the rural-urban continuum (Siwale 2014; Tapiador 2008; Woods 2011).

Reason 4 – Low crime rates in rural areas do not mean "no problems"
Far too often we take for granted that "because there is less crime in the countryside, crime is not a problem for people living there" (Yarwood 2001, p. 206). In rural areas, lower crime rates alone do not measure the impact crime has on those living in the countryside. A homicide (or any serious crime) in a rural area may have a stronger and more long-term impact on residents than it would have had in a metropolitan area. Even if such impacts could be measured with a metric, crime rates alone may be a poor indicator of the problems encountered in rural areas, as some crimes may impact particular groups such as employees and families (Ceccato et al. 2021b). The quality of life and health of such groups can be highly affected (see reason 12). Moreover, the 80/20 rule in which a large majority of crimes occur at a small minority of places (e.g., 80 percent of crimes at 20 percent of places, such as street segments) may not be appropriate as a reference for crime prevention in areas on the rural-urban continuum. Crime in rural areas may not be as concentrated as it is in large cities, or even if it is, crime underreporting (see reason 13) makes safety interventions based solely on police records problematic. Collapsing crime data over several years and aggregating them into appropriate sized-zones might be useful in sparsely populated areas to create a more reliable basis for crime and safety interventions. The development (and the testing) of methods that can better capture the nature of crime and safety in rural areas is emerging as an area of research in its own right (see e.g., Weisheit et al., 2022)

Reason 5 – Crime is influenced by the very nature of rural areas
Certain crime opportunities may only be present in rural areas, as low population density affects crime opportunities and detection. It is no surprise that hot spots of diesel theft from tractors are concentrated in farm-based municipalities; similarly, harassment and attacks against ranchers (e.g., of mink or cattle) are found only on farms that specialize in animal production (Ceccato et al. 2021). If people are not present in a place, a crime may go undetected for some time, for instance, the dumping of waste in forests (Ceccato 2013). Other conditions that may promote crime in rural areas include, for example, the high tolerance for certain types of behavior and crime itself among individuals of the local community (Barclay et al. 2004; Barclay et al. 2007). Hot spots of crime may be found in particular "towns marketed as centers for mass tourism and youth tourism" and "those where poverty combines with tourism" (Mawby 2007, p. 21). Fossil energy extraction operations are increasingly more common in rural areas, and the resulting population inflows may also lead to increases in crime (Ruddell 2017). In addition, crimes in the rural include cases in

which farmers are the offenders; a perspective which has been generally ignored by mainstream criminology (Collins 2016). Other examples include illegal criminal enterprises, such as in the meat trade (Smith and McElwee 2013); environmental wildlife crimes (Caniglia et al. 2010; Fyfe and Reeves 2011; Loeffler 2013; Maingi et al. 2012; Wellsmith 2011); and the illegal killing of predators or "pests" (Enticott 2011; Gargiulo et al. 2016). Brisman et al. (2014, p. 482) suggest, for example, that the study of the rural and the subject of rural criminology create a fertile ground for the development of a "green-cultural criminology of the rural," which could include connections between the global and the rural; agribusiness and the food/profit chain; farming the land and polluting the water and air; the cultural and media images and narratives of rural life; and forms of resistance to environmental damage. For other examples, see, for instance, Donnermeyer (2016).

Reason 6 – Safety perceptions in rural areas are unequal
People living in rural areas often declare feeling safer overall than people living in urban areas. However, safety perceptions reflect unbalanced levels of victimization, such that the poor are overrepresented among crime victims (Brå 2014; Nilsson and Estrada 2006; Tseloni et al. 2010). Some of these feelings relate to an individual's lack of sense of order and continuity with regard to one's experiences in life (Giddens 1991). Research also shows that safety perceptions reflect people's sense of place, where "place" refers to the immediate settings and conditions of daily life, but also the sense of one's place in a larger societal context (Hope and Sparks 2000). International literature confirms that safety perceptions vary with long-term social and economic exclusion and discrimination that manifest differently by gender, ethnicity, and length of residency (Babacan 2012; Ceccato 2018; Chakraborti and Garland 2011; Jensen 2012; Scott et al. 2012).

Safety perceptions also relate to macro-level changes in communities, such as rapid population inflow and crime. For instance, in Sweden, half of the respondents to the Swedish Crime Survey who live in larger municipalities expressed a greater worry about crime than those living in more rural municipalities (Ceccato 2016). Nowadays, with access to the internet and social media, overall anxieties are also said to be generated by the individual's lack of embedded biography with a plurality of social worlds (Giddens 1991), beliefs and the diversification of lifestyles. Victimization becomes less dependent on location or proximity, and with that the fear of being a victim of crime may be fed by boundary-less "glocal" forces. For example, an individual living on Manhattan in New York may run the same risk of being targeted by computer fraud or any other cybercrime as an individual living in the remote, rural areas of Sweden (Ceccato 2013).

Reason 7 – Violence characterizes rural contexts in the Global South
Rural areas of the Global South are contested spaces where violence is part of daily life (Ceccato and Ceccato 2017; DeKeseredy and Hall-Sanchez 2018). This is particularly true in Central and South America, Africa, and most of Asia, where violence encompasses fights between spouses and neighbors, armed robbery, organized cargo theft, child labor, prostitution, slavery, human trafficking, smuggling, so-called honor killings, killings related to land-reform and environmental conflicts,

and police-related violence (Ceccato and Ceccato 2017). Examples of recent, related research topics include rural patterns of violence (Ceccato and Ceccato 2017; Steeves et al. 2015); the effects of lighting on homicide (Arvate et al. 2018); the case of Somalian pirates (Collins 2016); violence in Turkish rural regions (Çaya 2014); estimations of homicide rates in Cambodia (Broadhurst 2002); and violent farm crime in Zimbabwe (Rutherford 2004). The research also calls for more evidence on the relationship between poverty and violence in rural areas (Lee and Slack 2008; Melde 2006), and the violence related to Western commercial exploitation of the Global South (which, e.g., engages in bio-prospecting and bio-piracy, i.e., using plant and animal species from rural areas for the production of medicines or tonics) and practices that ignore the rights of indigenous peoples in regard to traditional knowledge and ownership (Brisman et al. 2014). In addition, there is a need for new theoretical frameworks capable of understanding differences in the dynamics of crime across the world, especially in countries in the southern hemisphere (Carrington et al. 2015). As suggested by Carrington and colleagues, there exists a vast body of significant criminological research and crime prevention experience in the Global South that is worthy of appreciation, with important implications for global security and justice.

Reason 8 – The commodification of security is affecting rural areas
The commodification of rural areas takes different shapes and affects levels of crime and safety. Commodities become goods when a monetary value is associated with observing a landscape, petting animals, or living in a safe, rural gated community. The commodification of the rural is visible with rural tourism and the inflows of temporary populations. Private security has become part of the same process of commodification of the rural areas as it has taken over several responsibilities that used to be associated with the public sector, such as law enforcement. Privatization of security (as a public good) potentially has a negative impact on the provision, distribution, and quality of security services, in particular for those who are not seen as obvious consumers (Goold et al. 2010).

In the United States, South Africa, and many countries of the Global South, planning models based on target hardening and territoriality have provided theoretical support for gated communities, which have recently become part of the countryside (Spocter 2013). In rural China, for instance, rural gated communities play a different role than in those found in urban areas. Zhang et al. (2020) indicate that rural gated communities in their contemporary form have emerged as a response to the problems resulting from the increasing working force/migrant inflow in peri-urban zones, while those gated communities found in urban areas reflect a collective pursuit of a better quality of life, at different price scales. Despite any good intentions behind eco-communities or sustainable rural villages (Landman 2007), there is no compensation for the negative impacts such housing developments have on the overall community as they reinforce segregation.

Reason 9 – Drug production, dealing, and use threaten rural areas
Due to their isolation, rural areas have long been associated with drug production (Weisheit et al. 1994). More recently, though, the countryside has also become associated with the distribution and consumption of illicit substances. In the United Kingdom, for example, there has been an increase in so-called "county line" drug

dealing (Harding 2020), namely, "the practice of urban gangs recruiting vulnerable young people in rural and coastal settlements to distribute drugs." Enabled by new technologies and social media, dealers can exert control over widening areas and so enroll young people into remote illicit networks (Yarwood 2021).

In Sweden, Stenbacka (2021) assesses the presence of drugs in rural places and the way this impacts rural residents and the challenges faced by professionals dealing with the problem, especially police officers. In rural America, several studies have reported on marijuana cultivation and methamphetamine production (Garriott 2016; Weisheit and Brownstein 2016) as well as organized drug production and related violence (van Dun 2014). In the Global South, Anderson (2018) reports on opium poppy cultivators among the Karen people in Thailand, providing insight on how the restrictions of ethnic minorities' rights can lead to drug production as a last means of survival. A commonality in these studies is the realization that rural areas are not sufficiently prepared to combat drug-related crime as a globalized process with local consequences from international drug flows into the community. This is due to numerous reasons but in particular to a combination of the transformation of access to and distribution of drugs (via the internet or "county lines") and the limited supply of police resources within large geographical areas of responsibility.

Reason 10 – The theoretical legacy is urban-centric and Global North-dominated

Most of the current theories in criminology are urban-centric with little or no reference to contexts outside the big cities. Empirically, they are based on "urban neighborhoods" as a model, often limited to the city borders, for example. These theories also tend to be dated, as they do very little to offer an understanding of the current complexity of crimes that happen in globalized rural areas. They fail to recognize differences in the dynamics of crime across the world, especially in countries of the Global South (Carrington et al. 2015).

More recently, criminologists have started to contest the theoretical urban-centric legacy. Donnermeyer et al. (2013), for instance, contest the assumption that places with low crime must manifest high levels of social organization, while areas with low social organization must inevitably display more crime. They suggest that there are multiple forms of social organization in the rural, allowing individuals to simultaneously participate in multiple networks, some of which may be criminal: "it is quite possible that many rural communities have a social or moral order which keeps some crimes such as violence in the 'dark'" (Donnermeyer et al. 2013, p. 71). Also of relevance is the pioneering work of scholars devoted to the so-called 'green criminology' (White, 2013) that since the 1990s involved a large array of criminal offences against the environment and wildlife. The term 'green criminology' has increasingly been used to denote generic interest in the study of environmental crime and/or environmetal harm but has extended to include issues related to, for example, eco-justice, eco-terrorism and climate change (Nurse and Wyatt, 2020; White, 2021).

Reason 11 – Rural-urban linkages are neglected issues in governance

Rural and urban areas are highly interdependent entities. While urban areas may provide employment opportunities, and development of technology and information systems, many societally critical resources are imported from the rural, for example, food, water, wood, energy and raw materials (Gebre and Gebremedhin 2019). The agricultural sector is nearly exclusively located in rural areas, where farms produce 80% of the world's food in value terms (Lowder et al. 2021), and the food demand is only expected to increase (Gebre and Gebremedhin 2019). Additionally, while its contribution to the global Gross Domestic Product (GDP) has decreased since the 1960s (World Bank 2020), the agricultural sector still constitutes an essential part of global growth; in 2018 it still represented 4% of global GDP and up to 25% in some developing countries (World Bank 2021). Additionally, while the environmental effects of more farming have been criticized from a sustainable perspective, recent evidence indicates that modern practices such as grazing cattle may lead to more open landscapes and increased biodiversity (SDG 15, United Nations n.d.), which is a prerequisite for a rich flora and fauna, especially in forest-dependent countries (Swedish National Food Agency 2021). Thus, rural areas may provide vital tools for achieving the United Nations' Sustainable Development Goals (United Nations n.d.)

In addition, particularly in countries of the Global South, the existent rural-urban linkages create rural empowerment and economic development even when infrastructure problems, institutional constraints, and trade barriers tend to discourage such linkages (Akkoyunlu 2015). Moreover, the political power of rural areas cannot be underestimated as it can change the paths of national governments; for example, Brexit in the United Kingdom (Neal et al. 2021) or new models of rural governance in Sweden (Arora-Jonsson and Larsson 2021). An alternative perception to the boundaries drawn between the rural and the urban is needed (Lohnert and Steinbrink 2005) as conventional approaches disregard their sociospatial structures of interdependency, which in turn, affects the governance of crime and safety on the rural-urban continuum. Such an alternative perspective is also lacking in research and policy practices regarding sustainable development given the current dominant focus on big city problems (see, e.g., Koch and Ahmad 2018; UN-Habitat 2019) and on large crime concentrations.

Reason 12 – Rural safety is a public health issue

In the past decades, farmers have become more exposed to extra stressors due to environmental, structural, and economic changes in agriculture and other related sectors (Brisman et al. 2014). Climate change introduces greater variability in weather patterns and therefore crop productivity is no longer reliable. Donnermeyer et al. (2013, p. 78) note that agriculture is now intensive, expansive and has been "transformed into a Fordist model of production." In some countries, farmers show higher levels of depression symptoms than the general working population and the differences increase with age (Torske et al. 2016). Suicide in rural agrarian communities is a universal phenomenon (Behere et al. 2020). Regardless of the type of production, stressors are bound to affect farmers' health and overall quality of life, for example, stressors generated by the physical environment, family structure, farming economy, bureaucracy, and other farming-related uncertainties.

The growth of veganism and an increasing awareness about the environmental impacts of consuming animal products are at the root of actions against farmers working with animal production. Farmers are particularly vulnerable to criticisms and threats which are becoming more common in a number of countries (Carson et al. 2012; Katz and McPherson 2020; Monaghan 2013). Carson et al. (2012) found that in the United States, even though attacks by environmental and animal rights groups had often universally been non-violent, farmers were concerned that this situation would change. In Sweden, for example, there may be aggressive demonstrations and actions by animal rights activists, for example, at open farm events, but there are also threats directed toward farmers, farm employees, and family living on the farm property. There are even accounts in which children have been threatened (Jansson 2019). Reports also cite unlawful intrusion, theft, and other minor crimes (in the United Kingdom, see, e.g., Pasha-Robinson (2018)). Other attacks on farmers working with animal production have been directed at the animals themselves, in various forms of abuse and injury, including threats via social media. Recent evidence indicates that these criminal acts have a strong impact on the farmers' personal safety, the safety of their family and trust in society in general (Ceccato et al. 2021), putting their businesses' survival at risk but also their health.

Reason 13 – Crime underreporting in rural areas is a problem
Reporting rates in rural areas may be affected several factors. Distance to the police station contributes to differences in the willingness to report a crime to the police (Stassen and Ceccato 2019). In Australia, Barclay et al. (2004) show that the reporting rate is lower because farmers have a high tolerance for several criminal behaviors. Some illegal acts have become normalized and part of "doing business" (Stassen and Ceccato 2019). In Sweden, farmers avoid reporting an offense if it is not serious (LRF 2020) because there is a perception that "it does not lead to anything". Fear can be revealed by silence in rural areas. One example is the lack of trust in authorities and the criminal justice system, as victims and witnesses refrain from witnessing in court and revealing local criminal groups in fear of retaliation (Ceccato and Ceccato 2017) or in fear of ostracism if the violence on the part of the perpetrators were to become public (DeKeseredy et al. 2012).

Low rates of reported violence against women can be associated with a code of silence imposed by patriarchal community values. Websdale (1998) showed how some women are afraid to call the police because they know that their abuser is socially networked with police personnel and that little or no action would be taken in their defense if it were reported. In other cases, other local women do not help because they themselves are experiencing similar problems and their own struggles prevent them from helping others (DeKeseredy and Schwartz 2008, p. 112). In addition, the literature suggests that social and geographical isolation in rural areas can be particularly problematic for ethnic minority groups when seeking advice and reporting racial discrimination and abuse (Chakraborti and Garland 2011; Garland and Chakraborti 2006, 2012; Greenfields 2014; Robinson and Gardner 2012).

Reason 14 – Policing and crime prevention models neglect rural challenges
In recent decades, a wide variety of agencies and agents, including the volunteer sector, has attempted to deliver policing in pluralistic or autonomous ways (Loader 2000). It is therefore no surprise that the police and policing reveal the nature of rural societies in which they are embedded. As Mawby and Yarwood (2011) suggest, this includes the way that the police, the public and other agencies regulate themselves and each other according to the dominant ideals of society; both formally, through the growing spectrum of policing partnerships, and informally, through the enforcement of moral codes and values. Neighborhood watch schemes

and safety audits, for example, have been important examples of community safety practices in rural areas (Yarwood and Edwards 1995).

In most countries, rural policing is often under-resourced, exclusionary, and too parochial to deal with increasingly globalized, multiscalar threats (Yarwood 2015). Furthermore, most crime prevention models have been imported from urban areas to rural ones, with little concern about potential differences among contexts or if and how they actually work in rural areas (Ceccato 2013; Ceccato et al. 2019). The search for new models of crime prevention and for "an external silver bullet" for local problems may, in the long run, undermine agency of stakeholders and civial society in rural areas. The image of safety strategists from rural municipalities being "spoon-fed" by their urban counterparts can be observed in far too many criminology conferences that rarely focus on issues relevant to those living in areas of rural-urban continuum.

Reason 15 – Technology can become an asset in situational rural crime prevention
Although still in its infancy, technology in situational crime prevention in rural areas is attracting more attention. Aransiola and Ceccato (2020) reviewed the literature searching for applications of modern technologies in situational crime prevention and found that traditional crime prevention (locking doors, using guard dogs, raising fences, and so on) are still the most common in rural areas, while modern measures (CCTV, security lights, alarms, and drones) are generally more supplemental. CCTV and alarms have been shown to have little to no effect on crime prevention, especially on farms, although they are better at detecting and monitoring wildlife crime (Aransiola and Ceccato 2020; Liedka et al. 2019). Other studies explore how different technologies have been used to prevent farm theft (Harkness and Larkins 2020) and housebreaking (Hamid and Yusof 2013) and to reduce violent crime (Arvate et al. 2018). Research about the role of technology in crime commission in rural contexts is also lacking as well as about inequities in access to technology in situational crime prevention in rural contexts.

Reason 16 – Gendered and intersectional perspectives on rural safety are critical
Traditionally, studies on domestic violence in rural areas have adopted a gendered approach, providing a more nuanced perspective compared to studies that historically treated women as having universal safety needs, usually patterned after white males (e.g., DeKeseredy et al. 2012; DeKeseredy and Joseph 2006; DeKeseredy and Schwartz 2008). Yet, much remains to be done on the intersectionality of safety (Crenshaw 1989) in rural contexts, both in research and in practice. Using references from rural contexts, studies should devote more attention to how, when, and why gender intersects with age, class, and ethnic belonging, which together may result in multiple dimensions of disadvantage, victimization, and/or poor safety perceptions. Steps in this direction are already being taken; see, for instance, the research by DeKeseredy (2020).

Reason 17 – There is a need for including trans and nonbinary experiences of safety in rural contexts.
Rurality has become to be understood as a site of oppression for Queer individuals, where Queer is used here as an umbrella term for the LGBTQ+ community, namely,

lesbian, gay, bisexual, transgender, queer, or questioning (Gorman-Murray et al. 2008). Queer people have been presented as "the other" in a number of studies that deal with sexuality and safety in rural contexts. The imposition of binary gender norms in rural environments is not yet well researched but is becoming an area of interest (Atalay and Doan 2019). Queer people are more exposed to discrimination, crime, and violence than the rest of the population (Angeles and Roberton 2020; Brå 2017), throughout the rural-urban continuum and on digital platforms. Research shows that the context of discrimination and victimization matters, and that stressors impact individuals' mobility, health, and life chances (MUCF) – The Swedish Agency for Youth and Civil Society (2020). Some small rural communities can be restrictive toward Queer people, see Misgav and Hartal (2019) reporting the experiences of sexual minorities and their fight to the right to be different, while other rural areas can be inclusive and welcoming (Rosenberg 2021); see, for instance, Conner and Okamura (2021) who illustrate the advantages of living in rural areas for LGBTQ+ rights advocates.

Secluded settings within communities including dark streets and public toilets generate feelings of "fear and anxiety" as most LGBTQ+ individuals are assaulted in such places (MUCF 2020; Nourani et al. 2020). However, secluded settings can also be perceived as "safe oases" by LGBTQ+ individuals, as they allow privacy for meetings, thus turning into arenas of everyday resistance and empowerment (Atalay and Doan 2019). Unfortunately, public safety and feminist planning literature still adopt static, heterosexist notions of men and women occupying urban spaces – a "tyranny of gender" (Angeles and Roberton 2020), that is said to disadvantage LGBTQ+ people, intersex, and trans populations (Doan 2007).

Reason 18 – Climate change is impacting crime on the rural-urban continuum

Researchers and policy analysts have argued that climate change will increase social conflict, especially due to competition over scarce resources, including fresh water, food, fuel, and land. Some of the impacts of climate change have already been observed in rural areas worldwide, such as flooding, drought, and heat. In addition, the migration produced by climate change is expected to foster conflict, particularly when migrants move to areas with scarce resources. Agnew (2012, p. 31 and 34) suggests that crime will be a coping mechanism, as "it may allow individuals and groups to obtain those resources that are in short supply, particularly food, water, shelter, fuel, and land. It may provide money, which aids in the adaptation to and recovery from climate change." In this context, "individuals may respond to economic hardship by engaging in acts that increase carbon emissions, such as the burning of low-grade coal and the raiding of forests for fuel." It is also suggested that an increase in the use of illicit drugs may be used to alleviate the negative emotions resulting from stressful situations.

Furthermore, it is expected that warmer weather will alter routine activities (Cohen and Felson 1979) with more people in public places, increasing the likelihood that motivated offenders will encounter victims and that more homes will be left unprotected (see previous evidence on temperature and crime Ceccato 2005; Cohn and Rotton 2000; Rotton and Cohn 2004). Research indicates that extreme weather events and blackouts may reduce guardianship, particularly by the police. Crime can become a means for revenge against those believed to be responsible for climate change and related targets, so acts of terrorism are likely, at the same time that white-collar crimes may increase as corporations and the wealthy attempt to maintain their privileged position and evade regulation. As climate change continues to impact agriculture and access to food, calls from nation states of the Global North for increased food security are leading to new forms of exploitation of resources in countries of the Global South (Brisman and South 2017).

Reason 19 – Animal welfare is central to rural sustainability

The human-animal relationship has been changing over time with humans often wielding an oppressive and dominating power over animals (Philo and Wilbert 2000). Currently, the debate is split among those who defend the use of animals and those who condemn it as exploitation. The animal welfare movement, on the one hand, believes humans have an obligation to minimize animal suffering whenever possible, but that humans should be able to use animals for food, clothing, and entertainment. These acts exclude all types of animal abuse (Beirne 1995), but there are hierarchical differences in the spectrum of animal exploitation that are at the core of why certain animals are chosen to be "saved" and others are not. Research indicates that numerous animals perish each year as a result of abuse, while surviving animal victims are often left maimed, physically disabled, or suffering from chronic health problems (Hughes et al. 2020).

The animal liberation movement, on the other hand, argues that any unnecessary infliction of pain or suffering on animals is immoral, and that animals are not ours to eat, wear, or use for entertainment purposes since these uses are wants and not necessities. With a goal of animal protection at any cost, some animal rights activists consider violence to be a legitimate means of achieving this goal. The use of force is justified by the idea of an "extended right to self-defense," which means that they, on behalf of the animals, exercise the animals' alleged right to protect themselves from violence and abuse (Lovell forthcoming). These behaviors involve arson and vandalism against property but may also include violence directed at people (Ceccato et al. 2021a), which in turn may have serious consequences for farmers, their employees, and families.

Reason 20 – Crime and safety are intertwined dimensions of sustainable rural development

The United Nations' 2030 Agenda for Sustainable Development identifies crime and fear of crime as major threats to sustainability (UN-Habitat 2019). An unsustainable environment is commonly characterized by "images of poverty, physical deterioration, increasing levels of crime, and fear of crime" (Cozens 2002, p. 131). In rural areas of the Global North, from the United States and Canada to European countries, these characteristics can be found in different degrees (Donnermeyer et al. 2006; Moore et al. 2005; Mora-Rivera and García-Mora 2021). Populations living on the rural-urban continuum are more prone to chronic poverty, famine, social exclusion, and violence, particularly in Africa, Asia, and Latin America (Florin and Corneliu 2020). Therefore, accounting for the safety needs of those living on hybrid, rural-urban continua around the world is crucial for achieving a more sustainable future.

Fig. 2.1 UN-Sustainable Development Goals (SDG), 2030. Source: United Nations (2019). (The use of Fig. 2.1 (SDG icons) was permitted by UN-SDG permissions. The content of this publication has not been approved by the United Nations and does not reflect the views of the United Nations or its officials or Member States. https://www.un.org/sustainabledevelopment/)

On September 25, 2015, the United Nations General Assembly adopted the historic Agenda 2030 resolution on sustainable development. The agenda means that all 193 member states of the United Nations are committed to working to achieve a socially, environmentally, and economically sustainable world by 2030 (UN 2015). The agenda contains 17 goals and 169 sub-goals (Fig. 2.1). These goals balance the three dimensions of sustainable development – the environment, the economy, and the social conditions of people – in which crime and safety constitute an integral part of the agenda.

References

Agnew, R. (2012). Dire forecast: A theoretical model of the impact of climate change on crime. *Theoretical Criminology, 16*(1), 21–42. https://doi.org/10.1177/1362480611416843

Akkoyunlu, S. (2015). The potential of rural-urban linkages for sustainable development and trade. *International Journal of Sustainable Development & World Policy, 4*(2), 20–40.

Anderson, B. (2018). Zomia's vestiges: Illegible peoples and legible crimes in Omkoi, northwest Thailand. *South East Asia Research, 26*(1), 38–57. https://doi.org/10.1177/0967828X17752710

Angeles, L. C., & Roberton, J. (2020). Empathy and inclusive public safety in the city: examining LGBTQ2+ voices and experiences of intersectional discrimination. Women's Studies International Forum,

Aransiola, T. J., & Ceccato, V. (2020). The role of modern technology in rural situational crime prevention. A review of the literature. In *Rural Crime Prevention* (1st ed., pp. 58–72). Routledge. https://doi.org/10.4324/9780429460135-6

Arora-Jonsson, S., & Larsson, O. (2021, 2021/02/01/). Lives in limbo: Migrant integration and rural governance in Sweden. *Journal of Rural Studies, 82*, 19–28. https://doi.org/10.1016/j.jrurstud.2021.01.010

Arvate, P., Falsete, F. O., Ribeiro, F. G., & Souza, A. P. (2018). Lighting and Homicides: Evaluating the Effect of an Electrification Policy in Rural Brazil on Violent Crime Reduction. *Journal of Quantitative Criminology, 34*(4), 1047–1078. https://doi.org/10.1007/s10940-017-9365-6

Atalay, O., & Doan, P. L. (2019). Reading the LGBT Movement through its Spatiality in Istanbul, Turkey. *Geography Research Forum*. https://grf.bgu.ac.il/index.php/GRF/article/view/585

Babacan, H. (2012). Racism Denial in Australia: The power of silence. *Australian Mosaic, 32*, 1–3. http://researchonline.jcu.edu.au/22526/

Barclay, E., Donnermeyer, J. F., & Jobes, P. C. (2004). The Dark Side of Gemeinschaft: Criminality within Rural Communities. *Crime Prevention and Community Safety, 6*(3), 7–22. https://doi.org/10.1057/palgrave.cpcs.8140191

Barclay, E., Scott, J., Hogg, R., & Donnermeyer, J. (Eds.). (2007). *Crime in Rural Australia*. The Federation Press.

Behere, P. B., Mansharamani, H., Behere, A. P., & Yadav, R. (2020). Suicide and Self-Harms in Rural Setting. In S. K. Chaturvedi (Ed.), *Mental Health and Illness in the Rural World* (pp. 151–167). Springer Singapore. https://doi.org/10.1007/978-981-10-2345-3_21

Beirne, P. (1995). The use and abuse of animals in criminology: A brief history and current review. *Social Justice, 22*(1 (59), 5–31.

Bell, D. (1997). Anti-idyll: Rural horror. In P. Cloke & J. Litte (Eds.), *Contested Countryside Cultures: Otherness, Marginalisation and Rurality* (pp. 94–108). Routledge.

Bell, D. (2006). Variation on the rural idyll. In P. Cloke, T. Marsden, & P. Mooney (Eds.), *Handbook of Rural Studies* (pp. 149–160). Sage.

Brisman, A., McClanahan, B., & South, N. (2014). Toward a Green-Cultural Criminology of "the Rural". *Critical Criminology, 22*(4), 479–494. https://doi.org/10.1007/s10612-014-9250-7

Brisman, A., & South, N. (2017). Food, Crime, Justice and Security: (Food) Security for Whom? In P. Z. Werkheiser I. (Ed.), *Food Justice in US and Global Contexts. The International Library of Environmental, Agricultural and Food Ethics*. Springer. https://doi.org/10.1007/978-3-319-57174-4_16

Broadhurst, R. (2002). Lethal violence, crime and state formation in Cambodia [Review]. *Australian and New Zealand Journal of Criminology, 35*(1), 1–26. https://doi.org/10.1375/acri.35.1.1

BRÅ – Brottsförebyggande rådet (The Swedish National Council for Crime Prevention). (2014). *Nationella trygghetsundersökningen 2006–2013*.

BRÅ – Brottsförebyggande rådet (The Swedish National Council for Crime Prevention). (2017). Hatbrottsstatistik. https://www.bra.se/statistik/statistiska-undersokningar/hatbrottsstatistik.html

Caniglia, R., Fabbri, E., Greco, C., Galaverni, M., & Randi, E. (2010, 10//). Forensic DNA against wildlife poaching: Identification of a serial wolf killing in Italy. *Forensic Science International: Genetics, 4*(5), 334–338. https://doi.org/10.1016/j.fsigen.2009.10.012

Carrington, K., Hogg, R., & Sozzo, M. E. (2015). Southern Criminology. *British Journal of Criminology, 56*, 1–20.

Carson, J. V., LaFree, G., & Dugan, L. (2012, 2012/04/01). Terrorist and Non-Terrorist Criminal Attacks by Radical Environmental and Animal Rights Groups in the United States, 1970–2007. *Terrorism and Political Violence, 24*(2), 295–319. https://doi.org/10.1080/09546553.2011.639416

Castells, M. (1996). The space of flows. *The rise of the network society, 1*, 376–482.

Castells, M. (2015). Space of flows, space of places: Materials for a theory of urbanism in the information age. In *The city reader* (pp. 263–274). Routledge.

Çaya, S. (2014, 2014/02/21/). Violence in Rural Regions: The Case of ModernTurkey. *Procedia – Social and Behavioral Sciences, 114*, 721–726. https://doi.org/10.1016/j.sbspro.2013.12.774

Ceccato, V. (2005, 9//). Homicide in São Paulo, Brazil: Assessing spatial-temporal and weather variations. *Journal of Environmental Psychology, 25*(3), 307–321. https://doi.org/10.1016/j.jenvp.2005.07.002

Ceccato, V. (2013). Integrating geographical information into urban safety research and planning. *Proceedings of the ICE - Urban Design and Planning, 166*, 15–23. http://www.icevirtuallibrary.com/content/article/10.1680/udap.11.00038

Ceccato, V. (2016). *Rural crime and community safety*. Routledge.

Ceccato, V. (2018). Fear of crime and overall anxieties in rural areas : The case of Sweden. In G. M. Murray Lee (Ed.), *The Routledge International Handbook on Fear of Crime* (1 ed.). Routledge. http://urn.kb.se/resolve?urn=urn:nbn:se:kth:diva-233897

Ceccato, V., Abraham, A., & Lundqvist, P. (2021a). Crimes against animal production: Exploring the use of media archives. *International Criminal Justice Review*

Ceccato, V., & Ceccato, H. (2017, 2017/09/01). Violence in the Rural Global South: Trends, Patterns, and Tales From the Brazilian Countryside. *Criminal Justice Review, 42*(3), 270–290. https://doi.org/10.1177/0734016817724504

Ceccato, V., Lundqvist, P., Abraham, J., Göransson, E., & Svennefelt, C. A. (2021b, 2021/07/31). The Nature of Fear Among Farmers Working with Animal Production. *International Criminology*. https://doi.org/10.1007/s43576-021-00024-z

Ceccato, V., Abraham, J., Lundqvist, P. (2021). Crimes Against Animal Production: Exploring the use of Media Archives. *International Criminal Justice Review, 31*(4): 384–404. https://doi.org/10.1177/10575677211041915.

Ceccato, V., Vasquez, L., Langefors, L., Cannabarro, A., & Petersson, R. (2019). *Trygg stadsmiljö: Teori och praktik för brottsförebyggande & trygghetsskapande åtgärder*. KTH. https://www.boverket.se/globalassets/publikationer/dokument/2019/trygg-stadsmiljo.pdf

Chakraborti, N., & Garland, J. (Eds.). (2011). *Rural racism*. Routledge.

Cohen, L. E., & Felson, M. (1979). Social change and crime rate trends: A routine activity approach. *American Sociological Review, 44*, 588–608.

Cohn, E. G., & Rotton, J. (2000, 9//). Weather, Seasonal trends and property crimes in Minneapolis, 1987–1988. A moderator-variable time-series analysis of routine activities. *Journal of Environmental Psychology, 20*(3), 257–272. https://doi.org/10.1006/jevp.1999.0157

Collins, V. E. (2016). The nomadic pastoralist, the fisherman and the pirate. In J. F. Donnermeyer (Ed.), *The Routledge International Handbook of Rural Criminology* (pp. 93–100). Routledge.

Conner, C. T., & Okamura, D. (2021). Queer expectations: An empirical critique of rural LGBT+ narratives. *Sexualities*, 13634607211013280.

Cozens, P. M. (2002, 4//). Sustainable Urban Development and Crime Prevention Through Environmental Design for the British City. Towards an Effective Urban Environmentalism for the 21st Century. *Cities, 19*(2), 129–137. https://doi.org/10.1016/S0264-2751(02)00008-2

Crenshaw, K. (1989). Demarginalizing the Intersection of Race and Sex: A Black Feminist Critique of Antidiscrimination Doctrine, Feminist Theory and Antiracist Politics. 139–167.

DeKeseredy, W. S. (2020). *Woman abuse in rural places*. Routledge.

DeKeseredy, W. S., Dragiewicz, M., & Rennisson, C. M. (2012). Racial/Ethnic Variations in Violence Against Women: Urban, Suburban, and Rural Differences. *International Journal of Rural Criminology, 1*(2).

DeKeseredy, W. S., & Hall-Sanchez, A. (2018). Male violence against women in the Global South: What we know and what we don't know. In *The Palgrave handbook of criminology and the Global South* (pp. 883–900). Springer.

DeKeseredy, W. S., & Joseph, C. (2006, March 1, 2006). Separation and/or Divorce Sexual Assault in Rural Ohio: Preliminary Results of an Exploratory Study. *Violence against women, 12*(3), 301–311. https://doi.org/10.1177/1077801205277357

DeKeseredy, W. S., & Schwartz, M. D. (2008, 2008/07/09). Separation/Divorce Sexual Assault in Rural Ohio: Survivors' Perceptions. *Journal of Prevention & Intervention in the Community, 36*(1–2), 105–119. https://doi.org/10.1080/10852350802022365

Doan, P. L. (2007, 2007/02/01). Queers in the American City: Transgendered perceptions of urban space. *Gender, Place & Culture, 14*(1), 57–74. https://doi.org/10.1080/09663690601122309

Donnermeyer, J. F. (2016). *The Routledge international handbook of rural criminology*. Routledge.

Donnermeyer, J. F. (2018). The rural dimensions of a southern criminology: Selected topics and general processes. In *The Palgrave handbook of criminology and the global south* (pp. 105–120). Springer.

Donnermeyer, J. F., & DeKeseredy, W. S. (2008). Toward a rural critical criminology. *Journal of Rural Social Sciences, 23*(2), 2.

Donnermeyer, J. F., Jobes, P., & Barclay, E. (2006). Rural crime, poverty and rural community. In W. S. DeKeseredy & B. Perry (Eds.), *Advancing Critical Criminology: Theory and Application* (pp. 199–213). Lexington books.

Donnermeyer, J. F., Scott, J., & Carrington, K. (2013). How Rural Criminology Informs Critical Thinking in Criminology. *International Journal for Crime, Justice and Social Democracy, 2*(3), 69–91.

Doyle, A. C. (1981). *The adventure of the copper beeches*. Kartindo. com.

Enticott, G. (2011, 2011/04/01/). Techniques of neutralising wildlife crime in rural England and Wales. *Journal of Rural Studies, 27*(2), 200-208. https://doi.org/10.1016/j.jrurstud.2011.01.005

Eurostat. (2020). Urban and rural living in the EU *Europa-news*. https://ec.europa.eu/eurostat/web/products-eurostat-news/-/edn-20200207-1

Florin, M., & Corneliu, I. (2020). *Sustainable Rural Development under Agenda 2030* Sustainability As sessment at the 21st century, IntechOpen,

Fyfe, N. R., & Reeves, A. D. (2011). The thin Green line? Police perceptions of challenges of policing wildlife crime in Scotland. In R. Mawby & R. Yarwood (Eds.), *Rural policing and policing the rural: a constable countryside?* (pp. 169–182). Ashgate.

Gargiulo, F., Angelino, C. V., Cicala, L., Persechino, G., & Lega, M. (2016). Remote sensing in the fight against environmental crimes: The case study of the cattle-breeding facilities in southern Italy. *International Journal of Sustainable Development and Planning, 11*(5), 663–671. https://doi.org/10.2495/SDP-V11-N5-663-671

Garland, J., & Chakraborti, N. (2006, June 1, 2006). 'Race', Space and Place: Examining Identity and Cultures of Exclusion in Rural England. *Ethnicities, 6*(2), 159–177. https://doi.org/10.1177/1468796806063750

Garland, J., & Chakraborti, N. (2012). Another country? Community, belonging and exclusion in rural England. In N. Chakraborti & J. Garland (Eds.), *Rural racism* (pp. 122–140). Rotledge.

Garriott, W. (2016). Metamphetamine and the canging rhetoric of drugs in the United States. In J. F. Donnermeyer (Ed.), *The Routledge International Handbook of Rural Criminology* (pp. 275–282). Routledge.

Gebre, T., & Gebremedhin, B. (2019). The mutual benefits of promoting rural-urban interdependence through linked ecosystem services. *Global Ecology and Conservation, 20*. https://doi.org/10.1016/j.gecco.2019.e00707.

Giddens, A. (1991). *Modernity and self-identity : self and society in the late modern age*. Polity Press.

Goold, B., Loader, I., & Thumala, A. (2010, February 1, 2010). Consuming security?: Tools for a sociology of security consumption. *Theoretical Criminology, 14*(1), 3–30. https://doi.org/10.1177/1362480609354533

Gorman-Murray, A., Waitt, G., & Gibson, C. (2008). A queer country? A case study of the politics of gay/lesbian belonging in an Australian country town. *Australian Geographer, 39*(2), 171–191.

Greenfields, M. (2014). Gypsies and travellers in modern rural England. In G. Bosworth & P. Somerville (Eds.), *Interpreting rurality: Multiciplinary approaches* (pp. 219–234). Routledge.

Halfacree, K. (1993). Locality and social representation: Space, discourse and alternative definitions of the rural. *Journal of Rural Studies, 9*(1), 23–37.

Hamid, L. A., & Yusof, W. Z. M. (2013, 2013/12/11/). Experiential Approach as a Design Innovation Solution to Prevent House Breaking Crime. *Procedia - Social and Behavioral Sciences, 107*, 145–152. https://doi.org/10.1016/j.sbspro.2014.02.293

Harding, S. (2020). *County lines: Exploitation and drug dealing amongst urban street gangs*. Policy Press.

Harkness, A., & Larkins, J. (2020). Technological approaches to preventing property theft from farms. In A. Harkness (Ed.), *Rural Crime Prevention: Theory, Tactics and Techniques* (pp. 226–244). Routledge.

Hodgkinson, T., & Harkness, A. (2020). Introduction: Rural crime prevention in theory and context. In *Rural Crime Prevention* (pp. 1–16). Routledge.

Hope, T., & Sparks, R. (2000). *Crime, risk, and insecurity: law and order in everyday life and political discourse*. Routledge.

Hughes, L. A., Antonaccio, O., & Botchkovar, E. V. (2020, 2020/03/01). The Crime of Animal Abuse in Two Nonwestern Cities: Prevalence, Perpetrators, and Pathways. *Journal of Quantitative Criminology, 36*(1), 67–94. https://doi.org/10.1007/s10940-019-09417-w

Jansson, A. (2013, February 1, 2013). The Hegemony of the Urban/Rural Divide: Cultural Transformations and Mediatized Moral Geographies in Sweden. *Space and Culture, 16*(1), 88–103. https://doi.org/10.1177/1206331212452816

Jansson, M. (2019). Djuraktivister allt mer hotfulla mot bönder. *Landlantbruk*. https://www.landlantbruk.se/lantbruk/djuraktivister-allt-mer-hotfulla-mot-bonder/

Jensen, M. (2012). *Rasism, missnöje och "Fertile Grounds" Östergötland Sverige jämförs med Birkaland Finland: Sverigedemokraterna vs Sannfinländarna* Linköping University]. Linköping. http://www.diva-portal.org/smash/record.jsf?pid=diva2:479299

Katz, C., & McPherson, T. (2020). Veganism as a Food Ethic. In H. L. Meiselman (Ed.), *Handbook of Eating and Drinking: Interdisciplinary Perspectives* (pp. 1137–1155). Springer International Publishing. https://doi.org/10.1007/978-3-030-14504-0_85

Koch, F., & Ahmad, S. (2018). How to Measure Progress Towards an Inclusive, Safe, Resilient and Sustainable City? Reflections on Applying the Indicators of Sustainable Development Goal 11 in Germany and India. In S. Kabisch, F. Koch, E. Gawel, A. Haase, S. Knapp, K. Krellenberg, J. Nivala, & A. Zehnsdorf (Eds.), *Urban Transformations: Sustainable Urban Development Through Resource Efficiency, Quality of Life and Resilience* (pp. 77–90). Springer International Publishing. https://doi.org/10.1007/978-3-319-59324-1_5

Krannich, R. S., Luloff, E., & Field, D. R. (2011). *People, Places and Landscapes: Social Change in High Amenity Rural Areas*. Springer.

Landman, K. (2007). The storm that rocks the boat: the systemic impact of gated communities on urban sustainability. *Cybergeo: European Journal of Geography*.

Lee, M. R., & Slack, T. (2008). Labor market conditions and violent crime across the metrononmetro divide. *Social Science Research, 37*(3), 753–768. https://doi.org/10.1016/j.ssresearch.2007.09.001

Liedka, R. V., Meehan, A. J., & Lauer, T. W. (2019). CCTV and Campus Crime: Challenging a Technological "Fix". *Criminal Justice Policy Review, 30*(2), 316–338. https://doi.org/10.1177/0887403416664947

Loader, I. (2000, September 1, 2000). Plural Policing and Democratic Governance. *Social & Legal Studies, 9*(3), 323–345. https://doi.org/10.1177/096466390000900301

Lockie, S., & Bourke, L. (2001). *Rurality Bites: The social and environmental transformation of rural Australia*. Pluto.

Loeffler, K. (2013, 2013/10/01). Breeding Wildlife to Extinction in China. *Journal of Applied Animal Welfare Science, 16*(4), 387–387. https://doi.org/10.1080/10888705.2013.827933

Lohnert, B., & Steinbrink, M. (2005, 2005/09/01). Rural and Urban Livelihoods: A Translocal Perspecitve in a South African Context. *South African Geographical Journal, 87*(2), 95–103. https://doi.org/10.1080/03736245.2005.9713832

Lovell, J. S. (forthcoming) Animal rights and activism. In: Harkness, A., Peterson, J., Bowden, M., Pedersen, C., and Donnermeyer, J.F. (Eds.) *The Encyclopedia of Rural Crime*. Bristol, UK: Bristol University Press.

Lowder, S., Sánchez, M. V., & Bertini, R. (2021). Which farms feed the world and has farmland become more concentrated? *World Development, 142*, Article 105455. https://doi.org/10.1016/j.worlddev.2021.105455

LRF – Lantbrukarnas Riksförbund (The Federation of Swedish Farmers). (2020). *Grön entreprenör: Affärsmöjligheter i hela landet*. https://www.lrf.se/imagevault/publishedmedia/q29e0k2et35yvn1wzgba/Gr-n_entrepren-r_3_upplagan_sept_2018.pdf

Maingi, J. K., Mukeka, J. M., Kyale, D. M., & Muasya, R. M. (2012). Spatiotemporal patterns of elephant poaching in south-eastern Kenya. *Wildlife Research, 39*(3), 234–249. https://doi.org/10.1071/WR11017

Mawby, R., & Yarwood, R. (Eds.). (2011). *Rural policing and policing the rural: a constable countryside?* Ashgate.

Mawby, R. I. (2007). Crime, place and explaining rural hotspots. *International Journal of Rural Crime* (1), 21–43. http://pandora.nla.gov.au/pan/81506/20080212-1139/www.ruralfutures.une.edu.au/rurcrime/resources/IJRC/vol1/IJRCV1_3.pdf

Melde, C. (2006). MCJA student paper award winner: Social disorganization and violent crime in rural appalachia. *Journal of Crime and Justice, 29*(2), 117–140. https://doi.org/10.1080/0735648X.2006.9721651

Misgav, C., & Hartal, G. (2019). Queer urban movements from the margin (s)–Activism, politics, space: An editorial introduction. In *Geography Research Forum* (Vol. 39, pp. 1–18).

Monaghan, R. (2013, 2013/11/01). Not Quite Terrorism: Animal Rights Extremism in the United Kingdom. *Studies in Conflict & Terrorism, 36*(11), 933–951. https://doi.org/10.1080/1057610X.2013.832117

Moore, C. G., Probst, J. C., Tompkins, M., Cuffe, S., & Martin, A. B. (2005). *Poverty, stress, and violent disagreements in the home among rural families.*

Mora-Rivera, J., & García-Mora, F. (2021, 2021/03/01/). Internet access and poverty reduction: Evidence from rural and urban Mexico. *Telecommunications Policy, 45*(2), 102076. https://doi.org/10.1016/j.telpol.2020.102076

MUCF – Myndigheten för ungdoms- och civilsamhällesfrågor (Swedish Agency for Youth and Civil Society). (2020). *Uppdrag att stärka förutsättningarna att skapa mötesplatser för unga hbtq-personer.*

Neal, S., Gawlewicz, A., Heley, J., & Jones, R. D. (2021, 2021/02/01/). Rural Brexit? The ambivalent politics of rural community, migration and dependency. *Journal of Rural Studies, 82,* 176–183. https://doi.org/10.1016/j.jrurstud.2021.01.017

Nilsson, A., & Estrada, F. (2006, October 1, 2006). The Inequality of Victimization: Trends in Exposure to Crime among Rich and Poor. *European Journal of Criminology, 3*(4), 387–412. https://doi.org/10.1177/1477370806067910

Nourani, F., Antonello, S. L., Govone, J. S., & Ceccato, V. (2020). Women and LGBTI youth at target: Assessing transit safety in Rio Claro, Brazil. In M. V. Ceccato & Nalla (Ed.), *Crime and fear in public places: Towards safe, inclusive and sustainable cities.* Routledge.

NPCC – The National Police Chiefs Council. (2018). *Rural Affairs Strategy NPCC.*

Nurse, A., & Wyatt, T. (2020). Wildlife criminology. Bristol University Press.

Pasha-Robinson, L. (2018). Vegan animal rights activists are 'sending farmers death threats' branding them 'murderers'. *Independent.* https://www.independent.co.uk/news/uk/home-news/vegan-animal-rights-activists-farmers-death-threats-murderers-veganism-a8183091.html

Philo, C., & Wilbert, C. (2000). Animal Spaces, Beastly Places: An introduction. In C. Philo & C. Wilbert (Eds.), *Animals Spaces, Beastly Places* (pp. 1–36). Routledge.

Robinson, V., & Gardner, G. (2012). Unravelling a stereotype: The lived experience of black and minority ethnic in rural Wales. In N. Chakraborti & J. Garland (Eds.), (pp. 85–107). Routledge.

Rosenberg, R. D. (2021). Negotiating racialised (un) belonging: Black LGBTQ resistance in Toronto's gay village. *Urban Studies, 58*(7), 1397–1413.

Rotton, J., & Cohn, E. G. (2004). Outdoor temperature, climate control, and criminal assault: The spatial and temporal ecology of violence. *Environment and Behavior, 36*(2), 276–306. https://doi.org/10.1177/0013916503259515

Ruddell, R. (2017). *Oil, gas, and crime: The dark side of the boomtown* [Book]. https://doi.org/10.1057/9781137587145

Rutherford, B. (2004). Desired Publics, Domestic Government, and Entangled Fears: On the Anthropology of Civil Society, Farm Workers, and White Farmers in Zimbabwe [Review]. *Cultural Anthropology, 19*(1), 122–153. https://doi.org/10.1525/can.2004.19.1.122

Scott, J., & Biron, D. (2010, 2010/04/01). Wolf Creek, rurality and the Australian gothic. *Continuum, 24*(2), 307–322. https://doi.org/10.1080/10304310903576358

Scott, J., Carrington, K., & McIntosh, A. (2012). Established-Outsider Relations and Fear of Crime in Mining Towns. *Sociologia Ruralis, 52*(2), 147–169. https://doi.org/10.1111/j.1467-9523.2011.00557.x

Sethi, M., & Puppim de Oliveira, J. (2015, 2015/12/01/). From global 'North–South' to local 'Urban–Rural': A shifting paradigm in climate governance? *Urban Climate, 14,* 529–543. https://doi.org/10.1016/j.uclim.2015.09.009

Short, B. (2006). Idyllic Ruralities. In T. M. a. P. H. C. P. J. Marsden (Ed.), *Handbook of Rural Studies* (pp. 133–148). Sage.
Short, J. R. (1991). *Imagined Country : Environment, Culture, and Society*. Routledge.
Shortall, S., & Warner, M. (2012). Rural transformations: Conceptual and Polciy Issues. In M. Shucksmith, D. Brown, S. Shothall, J. Vergunst, & M. Warner (Eds.), *Rural transformations and rural policies in the US and UK* (pp. 3–18). Routledge.
Siwale, J. (2014). Challenging Western perceptions: a case study of rural Zambia. In G. Bosworth & P. Somerville (Eds.), *Interpreting rurality: Multidisciplinary approaches* (pp. 15–30). Routledge.
Smith, R., & McElwee, G. (2013). Confronting Social Constructions of Rural Criminality: A Case Story on 'Illegal Pluriactivity' in the Farming Community. *Sociologia Ruralis, 53*(1), 112–134. https://doi.org/10.1111/j.1467-9523.2012.00580.x
Spocter, M. (2013, 2013/12/01). Rural gated developments as a contributor to post-productivism in the Western Cape. *South African Geographical Journal, 95*(2), 165–186. https://doi.org/10.1080/03736245.2013.847801
Squire, S. J. (1993). Valuing Countryside: Reflections on Beatrix Potter Tourism. *Area, 25*(1), 5–10. https://doi.org/10.2307/20003206
Stassen, R., & Ceccato, V. (2019). Police Accessibility in Sweden: An Analysis of the Spatial Arrangement of Police Services. *Policing: A Journal of Policy and Practice*. https://doi.org/10.1093/police/paz068
Steeves, G. M., Petterini, F. C., & Moura, G. V. (2015, 2015/09/01/). The interiorization of Brazilian violence, policing, and economic growth. *EconomiA, 16*(3), 359–375. https://doi.org/10.1016/j.econ.2015.09.003
Stenbacka, S. (2021). Local policing in a global countryside – combating drugs in rural areas. *The Professional Geographer*.
Swedish National Food Agency. (2021). *Meat – beef, lamb, pork and chicken*. https://www.livsmedelsverket.se/en/food-habits-health-and-environment/food-and-environment/eco-smart-food-choice/meat%2D%2Dbeef-lamb-pork-and-chicken
Tapiador, F. J. (2008). *Rural Analysis and Management: An Earth Science Approach to Rural Science*. Springer.
Torske, M. O., Hilt, B., Glasscock, D., Lundqvist, P., & Krokstad, S. (2016, 2016/01/02). Anxiety and Depression Symptoms Among Farmers: The HUNT Study, Norway. *Journal of Agromedicine, 21*(1), 24–33. https://doi.org/10.1080/1059924X.2015.1106375
Tseloni, A., Mailley, J., Farrell, G., & Tilley, N. (2010, September 1, 2010). Exploring the international decline in crime rates. *European Journal of Criminology, 7*(5), 375–394. https://doi.org/10.1177/1477370810367014
UN-Habitat. (2019). *Safer Cities Programme*. UN-Habitat. Retrieved 12-02-2020 from https://unhabitat.org/safer-cities
UN – United Nations. (2015). *Transforming our World: The 2030 Agenda for Sustainable Development*. https://www.unfpa.org/resources/transforming-our-world-2030-agenda-sustainable-development
United Nations. (2019). *Communications material*. Retrieved November 5 from https://www.un.org/sustainabledevelopment/news/communications-material/
United Nations. (n.d.). *Sustainable Development Goals*. Retrieved 14 Oct from https://www.un.org/sustainabledevelopment/sustainable-development-goals/
van Dun, M. (2014). Exploring Narco-Sovereignty/Violence: Analyzing Illegal Networks, Crime, Violence, and Legitimation in a Peruvian Cocaine Enclave (2003–2007). *Journal of Contemporary Ethnography, 43*(4), 395–418. /https://doi.org/10.1177/0891241613520452
Wangüemert, M. M. (2001). La Pampa : Historia de una pasión argentina [The pampas: A Argentinian Passion]. *Escuela de Estudios Hispano-Americanos de Sevilla* 357–369.
Websdale, N. (1998). *Rural Woman Battering and the Justice System: An Ethnography*. Sage.
Weisheit, R. A., & Brownstein, H. (2016). Drug production in the rural context. In J. F. Donnermeyer (Ed.), *The Routledge International Handbook Of Rural Criminology* (pp. 235–241). Routledge.
Weisheit, R. A., Wells, L. E., & Falcone, D. N. (1994, October 1, 1994). Community Policing in Small Town and Rural America. *Crime & Delinquency, 40*(4), 549–567. https://doi.org/10.1177/0011128794040004005

Weisheit, R. A., Peterson, J. R., & Pytlarz, A. (Eds.). (2022). Research Methods for Rural Criminologists. Routledge.

Wellsmith, M. (2011). Wildlife Crime: The Problems of Enforcement. *European Journal on Criminal Policy and Research, 17*(2), 125–148. https://doi.org/10.1007/s10610-011-9140-4

White, R. (2013). The conceptual contours of green criminology. In Emerging issues in green criminology (pp. 17-33). Palgrave Macmillan, London.

White, R. (2021). Theorising Green Criminology: Selected Essays. Routledge.

Woods, M. (2005). Defining the rural. In *Rural Geography* (pp. 3–16). Sage.

Woods, M. (2007, 2007/08/01). Engaging the global countryside: globalization, hybridity and the reconstitution of rural place. *Progress in Human Geography, 31*(4), 485–507. https://doi.org/10.1177/0309132507079503

Woods, M. (2011). *Rural*. Routledge.

World Bank. (2020). *Agriculture, forestry, and fishing, value added (% of GDP)*. https://data.worldbank.org/indicator/NV.AGR.TOTL.ZS

World Bank. (2021, 2021-10-04). *Agriculture and Food – Overview*. Retrieved 14 Oct from https://www.worldbank.org/en/topic/agriculture/overview#1s

Yarwood, R. (2001). Crime and Policing in the British Countryside: Some Agendas for Contemporary Geographical Research. *Sociologia Ruralis, 41*(2), 201–219. https://doi.org/10.1111/1467-9523.00178

Yarwood, R. (2015, 2015/06/01/). Lost and hound: The more-than-human networks of rural policing. *Journal of Rural Studies, 39*, 278–286. https://doi.org/10.1016/j.jrurstud.2014.11.005

Yarwood, R. (2021). The Geographies of Crime and Policing in the Global Countryside. *The Professional Geographer*.

Yarwood, R., & Edwards, B. (1995, 1995/10/01/). Voluntary action in rural areas: the case of neighbourhood watch. *Journal of Rural Studies, 11*(4), 447–459. https://doi.org/10.1016/0743-0167(95)00030-5

Zhang, S., Tang, J., Li, W., & Zheng, G. (2020, 2020/06/01/). Does gating make residents feel safer? Evidence from the gated villages of Beijing. *Cities, 101*, 102676. https://doi.org/10.1016/j.cities.2020.102676

Open Access This chapter is licensed under the terms of the Creative Commons Attribution 4.0 International License (http://creativecommons.org/licenses/by/4.0/), which permits use, sharing, adaptation, distribution and reproduction in any medium or format, as long as you give appropriate credit to the original author(s) and the source, provide a link to the Creative Commons license and indicate if changes were made.

The images or other third party material in this chapter are included in the chapter's Creative Commons license, unless indicated otherwise in a credit line to the material. If material is not included in the chapter's Creative Commons license and your intended use is not permitted by statutory regulation or exceeds the permitted use, you will need to obtain permission directly from the copyright holder.

Chapter 3
Current Knowledge on Crime and Safety in Rural Areas

This chapter reports on the growing body of literature on crime and safety in rural areas. The international literature is quite definitive about the complexity of rural areas and how their nature affects crime, safety perceptions, policing, and practices of crime prevention. In order to show evidence of this rich and vast body of research, we have executed a systematic review of four decades of English-language publications (in Scopus, JSTOR, and ScienceDirect) from 1980 to 2020 (Moher et al. 2009),[1] including articles, books, and book chapters, and excluding so-called gray literature as much as possible. We characterize the research on crime and safety in rural areas; highlight some of the most important themes, such as policing and crime prevention; and emphasize the importance of the interdisciplinary nature of the field.

Out of the 840 initially identified publications in total, 410 were found to be eligible publications, of which 78% were journal articles and the remainder were books and book chapters. By assigning themes to each publication, we were able to categorize the research into 12 themes (Fig. 3.1). This review in general, and the identified themes in particular, illustrate that rural criminology is a rich field of research that contributes to both criminology and numerous other related disciplines, such as rural studies and policing. In this chapter, we summarize some of the main findings, while in Chap. 4, we discuss the research in more detail, including examples.

Most reviewed publications dealt with trends and patterns of crime, at different degrees, in one or more rural areas (21%), followed by studies on rural police,

---

[1] We adopted the systematic review protocol of type PRISMA-P 2015 (Moher et al. 2015) using a vast array of keywords; for more information about the methodology, see Abraham and Ceccato (forthcoming). We avoided studies dealing with emergency services overall and focused instead on the governance of safety issues, namely, the role of the police and policing. While we do include rural fears not solely based on crime but also on the "other," we do not include, for example, farmers' fear of GMO development, or safety perceptions in terms of fear and anxiety due to natural hazards such as hurricanes, and similar.

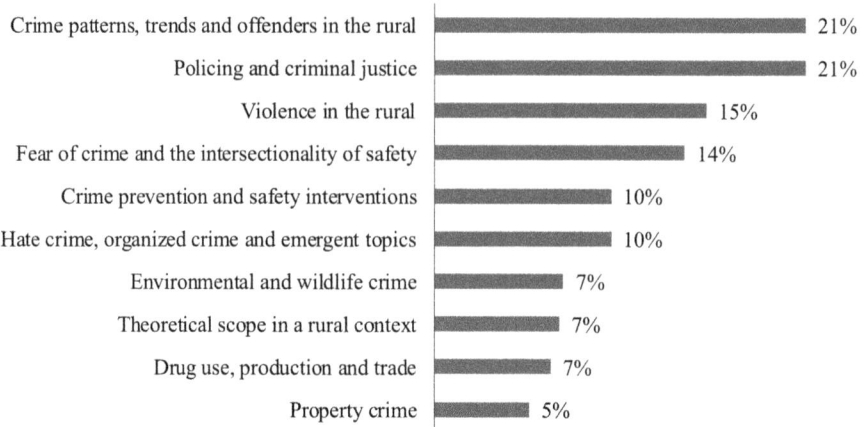

Fig. 3.1 Research on rural crime and safety 1980–2020 collected in Scopus, JSTOR, and ScienceDirect ($N = 410$), where each publication was assigned a maximum of two themes. Source: Based on Abraham and Ceccato (forthcoming)

policing, and the rest of the criminal justice system, including the court system and prison industry (21%) (Fig. 3.1).

This theme on crime trends in rural areas covered over a fifth (21%, $n = 85$) of the publications reviewed for this book, mainly from North America, followed by British and Australian cases. Most of these studies utilized secondary data and official records (56%), and/or performed statistical analyses (35%). Studies of crime trends in the Global South were often published more recently, for example, China (Cheong and Wu 2015), Brazil (Scorzafave et al. 2015), Haiti (Brewis et al. 2020), Zimbabwe (Mafumbabete et al. 2019), and Nigeria (Osakwe and Osakwe 2015).

Regarding the theme on policing and the criminal justice system, despite it being one of the earliest and most covered topics of research, systematic studies of rural policing were rare before the 1970s (Payne et al. 2005). Some of the more comprehensive studies were published in the late twentieth century, such as the studies by Weisheit et al. (1995) and Sims (1988). The methods used in these studies were mainly secondary data (34%), interviews (24%), surveys (17%), and statistical analyses (15%). These studies were affiliated with universities in the United States followed by the United Kingdom, but also a number of other countries, such as Canada, Sweden, Australia, and Tanzania.

Violence is the theme of 15% of the reviewed publications, often focusing on domestic violence and violence against women but some focusing on general "street violence" and other types of assaults in public places. Fear of crime was also a major theme with 57 publications, of which 78% were related to fear of crime in rural contexts, 10% to fear of "others," and 12% to both or other related anxieties. Rural crime prevention also appeared in a notable number of the studies (10%), of which 46% covered police-based prevention and community efforts, 22% focused on the use of different types of technologies in situational crime prevention, such security alarms and CCTVs, and the rest covered both types. Within our time frame, the earliest study in this theme of crime prevention appeared in 1986 (Shernock 1986), while 41% of this research were published after 2015. The most used methods were surveys (37%), followed by secondary data (34%), and interviews and statistical analyses (22%). Crime prevention in the United States was studied the most, followed by Australia, Sweden, and Tanzania.

Another common subject was perceptions of safety and fear of crime in rural contexts, accounting for 14% ($n = 59$) of our reviewed publications. Fear in rural areas has been written about comparably longer than other themes, as more publications were published before 2010 than after. Surveys (53%) followed by interviews (22%) were the most used methods. Although the sample was dominated by the northern hemisphere, studies of safety in rural contexts are also found in Australia and New Zealand, as well as countries of the Global South including India, Mexico and Central America, Pakistan, and Turkey.

Rural crime prevention and interventions for improving safety was identified as a theme in 10% of the publications. The earliest study within our time frame appeared in 1986 (Shernock 1986), while 41% of the studies were published after 2015. The most frequently used methods were surveys (37%), followed by secondary data (34%), and interviews and statistical analyses (22%). Most publications focused on preventing crime in rural America, while Australia, Sweden, and Tanzania were present in more studies than the United Kingdom.

The international literature from 1980 to 2020 shows that the theme Environmental and Wildlife Crime (EWC) covered 7% of all the reviewed publications ($n = 30$). Research on environmental crime has mainly been conducted in the past decade, with 94% having been published in 2011–2020. Among the methods identified ($n = 45$), most publications utilized secondary data in their analysis (27%), followed by interviews (19%) as well as reviews of other research and other theoretical pieces (14%). In this theme, the United States is the most studied area (22%), followed by the United Kingdom and Sweden (19% each). Studies on the Global South include examples from Brazil, Indonesia, and Ghana.

Drugs in rural areas were part of 7% of the publications in the literature review. While there have been several comprehensive studies on drugs within rural criminology, findings have to some extent been limited to the context of the United States, providing little perspective on drug behavior, production or markets in rural areas in, for example, Europe or the Global South. Exceptions to this were a handful of studies from Australia, the United Kingdom, Canada, Sweden, Norway, Brazil, Peru, Bolivia, and Thailand. Many of the studies used interviews as their main method (37%), followed by secondary data analysis (33%), and use of statistical analyses such as regression models (26%). The most common topic was substance abuse, especially related to the rural youth, although in studies in the Global South it is more common to examine rural drug production.

Several studies on crime trends may have included data on property crime, but only 5% ($n = 22$) of the reviewed publications covered rural property crime as a distinct theme. Of these, close to 60% were published in the span of 2010-2020. Surveys were the most common method, used in 32% of the studies, while statistical analyses such as regression models were applied in 26% of the articles. The most common study areas were the United States and the United Kingdom, followed by Sweden, Australia, and Malaysia. Studies would often investigate rural rates of property crime overall, but specific types such as burglaries and farm-related thefts were also common.

Among the minor topics, we find hate crime, organized crime, as well as other more emergent topics within rural criminology. Hate crime has been a largely unstudied area in rural criminology with only 18 identified publications (4%) in our selected time period. Secondary data (19%) and interviews (15%) were the most frequent methods among the studies, followed by surveys and literature reviews (11% each). Notably, India and the United Kingdom were the two most studied areas, followed by Brazil and the United States.

Organized crime constituted a similar size as hate crime, with total of 4% ($n = 17$) of the reviewed publications. Roughly two-fifths (41.7%) of the publications used interviews as a method for data collection, while nearly one-fifth (19%) employed field work. The United States was the most frequent studied area, followed by British examples. Other studies were mainly situated in Latin America, including Peru, Brazil, Mexico, and Cuba.

Other topics that could not be classified into the other themes and those considered more emergent comprised 2% of the reviewed publications ($n = 8$). All of these were published in 2011–2020. This research was dominated by examples from the Global South, including India, Bangladesh, Ghana, and China. Here secondary data were utilized in 38% of the publications, with interviews and literature reviews in a quarter each. This theme included rare topics such as rural corruption (Banerjee et al. 2014; Cheng and Urpelainen 2019) and rural prostitution, as in Scott (2016).

In most of these studies, there is a recognition that criminology has for decades relied on urban understandings of rural crime and rural offenders. Some recently published studies have expanded the urban-centric framework, calling for theoretical and empirical models that can better explain the mechanisms behind crime in areas on the rural-urban continuum. This research has also focused on understandings of the intersections of demographic, ethnic, and socioeconomic factors; cultural contexts; and situational conditions that are typical to rural areas.

Research findings from multiple studies indicate that, over the years, crime has decreased overall in many parts of the world, but there are major variations between indicators and crime types. Historically, rural areas in most countries exhibited lower crime rates than urban areas (with a few exceptions), but lately rural areas are showing higher increases than (some) urban areas for certain types of crime. During the past decades, there have been signs that rural and urban crime rates are converging (urban decreasing and rural increasing), but crime underreporting and definitional, theoretical, and methodological difficulties in comparing crime rates across geographies still limit the analyses of crime trends (e.g. Ceccato, 2016). In quantitative studies, the implementation of "rural" as an analytical category can vary significantly, not only between countries but also between studies in a single country; see examples in the United States, Sweden, and Brazil in the next chapter.

In addition, the reviewed publications show how crime prevention programs have been urban-centric as well, meaning they are often imported from urban areas and directly applied in a way that ignores the uniqueness of rural contexts. Therefore, studies indicate that there is need for comparative analyses based on more than *just* rural-urban dichotomies, in particular in relation to crime prevention and police practices. A future approach that recognizes rural-urban interlinkages would further cement the complexities of rural areas without the need for comparisons with the urban norm, which may not be an appropriate reference in the first place.

A small set of the reviewed studies examine the spatial and temporal characteristics of rural crime. The literature has also identified some of the typical offenders in rural areas, as well as how deviant behavior may be normalized among the local population. There have been studies on how globalization, organized crime, new ideological trends, and ICT have influenced criminogenic conditions in the countryside (e.g., computer-based fraud, illegal animal rights activism, animal abuse, drugs, wage theft, slavery, racism).

Authors were most frequently affiliated with universities and colleges in the United States (41%), while British institutions came second, followed by Australian, Swedish, and Canadian universities. More recently, book chapters and articles have also been published by authors in and about the Global South, namely, India, Malaysia, Brazil, China, and a few African countries. Publications by female lead authors ($n_{female} = 143$) were most common in the United States, Sweden, the United Kingdom, Australia, and Canada. Of the female lead authors *not* at universities and colleges in these five countries, most were in the Global South ($n_{female} = 26$) rather than other countries in the Global North ($n_{female} = 7$). Figure 3.2 shows the reviewed publications by (a) university affiliation (when the affiliation of the first author(s) could be identified) and by (b) study area.

In terms of methods, approximately half the reviewed publications utilized qualitative methods, a third quantitative methods, and the rest a mix of qualitative and quantitative methods (Fig. 3.3). Yet, studies showed major variations in methodology.

From 1980 to 2000, the number of publications grew slowly, but a major increase occurred after 2011. This review follows and complements the existent compilations of literature by Hubbard et al. (1980), by Marshall and Johnson (2005), and on rural policing by Tucker (2015), as these reviews were neither systematic (Higgins and Green 2011) nor comprehensive (see also Weisheit (2016)). Interestingly, one of the earliest publications in our time frame was a compilation of North American literature on rural crime prevention and criminal justice (Hubbard et al. 1980) that reviewed also studies dating back to the early nineteenth century on rural-urban differences in crime and victimization. Also of note is an early article written by Laub (1981) which assessed the variation in crime reporting to the police among victims in urban, suburban, and rural areas. And one of the most recent articles from 2020 by Arisukwu et al. (2020) reported examples of informal crime prevention practices in rural Nigeria, which showed (via surveys) that poor safety perceptions are linked to crime victimization and poor police presence.

Fig. 3.2 (**a**) Reviewed publications on rural crime and safety 1980-2020 by university affiliation (first author)

3 Current Knowledge on Crime and Safety in Rural Areas

Fig. 3.2 (**b**) Reviewed publications on rural crime and safety 1980-2020 by study area. Source: Based on Abraham and Ceccato (forthcoming)

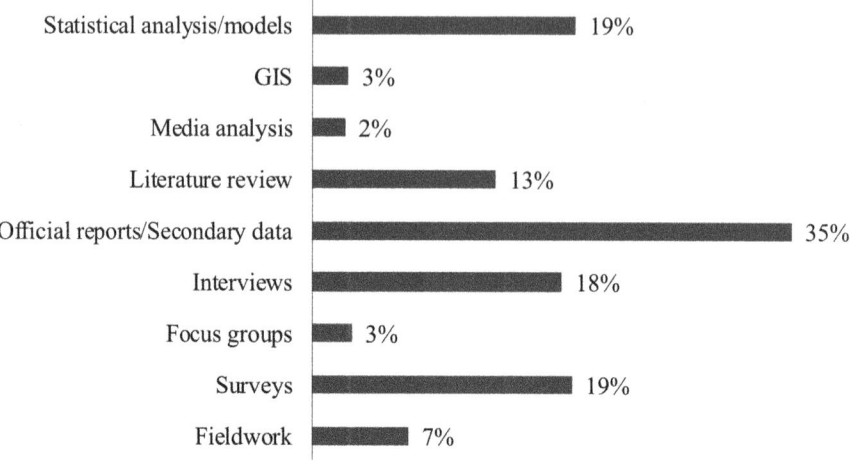

Fig. 3.3 Methods utilized in the reviewed publications on rural crime and safety 1980–2020 (*N* = 410). Studies were assigned one or more methods. Source: Based on Abraham and Ceccato (forthcoming)

Different theoretical traditions characterize the studies over these four decades. The theme encompassing theory in rural criminology covers 7% of the reviewed publications (Fig. 3.1). These studies have expanded on definitions, concepts, and theoretical models. Half of the studies were published between 2015 and 2020, and were often written by authors in the United States and the United Kingdom but also in France, Slovenia, and Australia (Barclay 2017; Harris and Harkness 2016; Hodgkinson and Harkness 2020; Meško 2020; Mouhanna 2016).

Social disorganization theory is among the most common criminological approaches to explain rural crime. Although contemporary criminology associates social disorganization with urban areas and the Chicago School, the concept actually emerged from studies of rural Europe (for an in-depth discussion, see Rogers and Pridemore (2016)). In its North American version, social disorganization theory suggests that structural disadvantage breeds crime and that offending occurs when impaired social bonds are insufficient to enforce legitimate behavior and discourage offending. The legacy of social disorganization (Bursik 1999; Kornhauser 1978; Sampson 1986; Shaw and McKay 1942) has been observed in many contexts. Population size, mobility and instability, income, unemployment, and degree of urbanization are conditions that have consistently been found to relate to crime (Allen and Cancino 2012; Barnett and Mencken 2002; Fafchamps and Minten 2006; Jobes 1999; Ukert et al. 2018). Although Jobes et al. (2004) found support for the theory in rural areas, economic factors showed weaker relationships with crime than social factors such as population diversity and family stability.

Other theories in environmental criminology also comprises an integral part of the reviewed rural crime literature, including applications of routine activity theory and situational crime prevention to rural areas in different countries (e.g., Aransiola and Ceccato 2020; Ceccato 2015; Harkness 2020; Harris and Harkness 2016). One example includes the analysis of environmental crime. While the first studies in this area were concerned with crime geography and prevention (e.g., Ceccato and Uittenbogaard 2013; Cowan et al. 2020; Maingi et al. 2012; Stassen and Ceccato 2020), new research of a more "tactical" nature is emerging, for example, detecting a place's equivalent to a "fingerprint," which is important information for crime investigation and prevention (Lega et al. 2014).

Finally, critical perspectives on rural criminology and the intersectionality of safety heavily dominated the past two decades of reviewed studies, with numerous contributions from North America, Australia, and the United Kingdom (Carrington et al. 2014; DeKeseredy et al. 2007; Donnermeyer 2007, 2012, 2017, 2018; Donnermeyer and DeKeseredy 2013; Donnermeyer et al. 2013; Garland and Chakraborti 2006; Robinson and Gardner 2012; Rogers and Pridemore 2016; Smith and McElwee 2013; Somerville et al. 2015; Yarwood 2010; Yarwood and Edwards 1995) and also from Green Criminology (White 2013; Nurse and Whyatt 2020).

In summary, although studies in rural criminology have been testing a diverse set of theoretical traditions, in the next chapter we show examples of how the discipline is slowly expanding to theoretical perspectives beyond the boundaries of criminology. Examples include, for instance, studies involving engineering, computer science but also psychology, architecture, and geography. An example of this trend is analyzing how police and voluntary organizations use social media to engage communities in sparsely populated areas. In Chaps. 4, 5, 6, and 7, we draw attention to a selection of research fields on crime and safety in areas on the rural-urban continuum.

References

Abraham, J., & Ceccato, V. (forthcoming). Crime and safety in rural areas: A systematic review of the English-language literature 1980–2020. *Journal of Rural Studies*.

Allen, J., & Cancino, J. M. (2012, 2012/03/01/). Social disorganization, Latinos and juvenile crime in the Texas borderlands. *Journal of Criminal Justice, 40*(2), 152–163. https://doi.org/10.1016/j.jcrimjus.2012.02.007

Aransiola, T. J., & Ceccato, V. (2020). The role of modern technology in rural situational crime prevention. A review of the literature. In *Rural Crime Prevention* (1st ed., pp. 58–72). Routledge. https://doi.org/10.4324/9780429460135-6

Arisukwu, O., Igbolekwu, C., Oye, J., Oyeyipo, E., Asamu, F., Rasak, B., & Oyekola, I. (2020, 2020/09/01/). Community participation in crime prevention and control in rural Nigeria. *Heliyon, 6*(9), e05015. https://doi.org/10.1016/j.heliyon.2020.e05015

Banerjee, A., Green, D. P., McManus, J., & Pande, R. (2014). Are poor voters indifferent to whether elected leaders are criminal or corrupt? A vignette experiment in rural India. *Political Communication, 31*(3), 391–407. https://doi.org/10.1080/10584609.2014.914615

Barclay, E. M. (2017). Rural crime. In *The Palgrave Handbook of Australian and New Zealand Criminology, Crime and Justice* (pp. 285–297). https://doi.org/10.1007/978-3-319-55747-2_19

Barnett, C., & Mencken, F. C. (2002). Social disorganization theory and the contextual nature of crime in nonmetropolitan counties. *Rural Sociology, 67*(3), 372–393. https://doi.org/10.1111/j.1549-0831.2002.tb00109.x

Brewis, A., Wutich, A., Galvin, M., & Lachaud, J. (2020, 2020/05/15/). Localizing syndemics: A comparative study of hunger, stigma, suffering, and crime exposure in three Haitian communities. *Social Science & Medicine*, 113031. https://doi.org/10.1016/j.socscimed.2020.113031

Bursik, R. J. (1999, 1999/02/01). The Informal Control of Crime Through Neighborhood Networks. *Sociological Focus, 32*(1), 85–97. https://doi.org/10.1080/00380237.1999.10571125

Carrington, K., Donnermeyer, J. F., & DeKeseredy, W. S. (2014). Intersectionality, rural criminology, and re-imaging the boundaries of critical criminology. *Critical Criminology, 22*, 463–477.

Ceccato, V. (2016) Rural crime and community safety. London and New York: Routledge.

Ceccato, V. (2015). Rural crime and community safety. *Journal of Rural Studies, 39*, 157–159. https://doi.org/10.1016/j.jrurstud.2015.04.001

Ceccato, V., & Uittenbogaard, A. C. (2013). Environmental and Wildlife Crime in Sweden. *International Journal of Rural Criminology, 2*(1), 23–50. http://kb.osu.edu/dspace/handle/1811/51122

Cheng, C. Y., & Urpelainen, J. (2019). Criminal Politicians and Socioeconomic Development: Evidence from Rural India. *Studies in Comparative International Development, 54*(4), 501–527. https://doi.org/10.1007/s12116-019-09290-5

Cheong, T. S., & Wu, Y. (2015). Crime rates and inequality: a study of crime in contemporary China. *Journal of the Asia Pacific Economy, 20*(2), 202–223. https://doi.org/10.1080/1354786 0.2014.964961

Cowan, D., Moreto, W. D., Burton, C., Nobles, M. R., & Singh, R. (2020, 2020/08/01). Applying Crime Pattern Theory and Risk Terrain Modeling to Examine Environmental Crime in Cambodia. *Journal of Contemporary Criminal Justice, 36*(3), 327–350. https://doi.org/10.1177/1043986220923467

DeKeseredy, W. S., Donnermeyer, J. F., Schwartz, M. D., Tunnell, K., & Hall, M. (2007, 2007/12/01). Thinking Critically About Rural Gender Relations: Toward a Rural Masculinity Crisis/Male Peer Support Model of Separation/Divorce Sexual Assault. *Critical Criminology, 15*(4), 295-311. https://doi.org/10.1007/s10612-007-9038-0

Donnermeyer, J. F. (2007). Rural Crime: Roots and Restoration. *International journal of rural crime, 1*, 2–20. http://dx.doi.org/

Donnermeyer, J. F. (2012). Rural crime and critical criminology. In W. S. DeKeseredy & M. Dragiewicz (Eds.), *Routledge Handbook of Critical Criminology*. Routledge

Donnermeyer, J. F. (2017). The place of rural in a southern criminology. *International Journal for Crime, Justice and Social Democracy, 6*(1), 118.

Donnermeyer, J. F. (2018). The rural dimensions of a southern criminology: Selected topics and general processes. In *The Palgrave handbook of criminology and the global south* (pp. 105–120). Springer.

Donnermeyer, J. F., & DeKeseredy, W. S. (2013). *Rural criminology*. Routledge.

Donnermeyer, J. F., Scott, J., & Carrington, K. (2013). How Rural Criminology Informs Critical Thinking in Criminology. *International Journal for Crime, Justice and Social Democracy, 2*(3), 69–91.

Fafchamps, M., & Minten, B. (2006). Crime, transitory poverty, and isolation: Evidence from Madagascar. *Economic Development and Cultural Change, 54*(3), 579–603. https://doi.org/10.1086/500028

Garland, J., & Chakraborti, N. (2006, June 1, 2006). 'Race', Space and Place: Examining Identity and Cultures of Exclusion in Rural England. *Ethnicities, 6*(2), 159–177. https://doi.org/10.1177/1468796806063750

Harkness, A. (2020). *Rural Crime Prevention: Theory, Tactics and Techniques*.

Harris, B., & Harkness, A. (2016). Introduction: Locating Regional, Rural, and Remote Crime in Theoretical and Contemporary Context. In *Locating crime in context and place: Perspectives on regional, rural and remote Australia*. Federation Press.

Higgins, J. P. T., & Green, S. (2011). *Cochrane Handbook for Systematic Reviews of Interventions* http://handbook.cochrane.org/

Hodgkinson, T., & Harkness, A. (2020). Introduction: Rural crime prevention in theory and context. In *Rural Crime Prevention* (pp. 1–16). Routledge.

References

Hubbard, R. D., Horton, D. M., & Duncan, S. T. S. (1980). *Rural crime and criminal justice: A Selected Bibliography*. https://www.ojp.gov/pdffiles1/Digitization/69221NCJRS.pdf

Jobes, P. C. (1999). Residential Stability and Crime in Small Rural Agricultural and Recreational Towns. *Sociological Perspectives, 42*(3), 499–524. https://doi.org/10.2307/1389700

Jobes, P. C., Barclay, E., Weinand, H., & Donnermeyer, J. F. (2004). A structural analysis of social disorganisation and crime in rural communities in Australia [Review]. *Australian and New Zealand Journal of Criminology, 37*(1), 114–140. https://doi.org/10.1375/acri.37.1.114

Kornhauser, R. (1978). *Social sources of delinquency*. University of Chicago Press.

Laub, J. H. (1981, 1981/01/01/). Ecological considerations in victim reporting to the police. *Journal of Criminal Justice, 9*(6), 419–430. https://doi.org/10.1016/0047-2352(81)90088-X

Lega, M., Ferrara, C., Persechino, G., & Bishop, P. (2014, 2014/12/01). Remote sensing in environmental police investigations: aerial platforms and an innovative application of thermography to detect several illegal activities. *Environmental Monitoring and Assessment, 186*(12), 8291–8301. https://doi.org/10.1007/s10661-014-4003-3

Mafumbabete, C., Chivhenge, E., Museva, T., Zingi, G. K., & Ndongwe, M. R. (2019). Mapping the spatial variations in crime in rural Zimbabwe using geographic information systems. *Cogent Social Sciences, 5*(1), Article 1661606. https://doi.org/10.1080/23311886.2019.1661606

Maingi, J. K., Mukeka, J. M., Kyale, D. M., & Muasya, R. M. (2012). Spatiotemporal patterns of elephant poaching in south-eastern Kenya. *Wildlife Research, 39*(3), 234–249. https://doi.org/10.1071/WR11017

Marshall, B., & Johnson, S. (2005). *Crime in rural areas: A review of the literature for the rural evidence research centre*.

Meško, G. (2020). Rural criminology–A challenge for the future. *European journal of crime, criminal law and criminal justice, 28*(1), 3–13.

Moher, D., Liberati, A., Tetzlaff, J., Altman, D. G., & The PRISMA Group. (2009). Preferred Reporting Items for Systematic Reviews and Meta-Analyses: The PRISMA
Statement. *PLoS Med, 6*(7), Article e1000097. https://doi.org/10.1371/journal.pmed1000097.

Moher, D., Shamseer, L., Clarke, M., et al. (2015). Preferred reporting items for systematic review and meta-analysis protocol (PRISMA -P) 2015 statement. *Syst Rev 4*(1). https://doi.org/10.1186/2046-4053-4-1.

Mouhanna, C. (2016). From myth to myth: Rural criminology in France. In *The routledge international handbook of rural criminology* (pp. 65–73). Routledge.

Nurse, A., & Wyatt, T. (2020). Wildlife criminology. Bristol University Press.

Osakwe, E., & Osakwe, M. (2015). Rural decay, resource control, and the dynamics of youth unemployment and crime in Nigeria. *International Journal of Interdisciplinary Global Studies, 10*(4), 1–14. https://doi.org/10.18848/2324-755X/CGP/v10i04/53386

Payne, B. K., Berg, B. L., & Sun, I. Y. (2005, 2005/01/01/). Policing in small town America: Dogs, drunks, disorder, and dysfunction. *Journal of Criminal Justice, 33*(1), 31-41. https://doi.org/10.1016/j.jcrimjus.2004.10.006

Robinson, V., & Gardner, G. (2012). Unravelling a stereotype: The lived experience of black and minority ethnic in rural Wales. In N. Chakraborti & J. Garland (Eds.), (pp. 85–107). Routledge.

Rogers, E., & Pridemore, W. A. (2016). Research on social disorganization theory and crime in rural communities. In *The Routledge international handbook of rural criminology* (pp. 23–31). Routledge.

Sampson, R. J. (1986). Crime in cities: the Effects of formal and informal social control. *Crime and Justice, 8*, 271–311.

Scorzafave, L. G., Justus, M., & Shikida, P. F. A. (2015, 2015/06/01/). Safety in the global south: Criminal victimization in Brazilian rural areas. *Journal of Rural Studies, 39*, 247–261. https://doi.org/10.1016/j.jrurstud.2014.12.002

Scott, J. (2016). Rural prostitution. In J. F. Donnermeyer (Ed.), *The Routledge International Handbook of Rural Criminology* (pp. 75–82). Routledge.

Shaw, C. R., & McKay, H. D. (1942). *Juvenile delinquency and urban areas*. University of Chicago Press.

Shernock, S. K. (1986, 1986/01/01/). A profile of the citizen crime prevention activist. *Journal of Criminal Justice, 14*(3), 211–228. https://doi.org/10.1016/0047-2352(86)90002-4

Sims, V. H. (1988). Small town and Rural Police. In. C. C. Thomas.

Smith, R., & McElwee, G. (2013). Confronting Social Constructions of Rural Criminality: A Case Story on 'Illegal Pluriactivity' in the Farming Community. *Sociologia Ruralis, 53*(1), 112-134. https://doi.org/10.1111/j.1467-9523.2012.00580.x

Somerville, P., Smith, R., & McElwee, G. (2015, 2015/06/01/). The dark side of the rural idyll: Stories of illegal/illicit economic activity in the UK countryside. *Journal of Rural Studies, 39*, 219–228. https://doi.org/10.1016/j.jrurstud.2014.12.001

Stassen, R., & Ceccato, V. (2020). Environmental and Wildlife Crime (EWC) in Sweden 2000-2017. *Journal of Contemporary Criminal Justice*.

Tucker, R. D. (2015). *R ural crime and policing: Literature Review*. http://www.dyfedpowys-pcc.org.uk/media/2694/ruralcrimeandpolicingliteraturereview2015.pdf

Ukert, B., Wiebe, D. J., & Humphreys, D. K. (2018, 2018/10/01/). Regional differences in the impact of the "Stand Your Ground" law in Florida. *Preventive Medicine, 115*, 68–75. https://doi.org/10.1016/j.ypmed.2018.08.010

Weisheit, R., Edward, L., & Falcone, D. N. (1995). *Crime and Policing in Rural and Small-Town America*. Waveland Pr Inc.

Weisheit, R. A. (2016). Rural Crime: A Global Perspective. *International Journal of Rural Criminology, 3*(1), 23.

White, R. (2013). The conceptual contours of green criminology. In Emerging issues in green criminology (pp. 17–33). Palgrave Macmillan, London.

Yarwood, R. (2010, 2010/03/01). An exclusive countryside? Crime concern, social exclusion and community policing in two English villages. *Policing and Society, 20*(1), 61–78. https://doi.org/10.1080/10439461003611500

Yarwood, R., & Edwards, B. (1995). Voluntary Action in Rural Areas: the Case of Neighbourhood Watch. *Journal of Rural Studies, 11*(4), 447–459. https://doi.org/10.1016/0743-0167(95)00030-5

Open Access This chapter is licensed under the terms of the Creative Commons Attribution 4.0 International License (http://creativecommons.org/licenses/by/4.0/), which permits use, sharing, adaptation, distribution and reproduction in any medium or format, as long as you give appropriate credit to the original author(s) and the source, provide a link to the Creative Commons license and indicate if changes were made.

The images or other third party material in this chapter are included in the chapter's Creative Commons license, unless indicated otherwise in a credit line to the material. If material is not included in the chapter's Creative Commons license and your intended use is not permitted by statutory regulation or exceeds the permitted use, you will need to obtain permission directly from the copyright holder.

Chapter 4
Crime, Offenders, and Victims

In this chapter, we discuss examples of crime trends in areas on the rural-urban continuum in several countries, illustrating the difficulties and possible danger of comparison between types of statistics and across countries. Types of offenders found in rural areas as well as the types of victimization that most affect those living in these areas are also discussed in this chapter, based on examples from the international literature. Victimization in rural areas includes a wide array of offences from farm crime, environmental and wildlife offences to violence against women, harassment, and discrimination against minority groups to drug and related organized crime, just to name a few.

Crime Trends

While the international literature is rich in comparisons of crime trends among countries, relatively few studies are devoted to exploring rural-urban differences in crime across countries. During the second half of the twentieth century, the Western world experienced increasing rates of crime, notably robbery, homicide, and assault (Eisner 2008). But by the mid-1990s, several countries started to observe a widespread drop in crime, most notably the United states where violent and property crime indexes fell by 34% and 29%, respectively (Ceccato 2015d; Levitt 2004). More recently, van Dijk et al. (2021) found, for instance, that rates of common crime as well as homicide have continued to drop in the Global North, in particular from 2006 to 2019, while Africa, South Asia, and Central America experienced an increase. However, not all forms of crime followed this trend; for instance, an exception being organized crime and corruption which decreased in sub-Saharan Africa and increased in North and Latin America, Australia, and parts of Europe. Some of these national trends can be observed when they are split by type of area, but methodological challenges still constitute a barrier for comparison among (and within) countries and areas (Deller and Deller 2010).

The mere comparison of crime rates between rural and urban areas may not reveal informative patterns because rural areas show, as a rule, lower rates of crime than urban areas (Ceccato 2015d; Kaylen et al. 2019; Laub 1983; Mawby 2015). Comparing crime trends over time would be more enlightening, as sparsely populated areas are governed by their own circumstances of crime dynamics (Cebulak 2004), and some areas have become more criminogenic for certain types of crime but less for others (Bachman 1992; Ceccato and Dolmen 2011). Disparities in crime trends may appear among various degrees of rurality as well. Alternative ways of depicting crime trends across areas on the rural-urban continuum are necessary to capture intra country comparisons. For example, a recent study by Shimada and Suzuki (2021) explored the use of principal component analysis on municipal-level census data in Japan to generate a rural index that represents the ecological characteristics of each municipality on the rural-urban continuum.

In some countries, trends of crime and fear of crime appear to follow similar patterns, although they are not the same (Moore and Trojanowicz 1988; Skogan 2011) as more commonly, there is a discrepancy between actual crime and the public's perception of crime (see, e.g., Larsen and Olsen 2020; Office for National Statistics 2017; Roberts and Stalans 2000). The most fearful are not necessarily the most victimized; often the reverse is true (Moore and Trojanowicz 1988). For example, McPhail et al. (2017) found that while official crime rates had been declining in Canada during the previous two decades, residents of the province of Saskatchewan commonly perceived that crime levels were either stagnant or rising. Skogan (2011, p. 102) cites the National Reassurance Policing Program, which expresses how this kind of mismatch in trends of actual and perceived crime can be of serious concern for the police, as they ultimately rely on public support for funding and legitimacy. Notably, these discrepancies in trends may be particularly prominent within rural communities as illustrated in recent research, such as (McPhail et al. 2017).

The following subsection exemplifies how crime fluctuates over time in areas on the rural-urban continuum, using examples from the literature and updated statistics for a selection of countries. The United States presents an interesting case, due to the size of the country and of its rural territory: 97% of the country's land mass is 'rural' and home to around 20% of the total population (U.S. Census Bureau 2017). In Europe we look at Sweden, while Australia and Brazil provide us with references from the southern hemisphere, with Brazil as part of Global South. Although these figures are not strictly comparable across countries (e.g., some are police statistics, others are victimization survey data), these examples are illustrative of the trends in particular national contexts. The aim is to show differences in criminogenic conditions and safety needs by area.

Crime Trends on the Rural-Urban Continuum: Selected Countries

In the United States, violent and property crime decreased relatively steadily in all areas between 1993 and 2019 according to the National Crime Victimization Survey (Fig. 4.1). Kneebone and Raphael (2011) provide evidence of the apparent

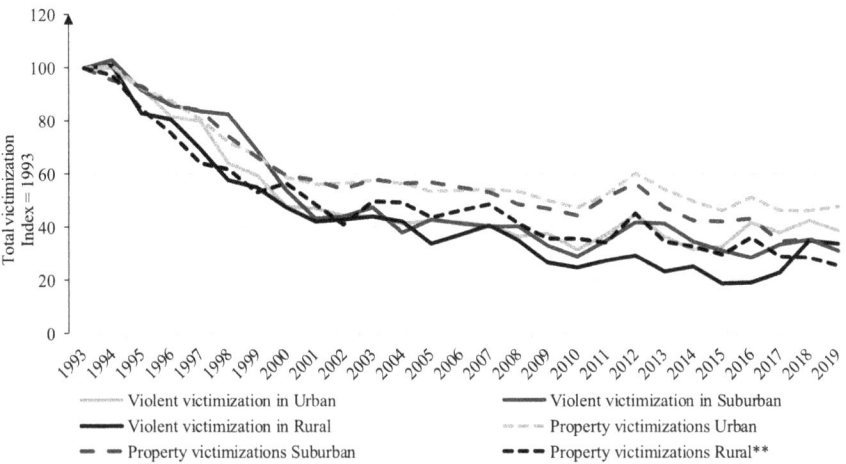

Fig. 4.1 Index of violent and property victimization in the United States, 1993 = 100; 1993–2019 (Data source: NCVS data, Bureau of Justice Statistics (2021)). (Notes regarding Fig. 4.1: (i) Urban = within a principal city of a Metropolitan Statistical Area (MSA). Suburban = within an MSA but not within a principal city of the MSA. Rural = outside of an MSA (Anderson, 2020). (ii) ** = For the years 1996–2019, the data should be interpreted with caution, as it is based on 10 or fewer sample cases or the coefficient of variation is greater than 50. (iii) The number of victimizations for the year of 2006 has been calculated as the mean of 2005 and 2007 numbers. The reasoning behind this is that methodological changes when conducting the NCVS of 2006 led to a variation in victimization that could not be attributed to actual year-to-year changes, mainly affecting rural sample areas. For more information, see Rand (2007))

convergence between rural and urban crime trends. In a study covering 5400 communities located within the 100 largest metropolitan areas in the United States, both violent and property crime were found to have significantly declined between 1990 and 2008, with the largest decreases occurring in cities. Cities and high-density suburbs saw violent crime rates decline, but predominantly rural communities experienced slight increases that could not be explained by their changing demographics. This trend falls in line with other international trends (e.g., Carcach 2000; Marshall and Johnson 2005; Osgood and Chambers 2003). Deller and Deller (2010) reports that between 1987 and 2002, both violent and total crime rates increased in rural counties but decreased in urban counties. Research showed that non-lethal violence has increased on average in exurban (rural) and some suburban areas (Kneebone and Raphael 2011).

Crime trends also vary among different types of areas on the rural-urban continuum. There is evidence that rural towns experiencing fast growth – often called "boomtowns" – are especially vulnerable to increasing crime rates (see, e.g., Archbold 2015; Park and Stokowski 2009; Park and Stokowski 2011; Ruddell 2017; Stokowski 1996). For example, Ruddell et al. (2014) found that in 2010–2012, violent crime dropped by 25.6% in non-"boom counties," but increased by 18.5% in counties that had been affected by oil expansion.

Crime trends often vary across different levels of population density. In the United States, for instance, the variance among highly non-metropolitan areas has been shown to be equal to or greater than that among metropolitan areas in terms of crime rates and contextual variables (Wells and Weisheit 2004). Offenders too, regardless of age, race, or gender, have shown similar offending patterns in both urban and rural areas (Laub 1983). Efforts to predict crime are of limited use in areas with low population density (Kadar et al. 2019). Previous research has shown that the idea of higher population densities being associated with higher crime levels may simply not be applicable for all types of crime. For example, Battin and Crowl (2017) found a significant, negative relationship between population density and property crimes, and little to no significant relationship with violent crimes.

Similar to the case of the United States and NCVS data (Fig. 4.1), the Swedish Crime Survey (NTU) shows that residents of smaller towns and rural municipalities appear to experience lower levels of victimization of crimes such as assault and burglary, compared to larger and more urban municipalities (Table 4.1). Interestingly, the rest of the country seems to be not simply conforming to the trends of larger municipalities: the share victimized of burglary decreased in larger cities between 2017 and 2018, while it increased slightly in small towns. Previous research showed that inter-municipal population changes (between remote rural areas to accessible rural) were in the past associated with these shifts in victimization, see, for example, Ceccato and Dolmen (2011).

Other data sources can show a slightly different trend for Sweden. For one, in rural areas in the 2010s, rates of violent crime recorded by police statistics were higher than if they had followed the national trend from the 1990s and 2000s (Ceccato and Dolmen 2011). From 1996 to 2010, urban and accessible rural areas had a higher risk of total crime than remote rural areas, but later the crime trend lines started to converge (Ceccato and Dolmen 2013). More recently, while urban and accessible rural areas have consistently shown larger rates of total reported crime than remote rural areas, rural areas have recently experienced relatively larger increases of levels of violent crime (Brå 2021a). Note however that current figures show that the percentage of increase, not the actual rates of crime.

Table 4.1 Self-reported victimization of assault and burglary 2016–2020 type of residence, share victimized people/households, respectively

		2016	2017	2018	2019	2020
Assault	Large cities and municipalities near large cities	3.5	3.7	3.7	4.0	3.1
	Medium-sized towns and municipalities near medium-sized towns	3.0	3.1	3.6	3.5	2.8
	Smaller towns/urban areas and rural municipalities	2.9	2.9	3.2	3.2	2.5
Burglary	Large cities and municipalities near large cities	2.4	2.5	2.3	2.0	1.5
	Medium-sized towns and municipalities near medium-sized towns	1.4	1.5	1.5	1.6	1.1
	Smaller towns/urban areas and rural municipalities	1.4	1.2	1.5	1.4	1.1

Source: Brå (2021b)

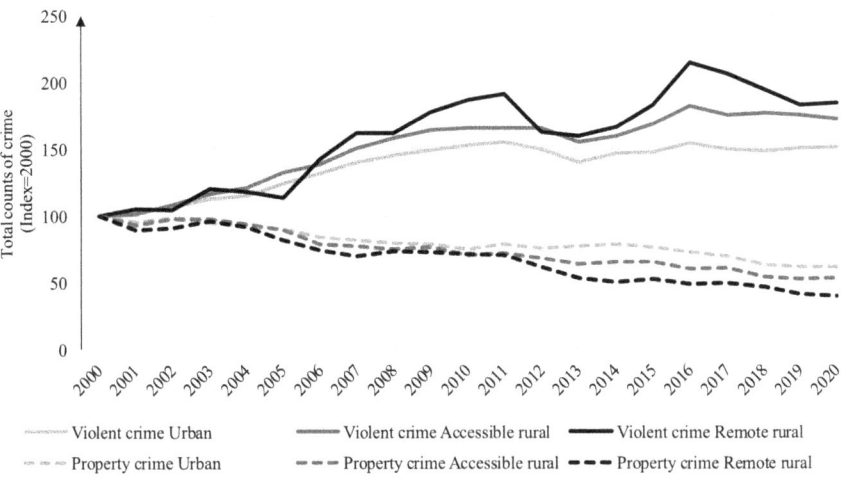

Fig. 4.2 Index of total violent and property crime in Sweden, 2004 = 100, 2004–2020. (Note: "Violent crime" includes all crimes under the Swedish Criminal Code Chap. 3 – "On offenses against life and health" and Chap. 6: "Sexual offenses." "Property crime" includes all offenses described within Chap. 8: "Theft, robbery and other appropriative offenses"). (Data source: Brå (2021a))

Although violent crimes in rural areas comprise significantly fewer cases than those found in other areas in Sweden, the total number of reported violent crimes in rural areas was more than the double in 2020 than those reported in 2000 (Fig. 4.2), where this increase was associated with assault and sexual violence, including rape.

Australia and Canada provide additional examples of countries where several rural areas are relatively more criminogenic than some metropolitan areas (Barclay 2017; Rudell and Lithopoulos 2016; Tyler 1998). In the Global South, other, yet similar trends have been observed. For example, the nature of violent crime in the Turkish countryside has differed from inner-city violence, with offenses like honor killings, land disputes, and family feuds (Cayli 2014). Residential burglary in the rural parts of the Malaysian state of Johor has been noted to be at the highest levels in the country (Hamid and Toyong 2014).

In Brazil, violent crimes have been on the rise nationally but have undergone a much steeper increase in rural areas, especially the most remote ones (Ceccato and Ceccato 2017; Justus et al. 2016; Scorzafave et al. 2015). Furthermore, violence rates can vary greatly in rural areas. The median of the rates of homicide in rural municipalities (accessible and remote) was found to be significantly different from the other areas. These rural municipalities comprise 3363 municipalities or 60% of the country's total municipalities (IPEA 2020).

The variation in the overall homicide rate in Brazil was smaller than the growth in the median of homicide rates in rural municipalities over the 11 years 2007–2017

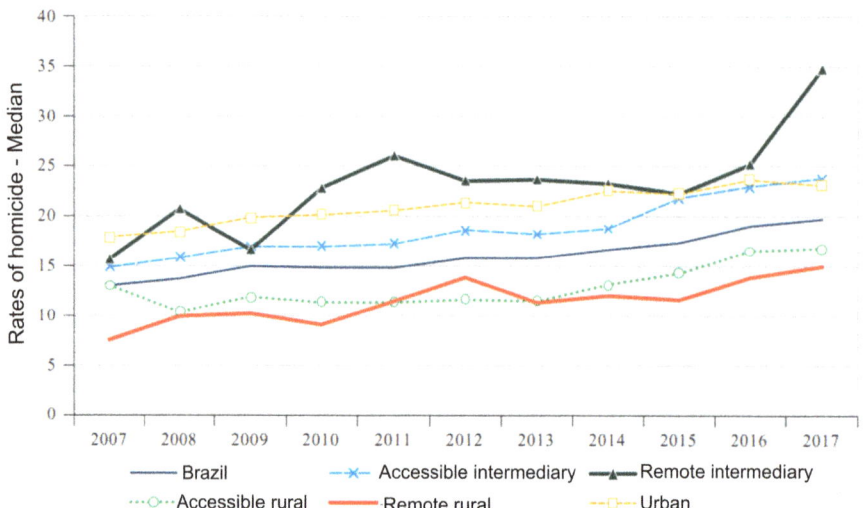

Fig. 4.3 Median of rates of homicide in Brazil; police-registered data, 2007–2017. Rate per 100,000 inhabitants per municipality. (Source: IPEA (2020))

(Fig. 4.3), especially in municipalities with conflicts related to land reform and including indigenous territories. The increase in violence in the countryside coincided with an increase in the variation of homicide rates within rural municipalities, which implies that rural municipalities remained more unequal in terms of the prevalence of lethality, particularly in the north, center, northeast regions (IPEA 2020).

Rural areas clearly show signs that their criminogenic conditions are distinct from those of urban areas, emphasizing the need for the continued study of crime trends across the rural-urban continuum. Although we advise against drawing conclusions across the previously illustrated examples, there is growing evidence that some areas on the rural-urban continuum are becoming more criminogenic. However, the rural-urban dichotomy imposes a number of limitations when illustrating these crime trends within and across countries because of the differences in rural-urban categories. Differences by crime type and data sources are also important to be considered before drawing any conclusions between rural and urban areas. Below we further discuss a few of other challenges when comparing crime trends across the rural-urban continuum.

Challenges in Identifying Crime Trends

One major obstacle when predicting crime trends is the underreporting of crime to the police. In general, the seriousness and type of the offense dictates the likelihood of reporting. Studies have presented several factors which influence the willingness and ability to report crime in rural areas. These include the physical characteristics of the area, such as a higher degree of isolation and remoteness in terms of accessing services, which constitute barriers to reporting, as many support networks are centered in urban areas and on urban victims (Owen and Carrington 2015). Laub (1981) indicated that in the United States, for crimes such as rape, assault, and personal larceny, no significant difference was found in reporting rates between urban and rural areas. However, the reasons for not reporting differed. As for rape, urban residents felt there was "nothing to be done" or mentioned a lack of proof, while rural populations more often referred to it being a "private or personal matter." Victims can also be "silenced" through informal social controls such as gossip, and feelings of dishonor and shame at being a domestic violence victim, all of which threaten the victim with ostracization by the community (Abrahams and Jewkes 2010; Owen and Carrington 2015). The real or perceived lack of anonymity can also decrease the likelihood of reporting crime, especially when the police may be acquainted with the victim and/or offender and spread sensitive information (Ceccato and Dolmen 2011; DeKeseredy and Hall-Sanchez 2016). In general, the close-knit communities of rural areas can be associated with lower reporting rates of highly interpersonal offenses such as domestic violence. Some other crimes, however, such as burglary and auto theft, are reported to a greater extent, mainly for the purpose of collecting insurance (Ceccato 2015a).

Offenders

Offenders in the Rural

Research has shown that typical characteristics of offenders in the rural include being male, a newcomer, travelling stranger, or tourist (see, e.g., Smith 2010; van Daele and Beken 2010); local, and young (Baldwin 1994); and working in the farming industry (Smith and McElwee 2013). This profile shows the difficulty in identifying "a typical rural offender," as it is only those who are caught by the police who are represented in research, which misses those who hide behind unreported crime. Mawby (2015) found, for instance, that offenders in rural areas could be divided into two categories: residents or visitors. Among the residents, one finds both long-term residents and newcomers, as well as temporary residents (e.g., seasonal workers). Visitors who commit crimes include vacationers, travelling criminals, and commuter criminals. While seasonal workers and vacationers may offend when living in or visiting the areas, commuter and travelling criminals travel to the area with the explicit aim of committing crime.

Changes in rural-urban dynamics, such as population shifts from cities to suburbs, may be associated with the mobility of criminals through migration or commuting (Porter 2011). Smith (2010) reports on how farm equipment, for example, is an attractive target for urban criminal gangs, as well as urban criminals relocating to and settling in rural communities where it is easier to avoid police detection. Ceccato et al. (2021) found that some travelling offenders target farms for reasons other than monetary gain, as is the case with criminal animal rights activists where their oppositional activities translated to trespassing, harassment, theft, vandalism, and violence against farmers working in animal production. Also, more persistent structural problems can also shape rural offenders; patriarchal marginalization of women has led to restrictions on mobility and both social and economic freedoms, with varying experiences for urban and rural female offenders (Parker and Reckdenwald 2008).

Prison inmates and repeat offenders have been studied in order to create profiles of rural offenders (see, e.g., Blurton and Copus 2003; Lilliott et al. 2017). For example, the rural career criminal has often been found to be relatively harmless, but mental health issues, drug abuse, and low levels of education are often linked to repeat offending (Berg and DeLisi 2005). Rural youth as offenders has also been a common topic within rural criminology. Baldwin (1994) studied alcohol-abusing, young offenders; Bouchard and Nguyen (2010) examined how criminal networks help the juvenile offender avoid the criminal justice system; and at-risk rural and non-rural minority youths were compared in Gale and Wundersitz (1986) and Vazsonyi and Trejos-Castillo (2006).

Farmers as Offenders

Farming and farmers are essential to rural areas and the discourse on rural crime. Donnermeyer (2016a, p. 147) defines farmers as "anyone who produces food, ranging from those who grows crops, fruits and vegetables to those who raise livestock [...], from small labor-intensive landholders to capital intensive large-scale industrialists...". Farmers' illegal behaviors can be associated with farming practices and violating environmental regulations. For example, the abuse and neglect of farm animals is, perhaps intuitively, one of the ways farmers can easily take on the role as offenders (Lovell 2016). Also, farming and related facilities can produce large amounts of environmentally hazardous materials, such as pollutants from manure, litter, and process wastewater, and regulating their proper disposal may be difficult due to, for example, large numbers of unrecorded small facilities, such as in the case of buffalo farm factories (Gargiulo et al. 2016). Additionally, the illegal killing of predators or "pests" is a common practice among farmers and other rural inhabitants, and often justified as protecting themselves or their businesses (Enticott 2011). In desperation during droughts, farmers may also steal water from irrigation channels (Barclay and Bartel 2015).

Monetary gain is, as with other types of offenders, also a motivation of criminal farmers. There is the case of "illegal pluriactivity" (McElwee et al. 2017; Smith and McElwee 2013), which involves farmers using alternative income generation strategies through engaging in, for example, the illegal meat trade, medicine trade, and wildlife and dog breeding. Furthermore, the forced labor trafficking industry is strongly connected to the farming industry, where farmers may subject trafficked workers (who are often foreign, poor, and disenfranchised), to, for example, poor living conditions, environmental hazards, threats, violence, and sexual assault (Barrick 2016).

Research has also found that while drug use is comparably lower among rural versus urban residents, rural areas are very prominent places of cultivation of drugs such as cannabis (Ceccato 2015b; Weisheit and Brownstein 2016; Weisheit et al. 1993).

Offenders of Environmental and Wildlife Crime (EWC)

Environmental crime can often be viewed as victimless or less offensive crimes that are committed by offenders with various and complex underlying motivations. One often imagines typical offenders of environmental crime to be larger corporations or industries (see, e.g., Brisman et al. 2016; Opsal and O'Connor Shelley 2014; Perdue 2018), such as mining companies, or hazardous waste facilities that are often deliberately located in poor and rural areas in order to protect the owners' economic interests (McDowell 2013). In fact, rural EWC such as illegal dumping is often committed by local residents (Ceccato 2015b). As previously mentioned, farmers have been found to be responsible for water theft or of offenses including polluting water and wetlands; illegal treatment, storage, or disposal of hazardous waste; illegal land clearance and farm animal abuse (see, e.g., Barclay and Bartel 2015; Gargiulo et al. 2016; Lin 2015; Lovell 2016; Lowe et al. 1996). Historically, hunters and other rural residents have also been associated with poaching (Archer 1999; Osborne 2016), which includes the illegal killing of animals perceived as threats and pests, for food or for recreational value. Furthermore, there appears to be patterns of rural residents becoming offenders of EWC when criminal law comes into conflict with local hunting practices. For example, cultural subsistence hunting among indigenous peoples in, for example, Brazil has come into clash with governmental authorities' conservation efforts (Antunes et al. 2019). Additionally, forest fires are an annual problem for many countries and in Europe they are provoked by human activities in 95% of cases (Salvador 2016). But laws restricting the use of fire may disregard the cultural and historical importance as well as the utility of intentional fire use, as in the cases of regenerating pastures and clearing agricultural residue (Carmenta et al. 2019; Salvador 2016). Certain activities considered environmentally harmful, for example, small-scale and artisanal mining, can also be the main source of income for less affluent households (Eduful et al. 2020). For more details, see section devoted to EWC.

Victimization

Property Crime

People living in rural areas can be said to be exposed to two types of property crimes – property crime in the rural and rural property crime. *Property crime in the rural* refers to all types of offenses that take place in rural areas, such as, residential burglary; as opposed to *rural property crime* which are those that are explicitly linked to rural situational conditions, such as, theft of livestock. Rural areas are not free from crimes such as thefts, burglaries, robberies, and vandalism. Urban areas have higher rates of property crime, which is largely due to providing more opportunities in the form of stock of goods than rural areas (Ceccato 2015d). These goods can often be money, personal objects of value, or even utilities such as water or electricity (see, e.g., Jamil 2018). However, there are certain goods and forms of property crime that are virtually only found in rural areas as discussed below.

Certain property crimes can appear to be more or less prevalent in rural areas. For example, Clarke and Harris (1992) noted a much higher disparity of auto theft between urban and rural areas in the United States (a ratio of 6.6 to 1) compared to most other property crimes, although robberies had the highest disparity (a ratio of 19 to 1). Ceccato (2015d) presents previous research with similar findings, although the author also notes that theft from motor vehicles in the United Kingdom has been disproportionately higher in rural areas. Furthermore, while the overall rates of property crimes have decreased in most countries, there are exceptions, and different types of crimes can follow different patterns in the same country. In Japan, a linear pattern of victimization was found for bicycle theft, with one-thirtieth the risk in the most rural municipalities compared to the most urban municipalities, while for motor vehicle theft the pattern was nonlinear. The same analysis also revealed that victims in rural areas were less likely to have locked their belongings before they were stolen than those living in urban areas (Shimada and Suzuki 2021). In Sweden, robbery, car theft, and burglary have increased in rural areas and decreased in urban areas (Ceccato 2015d), and housebreaking crime in the rural parts of the Malaysian state of Johor has been noted to be at the highest levels in the country (Hamid and Toyong 2014). Also, no matter how relatively low the rural rates are, the impacts of property crimes on rural areas and residents are significant, as demonstrated by the research. For example, Wilhelmsson and Ceccato (2015) found that burglaries have a strong negative effect on Swedish housing prices in non-metropolitan areas.

Allen and Cancino (2012) found that certain social structural conditions have different effects on property crimes in urban versus rural areas, such as ethnic heterogeneity and percentage foreign-born population. In the United States, resource disadvantage has been positively correlated with violent and property crime rates in rural counties with a population loss (Barnett and Mencken (2002). While Arthur (1991) successfully explained property crime with socioeconomic predictors, Stack (1995) applied routine activity theory to burglary and found crime opportunity to be positively correlated with burglaries in rural areas, independent of social disorganization conditions.

Rural property crime includes crimes that are endemic to rural areas, such as theft of tractors, agricultural equipment, fuel and livestock, which is commonly categorized as farm or agricultural crime (Barclay 2016). Notably, most research on agricultural crime has found that it is largely property related (Barclay and Donnermeyer 2002). Farms appear to provide opportunities for property crime, due to the presence of both valuable and easily accessible goods as well as to situational conditions that can be exploited by offenders, such as lack of guardianship on large properties (see, e.g., Barclay and Donnermeyer 2002; Jones 2012; Mears et al. 2007). In the United Kingdom, the annual economic cost of farm crime has been estimated at 45 million pounds (Morris et al. 2020). Furthermore, while on a local level there are obvious impacts such as economic losses due to theft and loss of work time, farm crime can also affect farmers' mental health and disrupt the cohesiveness of rural communities by undermining trust between neighbors (Barclay 2016; Ceccato 2015b; Saltiel et al. 1992; Smith 2020).

The perceptions of farmers and other rural residents regarding property crime can substantially differ from those of urban residents, although this has varied over time and place. Jones (2016, p. 172) quotes James T. Hammick about how in the nineteenth century rural crime was considered less serious with theft being more small-scale, and with criminals only occasionally committing crop or livestock theft once or twice a year. Kilday (2014) found that in eighteenth-century Oxfordshire County, England, petty thefts mainly involved food or livestock that could quickly be converted into food. In Africa, agricultural theft has long been expected and even tolerated by farmers, where the motivations for the thefts could often be obtaining food or even following cultural traditions (Bunei et al. 2016; Donnermeyer 2017). However, after the colonization era and other global and local socioeconomic and cultural shifts in society, the tolerance for agricultural theft has decreased while at the same time both the scale of and motivations for the thefts have changed, as monetary gain is now the main driver and violence is also more common (Bunei et al. 2016; Fleisher 2002).

Compared to other rural groups, farmers may be more vulnerable to and fearful of crime (Bankston et al. 1987). Farming has become an increasingly large-scale and capital-intense business globally, with new technology replacing labor for reasons of efficiency and increased economic viability (Barclay and Donnermeyer 2011). This has also increased the volume and scale of farm crime, for example, entailing the organized theft of crops and farm equipment that are smuggled into other countries (Jones 2012; Swanson 1981). Also, improved infrastructure, both in terms of transportation and internet access, has greatly facilitated the targeting of farmers. Cattle theft, for example, can be committed more easily with better roads and greater accessibility to highways, which also facilitate an easier escape (Justus et al. 2018). Crimes such as fraud and unlawful threats are increasingly committed via telephone, computer, and social media, where offenders hide behind the cover of anonymity (Ceccato 2016).

In summary, property crime has been shown to be a chronic problem in rural areas, both property crime that happens to occur in the rural, as discussed in the previous subsection, and property crime unique to the rural. However, the property crimes intrinsically tied to rural life (such as farm crime) decidedly demonstrate the need for contextualizing property crimes in the rural. While property crimes generally involve the theft of goods such as valuable objects and money, the definition could be expanded to the organized trade of, for example, people, as much of human trafficking takes part in rural areas (see, e.g., Barrick 2016; Byrne and Smith 2016; Kumar et al. 2020). Environmental crimes such as the trade of exotic or endangered species (Korsell and Hagstedt 2008; Smith and McElwee 2013) could also be considered theft of goods and property crime, but such crimes have not been explored within the scope of this study. However, with the increasingly larger scale and greater organization of crime in rural areas, property crime remains an important issue to tackle.

Violent Crime

Violence is among the subjects that garner the most attention within rural criminology, although it is not fully understood. While rural and suburban areas have generally experienced lower rates of violence than urban areas, the notion that rural residents around the world are safe from the impacts of violence is one of the persistent myths about rural violence (Donnermeyer 2016b). Conversely, various media have also contributed to stereotyping of rural areas as dangerous places where urban people may be violently victimized by "demented, in-bred locals without conscience or constraint" (DeKeseredy et al. 2014, p. 179). In this section, violent crime is discussed under two main categories: *general violence* which often means crimes like assault, murder, gun violence, and gang-related violence that mainly happen in public places, and *domestic violence and violence against women*, which involve violence against the offender's current, former, or potential partners and children that mainly occurs in the home. What follows here is first an overview of the historical and current violent crime trends across the world, and what violence means in a rural context.

General Violence

In most countries, violent crime rates have historically been relatively low in rural areas compared to other types of areas. For instance, in the United States during the 1970s, violence rates per 100,000 persons were 1568, 924, and 793 for urban, suburban, and rural areas, respectively (Laub 1983). Kaylen et al. (2019) similarly provide a comparison of aggravated assault rates in areas of different levels of urbanization between 1988 and 2005, which once again showed that urban areas experienced higher rates. As Kowalski and Duffield (1990) found for rural areas, this may be because the risk for violence decreases as individualism is reduced and cohesion is strengthened. Religion has been found to have a positive effect on violent crime reduction in rural areas through establishing social networks in churches (Lee 2006), although the detailed mechanisms between religion and violence are not fully known.

Kaylen et al. (2019) also observed that the decline in crime has been much greater in urban areas than in rural areas. The rural-urban gap has narrowed over time for certain crime types, for example, murder rates in Russia (Chervyakov et al. 2002), and in Sweden certain trends have shown higher than expected levels of violence in rural areas compared to if they had followed the national average (Ceccato 2015c). In fact, certain types of violence seem to be increasing in rural spaces, such as non-lethal violence and when the offender is an intimate (Ceccato 2015d). In the provinces of Canada, there exist patterns demonstrating tendencies for rural areas to specialize in violent crime (Carleton et al. 2014). However, there is also some controversy in the measurement of violent crime, as the choice of data sources may lead to inconsistent results, especially for rural areas (Berg and Lauritsen 2016).

In certain countries, like Australia, violent crime rates have been higher than average in rural and regional areas (Hogg and Carrington 2016). This is also true in the Global South, for example, in post-war Cambodia where rates of homicide were higher in rural areas (Broadhurst 2002). As previously discussed, in Brazil, violence has decreased in metropolitan areas and shown signs of dispersing to rural areas, as it is significantly rising in less urbanized rural areas (Justus et al. 2016; Steeves et al. 2015). With increased modernization (e.g., through electrification), poorer rural regions may experience decreased homicide rates as well, although the dispersion to other regions may persist (Arvate et al. 2018).

Studies have found some support for the generalizability of urban-based models to explain patterns of violence, such as social disorganization theory, although it is important to recognize that a separate rural contextualization of this theory may be needed (Barnett and Mencken 2002; Petee and Kowalski 1993). Rural violence has been explained through different mechanisms compared to urban violence, for example, residential (in)stability and ethnic heterogeneity not being predictive of violence, and poverty being inversely related to rape in rural areas (Melde 2006). While, for example, Lee and Slack (2008) found a consistent relationship between violent crime and labor market conditions throughout the rural-urban continuum, other studies have found less support, with, for example, Arthur (1991) finding that socioeconomic factors are better suited for predicting property crime than predicting violence.

Current theories and models appear to be insufficient to fully explain rural violence, for one must also understand the context of rural society. For example, an important part of the rural culture of violence in some countries is the availability of guns. Numerous studies have researched rural gun violence in the form of homicides, school shootings, police shootings, self-defense, and suicide (e.g., De Angelis et al. 2017; Hemenway et al. 2020; Hemenway and Solnick 2015; Kalesan et al. 2020; Rocque 2012; Singh and Singh 2005). In the international literature, guns are especially associated with North American rural communities due to the higher rate of gun ownership compared to urban areas. Although using guns as a means of committing homicide is actually rare in rural areas, lethal gun accidents are fairly common in the United States (Reid and Cesaroni 2016). DeKeseredy et al. (2016) cite Websdale (1998) who argues that it is easier to fire a gun undetected in rural areas, as rural residents often associate gunshots with hunting. The higher acceptance of guns for hunting and self-protection also increases the acceptance for using guns for intimidation, for example, of intimate partners, see more regarding domestic violence in the coming section.

Gendered Violence

A whole branch of rural criminology literature specializes in domestic violence (against partners and children) and in intimate partner violence (IPV) in particular, which includes physical and sexual violence, stalking, or psychological harm by a current, former, or potential partner or spouse. In the United States, for instance, intimate feminicide, or the murder of women by a current, former, or potential partner, is one specific crime type that tends to be increasing as well as be proportionally higher (in percentage) in rural areas than in urban and suburban areas (DeKeseredy et al. 2016). Yet the issue lacks priority, which may be due to lack of awareness and education (DeKeseredy 2020) and to an overall normalization of the problem. Underreporting domestic violence is not only the result of the victims' silence but also of the silence, tolerance, and negligence of those close to the victim (Gracia 2004). Neighbors in rural areas may have a higher tolerance for particular behaviors than in urban areas (Anderson 1999), and privacy norms dictate that they "keep their mouths shut" or "keep out of other people's business."

Barriers to reporting crime and/or receiving support can be more tangible in rural areas, particularly for women that have been victims of violence. Examples of barriers include the higher degree of isolation due to long distances, poverty, and the gender-role dynamics within couples (Ceccato 2015e). Women often have little access to cash, property, or other assets, with men or their extended family often controlling these resources either directly or indirectly through family trusts (Wendt 2016). Distances between houses in rural areas are often greater than in urban centers, which makes it more difficult for neighbors to discover any violence that occurs (DeKeseredy et al. 2004). If victims of violence decides to seek help, it is not always easy to leave the house (Websdale 1998). The nearest women's shelter may be many miles away, and the distance may be exacerbated by poor or no public transportation (Lewis 2003), or limited or sporadic access to the internet or mobile phones (DeKeseredy and Joseph 2006). Therefore, official data on domestic violence and/or violence against women in rural areas can be problematic. Systematic analyses published as articles about violence against women in the Global South are scarce, but examples can be found in DeKeseredy et al. (2018), Jewkes et al. (2005), and Abrahams and Jewkes (2010).

Most studies on rural violence research have been recently published, in other words, 68% were published in 2010 or later (violence is the theme in 15% of the publications). Secondary data such as official records were the most used method together with statistical analysis, followed by interviews. While studies focusing on the United States were dominant, Brazil was the second most studied country. Other contributions from the Global South included cases of violence in Turkish rural regions (Çaya 2014), racialized farm worker violence in Zimbabwe (Rutherford 2004), Somalian piracy (Collins 2016), and violent land reform in China (Meng 2016). Overall, 62% of the publications on violence were about "street violence," while the rest of the publications were dedicated to domestic violence and a larger focus on violence against women, but also to topics related to child abuse (Calvert and Munsie-Benson 1999; Dawson and Wells 2006; El-Hak et al. 2009). In summary, violence in rural areas is plentiful and takes many forms. Focusing on general trends can lead to ignoring variations among and within rural communities, missing areas of high risk. Understanding rural culture is essential to truly grasp the mechanisms of violent crime in rural areas, how it occurs and persists and, how to prevent it.

Hate Crime, Discrimination, and the Rural "Other"

The term "hate crime" has varying definitions among and within countries and has been criticized for not being sufficiently precise. Using a definition from Swedish law, it can involve incitement against ethnic groups, unlawful discrimination, and any crime where the motive to offend is "because of race, color, national or ethnic origin, creed, sexual orientation, transgender identity or expression or other similar circumstance" (Brå 2019, p. 14). Gerstenfeld (2003, p. 5) provides a simpler definition: "a criminal act that is motivated, at least in part, by the group affiliation of the victim." What can be generally agreed upon is that "hate crime" is a collective term for many different crimes, such as threats, harassment, and physical violence. And as with many other subjects within criminology, studies of hate crime have only recently turned to non-urban contexts (Lumsden et al. 2019). This urban bias can be problematic as it allows for ignoring worrying trends. For example, Ruback et al. (2018) found that in Pennsylvania, USA, the rate of hate crimes based on the Uniform Crime Report had been underestimated by a factor of 1.6 overall, but by factor of 2.5 for rural areas.

Due to the idea of the rural idyll, rural communities have persistently been viewed as tight-knitted and friendly, with residents having a deep sense of local identity and feeling of belonging (Garland and Chakraborti 2006a). However, this perspective marginalizes and neglects the experiences of the rural "other," which in certain contexts can be defined as "people other than white, middle-class, middle-aged, able-bodied, sound-minded, heterosexual men" (Philo 1992, p. 193). In numerous cases, rural communities have been observed to be very inclined to protect their self-defined identities and cultures against perceived threats (Yarwood and Gardner 2000). As such, the othering process usually targets strangers and "outsiders" as well as whoever else does not fit into the image of the community in terms of behavior and lifestyle and/or visual appearance (such as sexual orientation or racial/ethnic phenotype). Who is "othered" and who is considered "the same" is a result of broader configurations of power and systematic issues in society (Little 1999).

In this section, we report how those who are considered as non-conforming to the image and ideals of rural society are subjected to hate and discrimination, especially due to their racial and ethnic group affiliation and/or sexual orientation.

Racial and Ethnic-Based Hate and Discrimination

Even within the small body of reviewed studies on this topic, experiences of racist harassment have been largely neglected (Garland and Chakraborti 2006b). Garland and Chakraborti (2004) studied victims of racism in the United Kingdom, where they note that interviewees had a hard time breaking down their experiences into isolated incidents. They confirm previous research that racist harassment is better viewed as a process rather than a series of independent events. Furthermore, although the recorded rates of racist incidents were much lower in rural areas, only a fraction is ever reported to the police. Observed harassments included both "low-level racism" such as hostile exclusion and subjection of victims through an "othering"-process, as well as "high-level racism" by which victims experienced vandalism of their property, physical violence, and attempted petrol bombings. Additionally, victims rarely felt supported by state or voluntary agencies such as the police, due to their lack of sympathy and understanding of their victimization.

Rural areas have long been presented as homogenous in terms of social values as well as race and ethnicity; specifically, in countries of the Global North like the United States, the United Kingdom, and Australia, the notion of rural areas as "white" spaces has persisted (Forrest and Dunn 2013; Garland and Chakraborti 2006a; Lichter and Brown 2011). This notion has been increasingly contested following population shifts, such as in the United States and the diffusion of Latin American immigrants into rural areas (Lichter and Brown 2011). These changes may be interpreted by some as a potential threat to rural identity and culture, leading to the formation of hostile groups. Weisheit et al. (1995) outline how rural America has been the home and birthplace of several "hate groups" and far-right, extremist organizations connected to anti-Semitism, racism, fundamentalist Christian values, and a suspicion of government. Many such group members "seek to return to simpler times in a world they can create and control," which is why they are drawn to the remoteness of rural areas (Weisheit et al. 1995, p. 47). In Europe, the increased influence of far-right-wing political parties has also led to a higher prevalence of racist attitudes in the countryside (Schuermans and de Maesschalck 2010).

Research has demonstrated varying findings regarding rural attitudes toward immigration. For example, on the one hand, Palmer (1996) noted that Canadian rural residents were less concerned about immigrant crime than urban residents, while, on the other hand, Forrest and Dunn (2013) found that rural South Australians were less tolerant than those living in metropolitan areas. Any definition of "whiteness" has admittedly varied over time and may also vary by context. Lumsden et al. (2019) point out that there can be a racialized differentiation based on cultural differences rather than phenotypical. This reveals that even immigrants that can be considered "white," for example, eastern Europeans, can be racially marginalized.

Not only "outsiders" are subjected to discrimination or viewed as the "other"; both social structural systems and government institutions can target native rural residents. In India, multiple studies have focused on discrimination (based on the caste system), which appears to be prominent in the rural parts of the country (see, e.g., Akhtar 2020; Chandra and Pradhan 2001; Panda and Guha 2015). The othering process can take different shapes depending if it is the "old other" or the "new other"; see the example of Sami population and the temporary population of berry pickers in Sweden (Ceccato 2017). Notably, indigenous peoples of, for example, Thailand, Australia, Brazil, and Cuba have also been targeted by governmental discrimination and infringement on land, actions largely painted by colonialist mindsets (see, e.g., Anderson 2018; Canofre 2017; Cunneen 2016; García 2011; Jobes 2004), although this has occurred and continues to occur in many more places across the globe than are documented in the reviewed publications.

Discrimination and Hate Crimes Against LGBTQ+ Persons

No matter where they live, LGBTQ+ persons face similar struggles. Homophobic prejudice has led to discriminatory behaviors that impact the mental health and safety perceptions of gay and lesbian individuals, but also lead to verbal and physical harassment, and even murder (Lindhorst 1997). LGBTQ+ youth have been found to experience much higher rates of harassment and bullying than non-LGBTQ+ youth (Wike et al. 2021). Herek (1992, p. 89) points out that anti-gay hate crime is a result of heterosexism; "an ideological system that denies, denigrates and stigmatizes any non-heterosexual form of behavior, identity, relationship or community." Crimes with heterosexism as an underlying motivation may cause harm that goes beyond the actual victimization event by affecting psychological and emotional well-being as well as causing behavioral changes (Bell and Perry 2015).

Few studies have considered the rural experiences of homophobic and transphobic hate crime, despite evidence pointing to a higher probability of victimization in rural areas. According to a 2019 survey conducted by the Gay, Lesbian, Straight Education Network (GLSEN), 76.4% of rural LGBTQ+ students had been victimized based on their sexual orientation compared to 66.1% of suburban and 68.8% of urban LGBTQ+ students (Kosciw et al. 2020). Rural transgender students were also found to be more likely to experience gender-based harassment than their non-rural counterparts. But even when rural victimization rates are similar to the rates urban and suburban areas, rural LGBTQ+ may have less accessibility to various services and social support. The close bonds of rural communities may restrict individual privacy, and may complicate living in communities that are not as LGBTQ+-friendly (Wike et al. 2021). In Australia, Morandini et al. (2015) found that those residing in rural-remote areas concealed their sexuality at much higher rates than those living in metropolitan areas. They also had less involvement in the LGBTQ+ community and fewer friendships than other people with the same identity. The researchers also noted higher internalized homophobia among men. In Sweden, MUCF (2020) found that young LGBTQ+ people in rural areas have less access to meeting places with other youths and may avoid attending recreational events and activities due to the fear of being treated badly. However, there are cases in which rural areas can be inclusive and welcoming (Rosenberg 2021); see for instance, the case of Conner and Okamura (2021) who list the advantages of living in rural areas for LGBTQ+ people.

Drugs in Rural Areas

Drug-related offenses encompass a range of activities, from (ab)use to production, transportation, and trade; all of which may take different forms in rural contexts, especially in border regions. Relying mainly on evidence from North America, in this section we discuss who the rural substance users are, the types of drugs, the production and transportation of drugs, and their relation to the rural context.

Substance abuse is often viewed as primarily an urban issue, which may be true from some perspectives as most rural areas report lower levels of drug use (Weisheit and Brownstein 2016). However, studies have shown that among certain groups, especially rural youth, the rural-urban gap in substance abuse has been narrowing. In fact, since the early 2000s, the levels of substance abuse among rural youth have often been equal to or even exceeded those of their urban counterparts: mainly in the United States but also in the United Kingdom (Ceccato 2015f; Donnermeyer 2015a; Gomez and Pruitt 2016).

Certain rural characteristics may explain why rural youth (and other groups) may be at larger risk for turning to drug consumption and forming addictions. This includes more restricted access to local services such as treatment and recreation centers compared to urban areas, social stigma and a lack of anonymity deterring the use of mental health services (Gomez and Pruitt 2016). Factors such as bonding with family and school peers and integration into peer clusters may decrease or increase the probability of rural youth learning of illegal drugs, as per the theories of peer cluster theory and primary socialization theory (for a review, see Donnermeyer (2015b). Also, previous and current criminal engagement, especially involving violent crime, has been linked to higher rates of rural substance abuse in several studies (see, e.g., Nordfjærn et al. 2013; Oser et al. 2011; Webster et al. 2007, 2010). Rates of substance abuse may also differ based on drug type. Hakansson et al. (2008) found that Swedish amphetamine users are often older, less likely to be non-Nordic immigrants and members of a more rural population, compared to heroin users. Rural males have also been shown to abuse pain relievers, psychotherapeutics, and other illicit drugs (excluding marijuana) at higher rates than non-rural males (Gundy et al. 2016).

Largely located in rural areas, the domestic marijuana industry has grown rapidly in industrialized countries like the United States and Canada (Bouchard and Nguyen 2010; Weisheit et al. 1993). Methamphetamine is one of the more prominent and modern types of synthetic drugs, and, notably in the United States, it is unique as its epicenter of production was in rural communities when it first emerged in the early twenty-first century (Garriott 2016). Methamphetamine and amphetamine use continue to be a problem in large parts of Europe, Australia, and parts of Asia, and notably among the rural population in Sweden (Hakansson et al. 2008). In recent years, the use of opioids, including heroin as well as legal medical substances, have been part of the so-called 'overdose crises' largely in the rural areas of the United States (Kalesan et al. 2020; Orsi et al. 2018) but also found in rural Scotland (Hay and Gannon 2006). Furthermore, drugs that are legal in most countries are not necessarily detached from criminal behavior, such as alcohol, which has a long association with rural delinquency (see, e.g., Davis and Potter 1991; Martire and Larney 2011; Petrie et al. 2010).

Weisheit and Brownstein (2016) point out that rural areas are especially suited for drug production as they "provide a level of physical privacy...that is more difficult to find in an urban environment," and the detection of these sites is further impeded by the comparably limited resources of the rural police. Additionally, the lesser social and economic capital of rural areas may also be a strong factor affecting both drug use and production, which are the most prevalent in the poorest rural areas (Donnermeyer 2015a). Rural areas as sites of drug production (mainly marijuana and methamphetamine) have become common in not only the United States, but also in the United Kingdom, Australia, and Sweden (Ceccato 2015b; Weisheit and Brownstein 2016). Looking outside the Global North also reveals more of the social and cultural connotations of drug production within rural areas. For example, in the studies by van Dun (2014) and De Souza and Hoefle (1999) in Peru and Brazil, respectively, we find two historical pieces on organized drug production that look at both the illicit economies and social networks within the rural population, and the related violence. Anderson (2018) has examined how the restrictions of the civil rights of the Karen people in Thailand led to opium cultivation becoming their last means of survival. Stippel and Serrano-Moreno (2020) explored the importance of the coca leaf in the rural population in Bolivia and the interaction with the country's continuous adaptations of anti-drug policies.

Rural areas and border areas also play an important role in the transshipment of drugs; for example, in the United States where drugs like cocaine, heroin, and methamphetamine are still largely produced outside the country (Garriott 2016; Weisheit et al. 1993). Weisheit et al. (1993) found that rural areas that serve as transshipment points often develop problems with drug use as well, as interviews with marijuana growers revealed that some used their profits to support their cocaine habits. Findings have also shown links with other types of crime; for example, Ceccato (2004) noted that in Lithuania, certain border cities associated with drug and alcohol smuggling also had more assaults.

Environmental and Wildlife Crime

Environmental and wildlife crime (EWC) encompasses a range of possible transgressions against nature, including illegal dumping of waste, pollution, animal abuse, poaching, deforestation, and other environmental harms. Barclay and Bartel

(2015) outlined several reasons why there are currently no official definitions of environmental crime. First, the topic is relatively recent. Second, it is difficult to pinpoint individualized harm and causation, as incidents of environmental harm can happen at both global and local levels. Third, an incident may involve multiple acts and the effects may not be detected immediately, or even after several years. And last, that there can be ambiguity surrounding the (il)legality and (im)morality of many of the actions considered as EWC.

Traditional criminological theories have been applied to explain environmental crime. For example, factors associated with social disorganization have been found to increase the odds of forest fires in Indonesia (Saptawan et al. 2020). Rational choice theory has proven to be a useful basis for devising mitigation measures, as offenders of EWC adhere to cost-benefit assessments of the consequences of committing an offense (von Essen et al. 2016). Situational crime models such as routine activity and crime pattern theory have been utilized as well to explain levels and patterns of EWC (Stassen and Ceccato 2020; von Essen et al. 2016).

However, the aforementioned conflict between law and local practices, as well as morality and legal ambiguity, constitutes a large part of understanding EWC in the rural. White (2016) describes the idea of "folk crime," that is, illegal acts that are perceived by the offenders and the community as not so criminal, dangerous, or harmful. Illegal killings of animals by hunters and farmers may be considered less offensive by rural residents, especially of animals that are considered "pests" or threats to the offenders and their businesses (see, e.g., Enticott 2011; Ruiz-Suárez et al. 2015; Wagner et al. 2019; Wisniewski et al. 2019). However, offenders of EWC are not necessarily unaware or nonchalant regarding offending; rather, they utilize justifications to neutralize inner, moral conflicts; see, for example, neutralization theory (Sykes and Matza 1957). von Essen et al. (2017) found that hunters justify the killings of wolves in multiple ways, although the crimes are discussed through the "veil of anonymity" by which the hunters distance themselves from the offending. Further justification includes framing these acts as political protest against injustice and resistance against authorities (Holmes 2016; Højberg et al. 2017; Pohja-Mykrä 2016; von Essen et al. 2015). Additionally, Schoultz and Flyghed (2016) showed how environmental harm caused by corporations and industries is excused by appealing to higher loyalties, such as referencing the societal benefits their activities may provide; and this happens across the globe. Indeed, EWC is often considered a "cost of doing business," or even covered up to defend local economies or businesses (Ceccato 2015b; McDowell 2013).

Stassen and Ceccato (2020) suggested that EWC does not happen at random but follows people's routine activities. This in turn makes combating EWC in rural areas even more challenging than in urban areas, as the detection time increases due to comparably lower guardianship and likelihood of someone encountering the incident. Ceccato (2015b) found that the detection rate is heavily dependent on environmental inspectors, who in Sweden, for example, have the dual role of reporting crimes and develop many other functions. However, when there is difficulty proving that an incident is the result of a crime and the likelihood of prosecution is low, inspectors may choose not to report, which in turn makes police statistics of EWC a problematic source of data. Additionally, authorities are not actively searching for environmental crime, meaning that they are only notified of more obvious and visible incidents.

Organized Crime

Rural areas have increasingly been found to be locations of organized and larger-scale crime by groups and larger networks. Organized crime in rural areas can include illegal enterprises of, for example, drug production and dealing, food fraud, counterfeiting, as well as human trafficking and gang violence (see, e.g. Somerville et al. 2015). As rural areas are often places of social isolation and lower guardianship, they may have vulnerabilities that allow organized crime to more easily manifest in communities in different ways. Criminal organizations can, for example, establish themselves within communities through social networks in the local area, or outside communities through long-distance networks. Rural areas may also serve as both transshipment points and final destinations of trafficked goods and/or people. While perspectives of the rural United States have dominated the research topic thus far, organized crime is clearly present in, for example, the South American and Asian country sides as well. In the following section, this will all be explored in different contexts, focusing on drugs, "street crime," human trafficking as well as other, more unique cases.

Organized Drug Trade

Drugs may be the most (in)famous illicit or illegal products trafficked by organized crime, and a substantial portion of both drug production and distribution takes place in the rural. For instance, rural areas are especially viable for drug production, as they provide drug producers with higher level of physical privacy and lower detection rates, and with lesser police presence than in urban areas, as well as with soil and water access for cultivating organic drugs (Barclay et al. 2016; Weisheit and Brownstein 2016). While much of the rural drug production and distribution in the United States involves small-scale producers and dealers, international drug trafficking organizations are significant actors in the trans-national production and distribution of drugs, for example, methamphetamine and marijuana from Mexican cartels and alcohol from Canada and Jamaica flowing into rural areas of the United States (Weisheit and Brownstein 2016).

Nonetheless, organized drug networks are commonly originating from or manifesting within rural areas as well. The industry of bootlegging alcohol, for example, can be considered a notable rural criminal enterprise (Davis and Potter 1991). Other developments can be seen in Scotland, where drug organizations based outside rural communities maintain drug markets in rural areas by proxy, making it increasingly difficult for police to disrupt them (Clark et al. 2020). De Souza and Hoefle (1999) studied organized crime related to cannabis cultivation in northeast Brazil, and how it intensified local family feuds and envy-inspired violence. Similarly, the study by van Dun (2014) examined illegal networks and relationships between local cocaine producers, drug bosses, and the rural community in Peru, and how these shape the social organization of these communities. Here the author further observed how the organized drug production industry not only functions as a local economic system but also involves a range of social relations and networks between both legal and illegal actors. In fact, the dominance of smaller Peruvian criminal organizations and their involvement with villagers was found to lead to a certain level of social acceptance of drug production and distribution.

Gang Crime

Gang crime is mainly referring to street and youth gangs, involving a range of illicit activities such as violence, theft, and drug trading. Gangs are not a recent phenomenon in rural areas, but the topic only recently received the same attention as its urban counterpart (Glosser 2016); this despite the fact that the likelihood of young people joining a gang is equal among youth from urban, suburban, and rural areas (Watkins and Taylor 2016). Furthermore, studies such as Anderson et al. (2016) have revealed that some rural areas in the United States have disproportionately high levels of gang-related crime. Glosser (2016) reviewed previous research finding that gang structures are somewhat different in rural areas; there is a higher prevalence of "hybrid gangs", meaning gangs that cross cultural, ethnic, and racial boundaries, in contrast to traditional gangs. This is due to the lower population of rural communities and potential gang members, restricting the possibility of having a single, structural characteristic as in traditional gangs. Rural gang activities have also been shown to be more secretive and less visible than their urban counterparts. Social isolation, inequality and the disconnect between "migrant" and "native" rural community members have been highlighted as reasons why young people engage in gangs in rural areas.

Human Trafficking

A subject that has increasingly become relevant is the prevalence of human trafficking in rural areas. One form of human trafficking is sex trafficking, which in the United States is defined by the Trafficking Victims Protection Act (TVPA) of 2000 as "the recruitment, harbouring, transportation, provision, or obtaining of a person for the purpose of a commercial sex act," where the sexual act is induced by force, coercion, fraud, or where the victim is a legal minor (Cole and Sprang 2015). While sex traffickers appear to operate similarly along the rural-urban continuum, there is a persistent lack of knowledge and preparedness to tackle the issue in rural areas, as rural government officials and professionals are less aware of and less likely to have received training in the subject (Cole and Sprang 2015; Kumar et al. 2020). As rural areas are often characterized by financial instability and a lack of legitimate employment opportunities compared to urban areas, rural inhabitants may be more vulnerable to falling prey to the sex traffickers' strategies when trying to secure a livelihood for themselves and their families (Kumar et al. 2020).

While the sex trafficking of women and children may be the more well-known form of human trade, there has been an increased focus on trafficking in order to exploit labor, especially within the farming industry (Barrick 2016; Brisman et al. 2014; Brisman et al. 2016; Byrne and Smith 2016). In fact, estimations of the composition of the forced labor industry puts the share of sex work at 22%, while 68% involves agricultural and 10%, construction and domestic work, although the likelihood of experiencing sexual abuse is high in both categories (Byrne and Smith 2016). Labor trafficking involves transporting, forcing, or coercing someone into involuntary servitude, debt bondage, or slavery, while differing from smuggling. The abuse of farm workers involves a large system of exploiting poor, disenfranchised, and often foreign workers, who have limited legal protection and therefore are easier to control and coerce into compliance (Barrick 2016).

Other Forms of Organized Crime

An emergent subtopic under the umbrella of organized crime is food fraud and theft among farmers; for example, the illegal halal meat trade (McElwee et al. 2017; Smith and McElwee 2013). Food fraud involves any illegal activity related to tampering with, adding to, or misrepresenting food, and it can be considered a criminal enterprise due to involving both legitimate and criminal behaviors (McElwee et al. 2017). It has been compared to the cocaine trade in terms of profit, although with fewer risks and a lower likelihood of detection (Smith and McElwee 2013). Other rural criminal enterprises include the Chinese "cake uncles," who under the guise of delivering cakes commit petty fraud in rural villages, which later expanded into larger enterprises (Xi 2018). Mafias have also emerged as illegal suppliers of sand and oil in rural India (Michelutti 2019).

In summary, organized crime seems to have a relatively significant presence in rural areas, although this is thus far not reflected in the amount of literature dedicated to this topic. Organized crime involves a range of different types of crime and offenders, which may impact differently areas in the rural-urban continuum. Certain organized crimes such as those related to the agricultural industry are, by their nature, limited to rural areas, as previously discussed. As this is an emergent topic within rural criminology, we hope that this section has illustrated the need for greater attention to be placed on this subject by future research.

References

Abraham, J., & Ceccato, V. (forthcoming) Crime and safety in rural areas: A systematic review of the English-language literature 1980–2020. *Journal of Rural Studies*.

Abrahams, N., & Jewkes, R. (2010). Barriers to post exposure prophylaxis (PEP) completion after rape: a South African qualitative study. *Culture, Health & Sexuality, 12*(5), 471-484. http://www.jstor.org/stable/27806670

Akhtar, Z. (2020). Scheduled Castes, Dalits And Criminalisation By 'Descent'. *State Crime Journal, 9*(1), 71-99. https://doi.org/10.13169/statecrime.9.1.0071

Allen, J., & Cancino, J. M. (2012, 2012/03/01/). Social disorganization, Latinos and juvenile crime in the Texas borderlands. *Journal of Criminal Justice, 40*(2), 152–163. https://doi.org/10.1016/j.jcrimjus.2012.02.007

Anderson, B. (2018). Zomia's vestiges: Illegible peoples and legible crimes in Omkoi, northwest Thailand. *South East Asia Research, 26*(1), 38-57. https://doi.org/10.1177/0967828X17752710

Anderson, J. F., Remsmith-Jones, K., Dyson, L., & Langsam, A. H. (2016). Disproportionate gang crime and violence in the west zone of greenville (Pitt County) North Carolina [Review]. *Journal of Gang Research, 23*(2), 19-40. https://www.scopus.com/inward/record.uri?eid=2-s2.0-84964702259&partnerID=40&md5=a4ff4c7180aa5f011eea0dd67355f127

Anderson, J. H. (2020). *Classification of urban, suburban, and rural areas in the National Crime Victimization Survey* (Criminal Victimization, 2019, Issue.

Anderson, S. (1999). Crime and social change in Scotland. In G. Dingwall & S. Moody (Eds.), *Crime and Conflict in the Countryside*. University of Wales Press.

Antunes, A. P., Rebêlo, G. H., Pezzuti, J. C. B., Vieira, M. A. R. d. M., Constantino, P. d. A. L., Campos-Silva, J. V., Fonseca, R., Durigan, C. C., Ramos, R. M., Amaral, J. V. d., Camps Pimenta, N., Ranzi, T. J. D., Lima, N. A. S., & Shepard, G. H. (2019, 2019/05/01/). A conspiracy of silence: Subsistence hunting rights in the Brazilian Amazon. *Land Use Policy, 84*, 1–11. https://doi.org/10.1016/j.landusepol.2019.02.045

Archbold, C. A. (2015). Established-outside relations, crime problems, and policing in oil boomtowns in western North Dakota. *Criminology, Criminal Justice, Law and Society, 16*(3), 19-40. https://www.scopus.com/inward/record.uri?eid=2-s2.0-85025120416&partnerID=40&md5=998ea22a6913cbb876f72d1c2c8669fc

Archer, J. E. (1999). Poaching Gangs and Violence: The Urban—Rural Divide in Nineteenth-Century Lancashire. *The British Journal of Criminology, 39*(1), 25-38. http://www.jstor.org/stable/23638042

Arthur, J. A. (1991). Socioeconomic Predictors of Crime in Rural Georgia. *Criminal Justice Review, 16*(1), 29-41. https://doi.org/10.1177/073401689101600106

Arvate, P., Falsete, F. O., Ribeiro, F. G., & Souza, A. P. (2018). Lighting and Homicides: Evaluating the Effect of an Electrification Policy in Rural Brazil on Violent Crime Reduction. *Journal of Quantitative Criminology, 34*(4), 1047-1078. https://doi.org/10.1007/s10940-017-9365-6

Bachman, R. (1992). Crime in Nonmetropolitan America: A National Accounting of Trends, Incidence Rates, and Idiosyncratic Vulnerabilities. *Rural Sociology, 57*(4), 546-560. https://doi.org/10.1111/j.1549-0831.1992.tb00479.x

Baldwin, S. (1994, 1994/09/06/). Preliminary investigation: Brief Screening Interview (BSI) with young drinking offenders. *Forensic Science International, 68*(1), 33-43. https://doi.org/10.1016/0379-0738(94)90377-8

Bankston, W. B., Jenkins, Q. A. L., Thayer-Doyle, C. L., & Thompson, C. Y. (1987). Fear of criminal victimization and residential location: the influence of perceived risk (Louisiana). *Rural Sociology, 52*(1), 98-107. https://www.scopus.com/inward/record.uri?eid=2-s2.0-0023469009&partnerID=40&md5=5e7c2b6c8b09d74112015955be302775

Barclay, E. (2016). Farm victimisation. In J. F. Donnermeyer (Ed.), *The Routledge International Handbook of Rural Criminology* (pp. 107-113). Routledge.

Barclay, E., & Bartel, R. (2015). Defining environmental crime: The perspective of farmers. *Journal of Rural Studies, 39*, 188-198. https://doi.org/10.1016/j.jrurstud.2015.01.007

References

Barclay, E., & Donnermeyer, J. F. (2002). Property crime and crime prevention on farms in Australia. *Crime Prevention and Community Safety, 4*(4), 47-61. https://doi.org/10.1057/palgrave.cpcs.8140169

Barclay, E., & Donnermeyer, J. F. (2011). Crime and security on agricultural operations. *Security Journal, 24*(1), 1-18. https://doi.org/10.1057/sj.2008.23

Barclay, E., Meisel, J., DeKeseredy, W. S., & Nolan, J. (2016). Teaching rural criminology. In J. F. Donnermeyer (Ed.), *The Routledge International Handbook of Rural Criminology* (pp. 431-436). Routledge.

Barclay, E. M. (2017). Rural crime. In *The Palgrave Handbook of Australian and New Zealand Criminology, Crime and Justice* (pp. 285–297). https://doi.org/10.1007/978-3-319-55747-2_19

Barnett, C., & Mencken, F. C. (2002). Social disorganization theory and the contextual nature of crime in nonmetropolitan counties. *Rural Sociology, 67*(3), 372-393. https://doi.org/10.1111/j.1549-0831.2002.tb00109.x

Barrick, K. (2016). Human trafficking, labor exploitation and exposure to environmental hazards. In J. F. Donnermeyer (Ed.), *The Routledge International Handbook in Rural Criminology* (pp. 147–154). Routledge.

Battin, J. R., & Crowl, J. N. (2017). Urban sprawl, population density, and crime: An examination of contemporary migration trends and crime in suburban and rural neighborhoods. *Crime Prevention and Community Safety, 19*(2), 136-150. https://doi.org/10.1057/s41300-017-0020-9

Bell, J. G., & Perry, B. (2015, 2015/01/02). Outside Looking In: The Community Impacts of Anti-Lesbian, Gay, and Bisexual Hate Crime. *Journal of Homosexuality, 62*(1), 98–120. https://doi.org/10.1080/00918369.2014.957133

Berg, M. T., & DeLisi, M. (2005, 2005/07/01/). Do career criminals exist in rural America? *Journal of Criminal Justice, 33*(4), 317–325. https://doi.org/10.1016/j.jcrimjus.2005.04.002

Berg, M. T., & Lauritsen, J. L. (2016). Telling a Similar Story Twice? NCVS/UCR Convergence in Serious Violent Crime Rates in Rural, Suburban, and Urban Places (1973–2010). *Journal of Quantitative Criminology, 32*(1), 61-87. https://doi.org/10.1007/s10940-015-9254-9

Blurton, D. M., & Copus, G. D. (2003). Alaska Native Inmates: The Demographic Relationship Between Upbringing And Crime. *The Prison Journal, 83*(1), 90-104. https://doi.org/10.1177/0032885502250395

Bouchard, M., & Nguyen, H. (2010). Is it who you know, or how many that counts? criminal networks and cost avoidance in a sample of young offenders. *Justice Quarterly, 27*(1), 130-158. https://doi.org/10.1080/07418820802593386

Brisman, A., McClanahan, B., & South, N. (2014). Toward a Green-Cultural Criminology of "the Rural". *Critical Criminology, 22*(4), 479-494. https://doi.org/10.1007/s10612-014-9250-7

Brisman, A., Mclanahan, B., & South, N. (2016). Fractured earth, forced labour: A green criminological analysis of rights and the exploitation of landscapes and workers in rural contexts. In J. F. Donnermeyer (Ed.), *The Routledge International Handbook of Rural Criminology* (pp. 289-296). Routledge.

Broadhurst, R. (2002). Lethal violence, crime and state formation in Cambodia [Review]. *Australian and New Zealand Journal of Criminology, 35*(1), 1-26. https://doi.org/10.1375/acri.35.1.1

BRÅ – Brottsförebyggande rådet (The Swedish National Council for Crime Prevention). (2019). *Hate Crime 2018 Statistics on crimes reported to the police with identified hate crime motives.*

BRÅ – Brottsförebyggande rådet (The Swedish National Council for Crime Prevention). (2021a). *Anmälda Brott (Reported Crimes)*. https://statistik.bra.se/solwebb/action/index

BRÅ – Brottsförebyggande rådet (The Swedish National Council for Crime Prevention). (2021b). *Nationella trygghetsundersökningen 2021.*

Bunei, E. K., Auya, S., & Rono, J. K. (2016). Agricultural crime in Africa. In J. F. Donnermeyer (Ed.), *The Routledge International Handbook of Rural Criminology* (pp. 117-123). Routledge.

Bureau of Justice Statistics. (2021). *NCVS Victimization Analysis Tool (NVAT)*. https://www.bjs.gov/index.cfm?ty=nvat

Byrne, R., & Smith, K. (2016). Modern slavery and agriculture. In J. F. Donnermeyer (Ed.), *The Routledge International Handbook of Rural Criminology* (pp. 157-164). Routledge.

Calvert, J. F., & Munsie-Benson, M. (1999, 1999/07/01/). Public opinion and knowledge about childhood sexual abuse in a rural community. *Child Abuse & Neglect, 23*(7), 671-682. https://doi.org/10.1016/S0145-2134(99)00038-1

Canofre, F. (2017). Criminalizing indigenous rights: The battle for land in Brazil. *World Policy Journal, 34*(3), 64-68. https://doi.org/10.1215/07402775-4280016

Carcach, C. (2000). Size, accessibility and crime in regional Australia. In *Trends and issues in crime and criminal justice* (Vol. 175). Australian Institute of Criminology.

Carleton, R., Brantingham, P. L., & Brantingham, P. J. (2014). Crime specialization in rural British Columbia, Canada. *Canadian Journal of Criminology and Criminal Justice, 56*(5), 595-621. https://doi.org/10.3138/ccj.2014.0038

Carmenta, R., Coudel, E., & Steward, A. M. (2019). Forbidden fire: Does criminalising fire hinder conservation efforts in swidden landscapes of the Brazilian Amazon?. *Geographical Journal, 185*(1), 23-37. https://doi.org/10.1111/geoj.12255

Çaya, S. (2014, 2014/02/21/). Violence in Rural Regions: The Case of ModernTurkey. *Procedia – Social and Behavioral Sciences, 114*, 721-726. https://doi.org/10.1016/j.sbspro.2013.12.774

Cayli, B. (2014). Renewing Criminalized and Hegemonic Cultural Landscapes. *Critical Criminology, 22*(4), 579-593. https://doi.org/10.1007/s10612-014-9258-z

Cebulak, W. (2004). Why rural crime and justice really matter. *Journal of Police and Criminal Psychology, 19*(1), 71-81. https://doi.org/10.1007/BF02802576

Ceccato, V. (2004). Crime Dynamics at Lithuanian Borders. *European Journal of Criminology, 4*(2), 131–160. https://doi.org/10.1177/1477370807074845

Ceccato, V. (2015a). Definitions, theory, and research making in rural Sweden. In *Rural Crime and Community Safety* (pp. 28–58). Routledge.

Ceccato, V. (2015b). Farm crimes and environmental wildlife offenses. In *Rural Crime and Community Safety* (pp. 165–193). Routledge.

Ceccato, V. (2015c). The geography of property and violent crimes in Sweden. In *Rural Crime and Community Safety* (pp. 93–115). Routledge.

Ceccato, V. (2015d). Rural-urban cirme trends in international perspective. In *Rural Crime and Community Safety* (pp. 65–90). Routledge.

Ceccato, V. (2015e). Violence against women in rural communities. In *Rural Crime and Community Safety* (pp. 226–252). Routledge.

Ceccato, V. (2015f). Youth in rural areas. In *Rural Crime and Community Safety* (pp. 196-223). Routledge.

Ceccato, V. (2016). *Rural crime and community safety*. Routledge.

Ceccato, V. (2017). Fear of crime and overall anxieties in rural areas: The case of Sweden. In *The Routledge International Handbook on Fear of Crime* (pp. 354–367). https://doi.org/10.4324/9781315651781

Ceccato, V., & Ceccato, H. (2017, 2017/09/01). Violence in the Rural Global South: Trends, Patterns, and Tales From the Brazilian Countryside. *Criminal Justice Review, 42*(3), 270–290. https://doi.org/10.1177/0734016817724504

Ceccato, V., & Dolmen, L. (2011, 2011/01/01/). Crime in rural Sweden. *Applied Geography, 31*(1), 119–135. https://doi.org/10.1016/j.apgeog.2010.03.002

Ceccato, V., & Dolmen, L. (2013). Crime prevention in rural Sweden. *European Journal of Criminology, 10*(1), 89-112. https://doi.org/10.1177/1477370812457763

Ceccato, V., Abraham, J., Lundqvist, P. (2021). Crimes against animal production: Exploring the use of media archives. *International Criminal Justice Review, 31*(4): 384–404. https://doi.org/10.1177/10575677211041915.

Chandra, K. S., & Pradhan, S. N. (2001). Crimes against scs/sts in rural areas: A study of causes and remedies. *Journal of Rural Development, 20*(1), 113-129. https://www.scopus.com/inward/record.uri?eid=2-s2.0-0035034378&partnerID=40&md5=14160833a500f0ccccc200faa7591aef

Chervyakov, V. V., Shkolnikov, V. M., Pridemore, W. A., & McKee, M. (2002, 2002/11/01/). The changing nature of murder in Russia. *Social Science & Medicine, 55*(10), 1713–1724. https://doi.org/10.1016/S0277-9536(01)00299-4

References

Clark, A., Fraser, A., & Hamilton-Smith, N. (2020). Networked territorialism: the routes and roots of organised crime. *Trends in Organized Crime*. https://doi.org/10.1007/s12117-020-09393-9

Clarke, R. V., & Harris, P. M. (1992). Auto Theft and Its Prevention. *Crime and Justice, 16*, 1-54. http://www.jstor.org/stable/1147560

Conner, C. T., & Okamura, D. (2021). Queer expectations: An empirical critique of rural LGBT+ narratives. *Sexualities*, 13634607211013280.

Cole, J., & Sprang, G. (2015, 2015/02/01/). Sex trafficking of minors in metropolitan, micropolitan, and rural communities. *Child Abuse & Neglect, 40*, 113–123. https://doi.org/10.1016/j.chiabu.2014.07.015

Collins, V. E. (2016). The nomadic pastoralist, the fisherman and the pirate. In J. F. Donnermeyer (Ed.), *The Routledge International Handbook of Rural Criminology* (pp. 93-100). Routledge.

Cunneen, C. (2016). Indigenous people and rural criminology. In J. F. Donnemeyer (Ed.), *The Routledge International Handbook of Rural Criminology* (pp. 365-372). Routledge.

Davis, R. S., & Potter, G. W. (1991). Bootlegging and rural criminal entrepreneurship. *Journal of Crime and Justice, 14*(1), 145-159. https://doi.org/10.1080/0735648X.1991.9721430

Dawson, J., & Wells, M. (2006). Crimes involving child victims: Law enforcement reporting to child protective services in rural communities. *Journal of Public Child Welfare, 1*(4), 43-65. https://doi.org/10.1080/15548730802118272

De Angelis, J., Benz, T. A., & Gillham, P. (2017). Collective Security, Fear of Crime, and Support for Concealed Firearms on a University Campus in the Western United States. *Criminal Justice Review, 42*(1), 77-94. https://doi.org/10.1177/0734016816686660

De Souza, A. M., & Hoefle, S. W. (1999). From family feud to organised crime: The cultural economy of cannabis in Northeast Brazil. *Bulletin of Latin American Research, 18*(3), 343-360. https://doi.org/10.1016/S0261-3050(98)00033-3

DeKeseredy, W. S. (2020). Preventing violence against women in the heartland. In A. Harkness (Ed.), *Rural Crime Prevention: Theory, Tactics and Techniques* (pp. 12). Routledge.

DeKeseredy, W. S., & Hall-Sanchez, A. (2016). Adult Pornography and Violence Against Women in the Heartland: Results From a Rural Southeast Ohio Study. *Violence against women, 23*(7), 830-849.

DeKeseredy, W. S., Hall-Sanchez, A., Dragiewicz, M., & Rennison, C. M. (2016). Intimate violence against women in rural communities. In J. F. Donnermeyer (Ed.), *The Routledge International Handbook of Rural Criminology* (pp. 167–178).

DeKeseredy, W. S., Hall-Sanchez, A., Dragiewicz, M., & Rennison, C. M. (2018). Male violence against women in the global south: What we know and don't know. In K. Carrington, Hogg, R., Scott, J., Sozzo, M. (Ed.), *The Palgrave Handbook of Criminology and the Global South* (pp. 883-900). Palgrave Macmillan.

DeKeseredy, W. S., & Joseph, C. (2006, March 1, 2006). Separation and/or Divorce Sexual Assault in Rural Ohio: Preliminary Results of an Exploratory Study. *Violence against women, 12*(3), 301-311. https://doi.org/10.1177/1077801205277357

DeKeseredy, W. S., Muzzatti, S. L., & Donnermeyer, J. F. (2014, 2014/05/01). Mad Men in Bib Overalls: Media's Horrification and Pornification of Rural Culture. *Critical Criminology, 22*(2), 179–197. https://doi.org/10.1007/s10612-013-9190-7

DeKeseredy, W. S., Rogness, M., & Schwartz, M. D. (2004). Separation/divorce sexual assault: the current state of social scientific knowledge. *Aggression and Violent Behavior, 9*, 675–691.

Deller, S. C., & Deller, M. A. (2010). Rural Crime and Social Capital. *Growth and Change, 41*(2), 221-275. https://doi.org/10.1111/j.1468-2257.2010.00526.x

Donnermeyer, J. F. (2015a). Crime in the Rural Context. In J. D. Wright (Ed.), *International Encyclopedia of the Social & Behavioral Sciences (Second Edition)* (pp. 158–163). Elsevier. https://doi.org/10.1016/B978-0-08-097086-8.45049-X

Donnermeyer, J. F. (2015b, 2015/06/01/). The social organisation of the rural and crime in the United States: Conceptual considerations. *Journal of Rural Studies, 39*, 160–170. https://doi.org/10.1016/j.jrurstud.2014.11.014

Donnermeyer, J. F. (2016a). The other side of agricultural crime: When farmers offend. In *Greening Criminology in the 21st Century: Contemporary Debates and Future Directions in the Study of Environmental Harm* (pp. 147–161). https://doi.org/10.4324/9781315585949

Donnermeyer, J. F. (2016b). *The Routledge international handbook of rural criminology*. Routledge.

Donnermeyer, J. F. (2017). The place of rural in a southern criminology. *International Journal for Crime, Justice and Social Democracy, 6*(1), 118-132. https://doi.org/10.5204/ijcjsd.v6i1.384

Eduful, M., Alsharif, K., Eduful, A., Acheampong, M., Eduful, J., & Mazumder, L. (2020, 2020/10/01/). The Illegal Artisanal and Small-scale mining (Galamsey) 'Menace' in Ghana: Is Military-Style Approach the Answer? *Resources Policy, 68*, 101732. https://doi.org/10.1016/j.resourpol.2020.101732

Eisner, M. (2008). Modernity Strikes Back? A Historical Perspective on the Latest Increase in Interpersonal Violence (1960-1990). *International Journal of Conflict and Violence, 2*(2), 288-316.

El-Hak, S. A. G., Ali, M. A. M., & El-Atta, H. M. H. A. (2009, 2009/10/01/). Child deaths from family violence in Dakahlia and Damiatta Governorates, Egypt. *Journal of Forensic and Legal Medicine, 16*(7), 388-391. https://doi.org/10.1016/j.jflm.2009.04.010

Enticott, G. (2011, 2011/04/01/). Techniques of neutralising wildlife crime in rural England and Wales. *Journal of Rural Studies, 27*(2), 200-208. https://doi.org/10.1016/j.jrurstud.2011.01.005

Fleisher, M. L. (2002). 'War is good for thieving!' The symbiosis of crime and warfare among the Kuria of Tanzania. *Africa, 72*(1), 131-149. https://doi.org/10.3366/afr.2002.72.1.131

Forrest, J., & Dunn, K. (2013). Cultural diversity, racialisation and the experience of racism in rural Australia: the South Australian case. *Journal of Rural Studies, 30*, 8.

Gale, F., & Wundersitz, J. (1986). Rural and Urban Crime Rates Amongst Aboriginal Youth: Patterns of Different Locational Opportunity. *Australian Geographical Studies, 24*(2), 179-186. https://doi.org/10.1111/j.1467-8470.1986.tb00527.x

García, G. (2011). Urban Guajiros: Colonial Reconcentración, Rural Displacement and Criminalisation in Western Cuba, 1895–1902. *Journal of Latin American Studies, 43*(2), 209-235. https://doi.org/10.1017/S0022216X11000010

Gargiulo, F., Angelino, C. V., Cicala, L., Persechino, G., & Lega, M. (2016). Remote sensing in the fight against environmental crimes: The case study of the cattle-breeding facilities in southern Italy. *International Journal of Sustainable Development and Planning, 11*(5), 663-671. https://doi.org/10.2495/SDP-V11-N5-663-671

Garland, J., & Chakraborti, N. (2004). Racist Victimisation, Community Safety and the Rural: Issues and Challenges. *British Journal of Community Justice, 2*(3, . 12p.), v.

Garland, J., & Chakraborti, N. (2006a). 'Race', space and place: Examining identity and cultures of exclusion in rural England. *Ethnicities, 6*(2), 18.

Garland, J., & Chakraborti, N. (2006b). Recognising and Responding To Victims Of Rural Racism. *International Review of Victimology, 13*, 49-69. https://journals.sagepub.com/doi/pdf/10.1177/026975800601300103

Garriott, W. (2016). Metamphetamine and the canging rhetoric of drugs in the United States. In J. F. Donnermeyer (Ed.), *The Routledge International Handbook of Rural Criminology* (pp. 275-282). Routledge.

Gerstenfeld, P. B. (2003). *Hate crimes. Causes, Controls and Controversies*. Sage.

Glosser, A. M. (2016). Homies of the corn. In J. F. Donnemeyer (Ed.), *The Routledge International Handbok of Rural Criminology* (pp. 85-91). Routledge.

Gomez, D. G., & Pruitt, L. R. (2016). Rural adolescent substance use. In J. F. Donnermeyer (Ed.), *The Routledge International Handbook of Rural Criminology* (pp. 245-251). Routledge.

Gracia, E. (2004, July 1, 2004). Unreported cases of domestic violence against women: towards an epidemiology of social silence, tolerance, and inhibition. *Journal of Epidemiology and Community Health, 58*(7), 536–537. https://doi.org/10.1136/jech.2003.019604

Gundy, K. T., Tucker, C. J., Stracuzzi, N. F., Sharp, E. H., & Rebellon, C. J. (2016). The rural context of substance misuse in the United States. In J. F. Donnermeyer (Ed.), *The Routledge International Handbook of Rural Criminology* (pp. 253-262). Routledge.

Hakansson, A., Schlyter, F., & Berglund, M. (2008). Characteristics of primary amphetamine users in Sweden: A criminal justice population examined with the addiction severity index. *European Addiction Research, 15*(1), 10-18. https://doi.org/10.1159/000173004

References

Hamid, L. A., & Toyong, N. M. P. (2014, 2014/10/16/). Rural Area, Elderly People and the House Breaking Crime. *Procedia – Social and Behavioral Sciences, 153*, 443–451. https://doi.org/10.1016/j.sbspro.2014.10.078

Hay, G., & Gannon, M. (2006, 2006/06/01/). Capture–recapture estimates of the local and national prevalence of problem drug use in Scotland. *International Journal of Drug Policy, 17*(3), 203–210. https://doi.org/10.1016/j.drugpo.2004.07.005

Hemenway, D., Berrigan, J., Azrael, D., Barber, C., & Miller, M. (2020, 2020/05/01/). Fatal police shootings of civilians, by rurality. *Preventive Medicine, 134*, 106046. https://doi.org/10.1016/j.ypmed.2020.106046

Hemenway, D., & Solnick, S. J. (2015, 2015/10/01/). The epidemiology of self-defense gun use: Evidence from the National Crime Victimization Surveys 2007–2011. *Preventive Medicine, 79*, 22–27. https://doi.org/10.1016/j.ypmed.2015.03.029

Herek, G. (1992). The social context of hate crimes: Notes on cultural heterosexism. In G. Herek & K. Berrill (Eds.), *Hate crimes: Confronting violence against lesbians and gay men ()*. (pp. 89–104). Sage.

Hogg, R., & Carrington, K. (2016). Crime and violence outside the metropole. In J. F. Donnermeyer (Ed.), *The Routledge International Handbook of Rural Criminology* (pp. 181-188). Routledge.

Holmes, G. (2016). Conservation crime as political protest. In J. F. Donnermeyer (Ed.), *The Routledge International Handbook of Rural Criminology* (pp. 309-315). Routledge.

Højberg, P. L., Nielsen, M. R., & Jacobsen, J. B. (2017). Fear, economic consequences, hunting competition, and distrust of authorities determine preferences for illegal lethal actions against gray wolves (Canis lupus): a choice experiment among landowners in Jutland, Denmark. *Crime, Law and Social Change, 67*(4), 461-480. https://doi.org/10.1007/s10611-016-9670-2

IPEA – Instituto de Pesquisa Econômica Aplicada (The Institute for Applied Economic Research). (2020). *Atlas da violencia no campo do Brasil: Condicionantes socio-economicos e estruturais (Atlas of violence in rural areas in Brazil: Socio-economic and structural indicators)*. IPEA.

Jamil, F. (2018, 2018/12/01/). Electricity theft among residential consumers in Rawalpindi and Islamabad. *Energy Policy, 123*, 147–154. https://doi.org/10.1016/j.enpol.2018.04.023

Jewkes, R., Penn-Kekana, L., & Rose-Junius, H. (2005, 2005/10/01/). "If they rape me, I can't blame them": Reflections on gender in the social context of child rape in South Africa and Namibia. *Social Science & Medicine, 61*(8), 1809–1820. https://doi.org/10.1016/j.socscimed.2005.03.022

Jobes, P. C. (2004). Colonialization and Crime: Contemporary Consequences of Invasion on Indigenous Peoples in Rural Places [Review]. *International Review of Sociology, 14*(1), 51-71. https://doi.org/10.1080/0390670042000186761

Jones, J. (2012). Looking beyond the 'rural idyll': Some recent trends in rural crime: Jane Jones describes recent trends in the theft of livestock and agricultural machinery in the countryside. *Criminal Justice Matters, 89*(1), 8-9. https://doi.org/10.1080/09627251.2012.721964

Jones, R. (2016). Gender, Criminal Opportunity and Landscape in Nineteenth-Century Wales. *Rural History, 27*(2), 169-185. https://doi.org/10.1017/S0956793316000030

Justus, M., Ceccato, V., Moreira, G. C., & Kahn, T. (2018). Crime against trading: The case of cargo theft in Sao Paulo. In *Retail crime* (pp. 297-323). Springer.

Justus, M., Scorzafave, L. G., & Sant'anna, E. G. (2016). Crime and victimization in rural Brazil. In J. F. Donnermeyer (Ed.), *The Routledge International Handbook of Rural Criminology* (pp. 211-220). Routledge.

Kadar, C., Maculan, R., & Feuerriegel, S. (2019, 2019/04/01/). Public decision support for low population density areas: An imbalance-aware hyper-ensemble for spatio-temporal crime prediction. *Decision Support Systems, 119*, 107–117. https://doi.org/10.1016/j.dss.2019.03.001

Kalesan, B., Zhao, S., Poulson, M., Neufeld, M., Dechert, T., Siracuse, J. J., Zuo, Y., & Li, F. (2020, 2020/12/01/). Intersections of Firearm Suicide, Drug-Related Mortality, and Economic Dependency in Rural America. *Journal of Surgical Research, 256*, 96–102. https://doi.org/10.1016/j.jss.2020.06.011

Kaylen, M., Pridemore, W. A., & Roche, S. P. (2019). A comparison of aggravated assault rate trends in rural, suburban, and urban areas using the UCR and NCS/NCVS, 1988–2005. *Crime Prevention and Community Safety 21*, 18.

Kilday, A. M. (2014). 'Criminally Poor?': Investigating the Link Between Crime and Poverty in Eighteenth Century England. *Cultural and Social History, 11*(4), 507-526. https://doi.org/10.2752/147800414X14056862572023

Kneebone, E., & Raphael, S. (2011). *City and Suburban Crime Trends in Metropolitan America.* M. O. Press.

Korsell, L., & Hagstedt, J. (2008). *Illegal handel med hotade djur- och växtarter: En förstudie.* http://www.bra.se/bra/publikationer/arkiv/publikationer/2008-12-31-illegal-handel-med-hotade-djur%2D%2Doch-vaxtarter.html

Kosciw, J. G., Clark, C. M., Truong, N. L., & Zongrone, A. D. (2020). *The 2019 national school climate survey: The experiences of lesbian, gay, bisexual, transgender, and queer youth in our nation's schools.* https://www.glsen.org/sites/default/files/2020-10/NSCS-2019-Full-Report_0.pdf

Kowalski, G. S., & Duffield, D. (1990). The Impact of the Rural Population Component on Homicide Rates in the United States: A County-Level Analysis. *Rural Sociology, 55*(1), 76-90. https://doi.org/10.1111/j.1549-0831.1990.tb00674.x

Kumar, R., Mishra, N., & Mishra, P. S. (2020, 2020/12/01/). Human trafficking: A review of the crime in Odisha, India. *Children and Youth Services Review, 119*, 105532. https://doi.org/10.1016/j.childyouth.2020.105532

Larsen, M. V., & Olsen, A. L. (2020). Reducing Bias in Citizens' Perception of Crime Rates: Evidence from a Field Experiment on Burglary Prevalence. *The Journal of Politics, 82*(2), 747-752.

Laub, J. H. (1981, 1981/01/01/). Ecological considerations in victim reporting to the police. *Journal of Criminal Justice, 9*(6), 419–430. https://doi.org/10.1016/0047-2352(81)90088-X

Laub, J. H. (1983, 1983/01/01/). Patterns of offending in urban and rural areas. *Journal of Criminal Justice, 11*(2), 129–142. https://doi.org/10.1016/0047-2352(83)90048-X

Lee, M. R. (2006). The Religious Institutional Base and Violent Crime in Rural Areas. *Journal for the Scientific Study of Religion, 45*(3), 309-324. http://www.jstor.org/stable/3838287

Lee, M. R., & Slack, T. (2008). Labor market conditions and violent crime across the metro-nonmetro divide. *Social Science Research, 37*(3), 753-768. https://doi.org/10.1016/j.ssresearch.2007.09.001

Levitt, S. D. (2004). Understanding why crime fell in the 1990s: Four factors that explain the decline and six that do not. . *Journal of Economic Perspectives, 18*(1), 163-190.

Lewis, S. H. (2003). *Unspoken Crimes: Sexual Assault in Rural America.* P. Enola.

Lichter, D., & Brown, D. (2011, 08/01). Rural America in an Urban Society: Changing Spatial and Social Boundaries. *Annual Review of Sociology, 37.* https://doi.org/10.1146/annurev-soc-081309-150208

Lilliott, E. A., Trott, E. M., Kellett, N. C., Green, A. E., & Willging, C. E. (2017). Women, Incarceration, and Reentry The Revolving Door of Prisons. In C. C. Datchi & J. R. Ancis (Eds.), *Gender, Psychology, and Justice* (pp. 127-150). NYU Press. https://doi.org/10.2307/j.ctt1ggjjpm.9

Lin, D. (2015). Ag-gag laws and farming crimes against animals. In *The Routledge International Handbook of the Crimes of the Powerful* (pp. 466–478). https://www.scopus.com/inward/record.uri?eid=2-s2.0-84942236777&partnerID=40&md5=36f6318307046115a3f3a3f747b320dc

Lindhorst, T. (1997, 1997/11/01). Lesbians and Gay Men in the Country. *Journal of Gay & Lesbian Social Services, 7*(3), 1–11. https://doi.org/10.1300/J041v07n03_01

Little, J. (1999). Otherness, representation and the cultural construction of rurality. *Progress in Human Geography 23*(3), 437-442.

Lovell, J. S. (2016). Understanding farm animal abuse. In J. F. Donnermeyer (Ed.), *The Routledge International Handbook of Rural Criminology* (pp. 137-144). Routledge.

Lowe, P., Ward, N., Seymour, S., & Clark, J. (1996). Farm pollution as environmental crime. *Science as Culture, 5*(4), 588-612. https://doi.org/10.1080/09505439609526448

Lumsden, K., Goode, J., & Black, A. (2019). 'I Will Not Be Thrown Out of the Country Because I'm an Immigrant': Eastern European Migrants' Responses to Hate Crime in a Semi-Rural

Context in the Wake of Brexit. *Sociological Research Online, 24*(2), 167-184. https://doi.org/10.1177/1360780418811967

Marshall, B., & Johnson, S. (2005). *Crime in rural areas: A review of the literature for the rural evidence research centre.*

Martire, K. A., & Larney, S. (2011). Health outcomes, program completion, and criminal recidivism among participants in the Rural Alcohol Diversion program, Australia. *Journal of Substance Use, 16*(1), 50-56. https://doi.org/10.3109/14659891003706407

Mawby, R. I. (2015, 2015/06/01/). Exploring the relationship between crime and place in the countryside. *Journal of Rural Studies, 39*, 262–270. https://doi.org/10.1016/j.jrurstud.2014.12.003

McDowell, M. G. (2013). 'Becoming a waste land where nothing can survive': resisting state-corporate environmental crime in a 'forgotten' place. *Contemporary Justice Review: Issues in Criminal, Social, and Restorative Justice, 16*(4), 394–411. https://doi.org/10.1080/10282580.2013.857094

McElwee, G., Smith, R., & Lever, J. (2017, 2017/05/01/). Illegal activity in the UK halal (sheep) supply chain: Towards greater understanding. *Food Policy, 69*, 166–175. https://doi.org/10.1016/j.foodpol.2017.04.006

McPhail, I. V., Olver, M. E., & Brooks, C. (2017). Taking the Pulse: perceptions of crime trends and community safety and support for crime control methods in the Canadian Prairies. *Journal Of Community Safety & Well-Being, 2*(2), 43-50.

Mears, D. P., Scott, M. L., & Bhati, A. S. (2007). Opportunity theory and agricultural crime victimization. *Rural Sociology, 72*(2), 151-184. https://doi.org/10.1526/003601107781170044

Melde, C. (2006). MCJA student paper award winner: Social disorganization and violent crime in rural appalachia. *Journal of Crime and Justice, 29*(2), 117-140. https://doi.org/10.1080/0735648X.2006.9721651

Meng, Q. (2016). Corruption and land use expropriation in rural China. In J. F. Donnermeyer (Ed.), *The Routledge International Handbook of Criminology* (pp. 223-230). Routledge.

Michelutti, L. (2019). The inter-state criminal life of sand and oil in North India. In L. Michelutti & B. Harriss-White (Eds.), *The Wild East* (pp. 168-193). UCL Press. http://www.jstor.org/stable/j.ctvfrxr41.14

Moore, M. H., & Trojanowicz, R. C. (1988). Policing and the Fear of Crime. *Perspectives of Policing, 3*.

Morandini, J. S., Blaszczynski, A., Dar-Nimrod, I., & Ross, M. W. (2015). Minority stress and community connectedness among gay, lesbian and bisexual Australians: a comparison of rural and metropolitan localities. *Australian and New Zealand Journal of Public Health 39*(3), 260-266.

Morris, W., Norris, G., & Dowell, D. (2020). The business of farm crime: evaluating trust in the police and reporting of offences. *Crime Prevention and Community Safety, 22*(1), 17-32. https://doi.org/10.1057/s41300-019-00083-5

MUCF - Myndigheten för ungdoms- och civilsamhällesfrågor (Swedish Agency for Youth and Civil Society). (2020). *Uppdrag att stärka förutsättningarna att skapa mötesplatser för unga hbtq-personer.*

Nordfjærn, T., Dahl, H., & Flemmen, G. (2013). Social influence, health variables and criminal behaviours associated with substance use among rural Norwegian adolescents. *Drugs: Education, Prevention and Policy, 20*(1), 56-66. https://doi.org/10.3109/09687637.2012.696744

Office for National Statistics. (2017). *Public Perceptions of crime in England and Wales: year ending March 2016.* Retrieved 24 October from https://www.ons.gov.uk/peoplepopulationandcommunity/crimeandjustice/articles/publicperceptionsofcrimeinenglandandwales/yearendingmarch2016

Opsal, T., & O'Connor Shelley, T. (2014). Energy Crime, Harm, and Problematic State Response in Colorado: A Case of the Fox Guarding the Hen House?. *Critical Criminology, 22*(4), 561-577. https://doi.org/10.1007/s10612-014-9255-2

Orsi, R., Yuma-Guerrero, P., Sergi, K., Pena, A. A., & Shillington, A. M. (2018, 2018/12/01/). Drug overdose and child maltreatment across the United States' rural-urban continuum. *Child Abuse & Neglect, 86*, 358–367. https://doi.org/10.1016/j.chiabu.2018.08.010

Osborne, H. (2016). 'Unwomanly practices': Poaching Crime, Gender and the Female Offender in Nineteenth-Century Britain. *Rural History, 27*(2), 149-168. https://doi.org/10.1017/S0956793316000029

Oser, C., Leukefeld, C., Staton-Tindall, M., Duvall, J., Garrity, T., Stoops, W., Falck, R., Wang, J., Carlson, R., Sexton, R., Wright, P., & Booth, B. (2011). Criminality Among Rural Stimulant Users in the United States. *Crime and Delinquency, 57*(4), 600-621. https://doi.org/10.1177/0011128708325048

Osgood, D. W., & Chambers, J. M. (2003). Community Correlates of Rural Youth Violence. *Juvenile Delinquency Bulletin*(may), 12.

Owen, S., & Carrington, K. (2015, 2015/06/01/). Domestic violence (DV) service provision and the architecture of rural life: An Australian case study. *Journal of Rural Studies, 39*, 229–238. https://doi.org/10.1016/j.jrurstud.2014.11.004

Palmer, D. L. (1996). Determinants of Canadian attitudes towards immigration: more than just racism? *Canadian Journal of Behavioural Science, 28*(3), 12.

Panda, S., & Guha, A. (2015). *'Criminal Tribe' to 'Primitive Tribal Group' and the role of welfare state: The case of Lodhas in West Bengal, India* [Book]. https://www.scopus.com/inward/record.uri?eid=2-s2.0-84954155458&partnerID=40&md5=5cbe164983c72b68fa58496cf1d89ee0

Park, M., & Stokowski, P. A. (2009, 2009/12/01/). Social disruption theory and crime in rural communities: Comparisons across three levels of tourism growth. *Tourism Management, 30*(6), 905-915. https://doi.org/10.1016/j.tourman.2008.11.015

Park, M., & Stokowski, P. A. (2011). Casino Gaming and Crime: Comparisons among Gaming Counties and Other Tourism Places. *Journal of Travel Research, 50*(3), 289-302. https://doi.org/10.1177/0047287510363616

Parker, K. F., & Reckdenwald, A. (2008). Women and crime in context: Examining the linkages between patriarchy and female offending across space. *Feminist Criminology, 3*(1), 5-24. https://doi.org/10.1177/1557085107308456

Perdue, R. T. (2018). Linking environmental and criminal injustice: The mining to prison pipeline in central Appalachia. *Environmental Justice, 11*(5), 177-182. https://doi.org/10.1089/env.2017.0027

Petee, T. A., & Kowalski, G. S. (1993). Modeling Rural Violent Crime Rates: A Test of Social Disorganization Theory. *Sociological Focus, 26*(1), 87-89. http://www.jstor.org/stable/20831646

Petrie, D. J., Doran, C. M., Shakeshaft, A. P., & Sanson-Fisher, R. (2010, 2010/04/01/). The relationship between risky alcohol consumption, crime and traffic accidents in Australian rural communities. *Addictive Behaviors, 35*(4), 359–362. https://doi.org/10.1016/j.addbeh.2009.10.022

Philo, C. (1992). Neglected Rural Geographies: a Review *Journal of Rural Studies, 8*(2), 193-207.

Pohja-Mykrä, M. (2016, 2016/04/01/). Felony or act of justice? – Illegal killing of large carnivores as defiance of authorities. *Journal of Rural Studies, 44*, 46–54. https://doi.org/10.1016/j.jrurstud.2016.01.003

Porter, J. R. (2011). Identifying spatio-temporal patterns of articulated criminal offending: An application using phenomenologically meaningful police jurisdictional geographies. *Systems Research and Behavioral Science, 28*(3), 197-211. https://doi.org/10.1002/sres.1076

Rand, M. R. (2007). *Criminal Victimization, 2006* (National Crime Victimization Survey, Issue.

Reid, S., & Cesaroni, C. (2016, 2016/10/01/). Depictions of youth homicide: Films set in rural environments. *Journal of Rural Studies, 47*, 1–9. https://doi.org/10.1016/j.jrurstud.2016.07.022

Roberts, J. V., & Stalans, L. J. (2000). *Public opinion, Crime, and Criminal Justice* (1st ed.). Routledge. https://doi.org/10.4324/9780429497971

Rocque, M. (2012, 2012/09/01/). Exploring school rampage shootings: Research, theory, and policy. *The Social Science Journal, 49*(3), 304–313. https://doi.org/10.1016/j.soscij.2011.11.001

Rosenberg, R. D. (2021). Negotiating racialised (un) belonging: Black LGBTQ resistance in Toronto's gay village. *Urban Studies, 58*(7), 1397–1413.

Ruback, R. B., Gladfelter, A. S., & Lantz, B. (2018). Hate crime victimization data in Pennsylvania: A useful complement to the uniform crime reports. *Violence and Victims, 33*(2), 330-350. https://doi.org/10.1891/0886-6708.VV-D-16-00173

Ruddell, R. (2017). *Oil, gas, and crime: The dark side of the boomtown* [Book]. https://doi.org/10.1057/9781137587145

Ruddell, R., Jayasundara, D. S., Mayzer, R., & Heitkamp, T. (2014). Drilling down: An examination of the boom-crime relationship in resource-based boom counties. *Western Criminology Review, 15*(1), 3-17. https://www.scopus.com/inward/record.uri?eid=2-s2.0-84901422952&partnerID=40&md5=dde7fddb8f0f7f62415533c6a52e3944

Rudell, R., & Lithopoulos, S. (2016). Policing rural Canada. In J. F. Donnermeyer (Ed.), *The Routledge International Handbook of Rural Criminology* (pp. 398-407). Routledge.

Ruiz-Suárez, N., Boada, L. D., Henríquez-Hernández, L. A., González-Moreo, F., Suárez-Pérez, A., Camacho, M., Zumbado, M., Almeida-González, M., del Mar Travieso-Aja, M., & Luzardo, O. P. (2015, 2015/02/01/). Continued implication of the banned pesticides carbofuran and aldicarb in the poisoning of domestic and wild animals of the Canary Islands (Spain). *Science of The Total Environment, 505*, 1093–1099. https://doi.org/10.1016/j.scitotenv.2014.10.093

Rutherford, B. (2004). Desired Publics, Domestic Government, and Entangled Fears: On the Anthropology of Civil Society, Farm Workers, and White Farmers in Zimbabwe [Review]. *Cultural Anthropology, 19*(1), 122–153. https://doi.org/10.1525/can.2004.19.1.122

Saltiel, J., Gilchrist, J., & Harvie, R. (1992). Concern About Crime Among Montana Farmers and Ranchers. *Rural Sociology, 57*(4), 535–545. https://doi.org/10.1111/j.1549-0831.1992.tb00478.x

Salvador, R. (2016). Jumping from the frying pan into the fire. In J. F. Donnermeyer (Ed.), *The Routledge International Handbook of Rural Criminology* (pp. 339-348). Routledge.

Saptawan, A., Ammar, M., Erina, L., Ermanovida, E., & Alamsyah, A. (2020). Criminality and disaster: The case of forest fires in Sumatra Island, Indonesia. *Disaster Advances, 13*(1), 29–37. https://www.scopus.com/inward/record.uri?eid=2-s2.0-85078302733&partnerID=40&md5=a0da2b73855695bff7c57522f84806b2

Schoultz, I., & Flyghed, J. (2016). Doing business for a "higher loyalty"? How Swedish transnational corporations neutralise allegations of crime. *Crime Law Soc Change, 66*, 183–198. https://doi.org/10.1007/s10611-016-9619-5

Schuermans, N., & de Maesschalck, F. (2010). Fear of crime as a political weapon: Explaining the rise of extreme right politics in the flemish countryside. *Social and Cultural Geography, 11*(3), 247-262. https://doi.org/10.1080/14649361003637190

Scorzafave, L. G., Justus, M., & Shikida, P. F. A. (2015, 2015/06/01/). Safety in the global south: Criminal victimization in Brazilian rural areas. *Journal of Rural Studies, 39*, 247–261. https://doi.org/10.1016/j.jrurstud.2014.12.002

Shimada, T., & Suzuki, A. (2021). Using a Rural Index to Assess Crime Risk and Crime Prevention Behavior Across the Urban–Rural Continuum: A Japanese Case Study. *International Criminal Justice Review*, 10575677211039998. https://doi.org/10.1177/10575677211039998

Singh, B. P., & Singh, R. P. (2005, 2005/05/28/). Shotgun shooting in northern India—a review (1980–1999). *Forensic Science International, 150*(1), 103-111. https://doi.org/10.1016/j.forsciint.2004.09.126

Skogan, W. G. (2011). Trends in Crime and Fear: Lessons from Chicago, 1994–2003. In S. Karstedt, I. Loader, & H. Strang (Eds.), *Emotions, Crime and Justice*. Hart Publishing.

Smith, K. (2020, 2020/12/01/). Desolation in the countryside: How agricultural crime impacts the mental health of British farmers. *Journal of Rural Studies, 80*, 522–531. https://doi.org/10.1016/j.jrurstud.2020.10.037

Smith, R. (2010). Policing the changing landscape of rural crime: a case study from Scotland. *International Journal of Police Science & Management, 12*(3), 14. https://doi.org/10.1350/ijps.2010.12.3.171

Smith, R., & McElwee, G. (2013). Confronting Social Constructions of Rural Criminality: A Case Story on 'Illegal Pluriactivity' in the Farming Community. *Sociologia Ruralis, 53*(1), 112–134. https://doi.org/10.1111/j.1467-9523.2012.00580.x

Somerville, P., Smith, R., & McElwee, G. (2015, 2015/06/01/). The dark side of the rural idyll: Stories of illegal/illicit economic activity in the UK countryside. *Journal of Rural Studies, 39*, 219–228. https://doi.org/10.1016/j.jrurstud.2014.12.001

Stack, S. (1995). The effect of temporary residences on burglary: A test of criminal opportunity theory. *American Journal of Criminal Justice, 19*(2), 197-214. https://doi.org/10.1007/BF02885915

Stassen, R., & Ceccato, V. (2020). Environmental and Wildlife Crime in Sweden from 2000 to 2017. *Journal of Contemporary Criminal Justice, 36*(3), 403-427. https://doi.org/10.1177/1043986220927123

Steeves, G. M., Petterini, F. C., & Moura, G. V. (2015, 2015/09/01/). The interiorization of Brazilian violence, policing, and economic growth. *EconomiA, 16*(3), 359-375. https://doi.org/10.1016/j.econ.2015.09.003

Stippel, J. A., & Serrano-Moreno, J. E. (2020). The coca diplomacy as the end of the war on drugs. The impact of international cooperation on the crime policy of the Plurinational state of Bolivia. *Crime, Law and Social Change, 74*(4), 361-380. https://doi.org/10.1007/s10611-020-09891-5

Stokowski, P. A. (1996). Crime patterns and gaming development in rural Colorado. *Journal of Travel Research, 34*(3), 63-69. https://doi.org/10.1177/004728759603400309

Swanson, C. R. (1981, 1981/01/01/). Rural and agricultural crime. *Journal of Criminal Justice, 9*(1), 19-27. https://doi.org/10.1016/0047-2352(81)90048-9

Sykes, G. M., & Matza, D. (1957). Techniques of Neutralization: A Theory of Delinquency. *American Sociological Review, 22*(6), 664-670.

Tyler, W. (1998). Race, crime and region: The socio-spatial dynamics of Aboriginal offending. *Journal of Sociology, 34*(2), 152-169. https://doi.org/10.1177/144078339803400204

U.S. Census Bureau. (2017). *One in Five Americans Live in Rural Areas*. Retrieved 21 Oct from https://www.census.gov/library/stories/2017/08/rural-america.html

van Daele, S., & Beken, T. V. (2010). Journey to crime of "itinerant crime groups". *Policing, 33*(2), 339–353. https://doi.org/10.1108/13639511011044920

van Dijk, J., Nieuwbeerta, P., & Larsen, J. J. (2021). Global Crime Patterns: An Analysis of Survey Data from 166 Countries Around the World, 2006–2019. *Journal of Quantitative Criminology*. https://doi.org/10.1007/s10940-021-09501-0

van Dun, M. (2014). Exploring Narco-Sovereignty/Violence: Analyzing Illegal Networks, Crime, Violence, and Legitimation in a Peruvian Cocaine Enclave (2003-2007). *Journal of Contemporary Ethnography, 43*(4), 395-418. https://doi.org/10.1177/0891241613520452

Vazsonyi, A. T., & Trejos-Castillo, E. (2006). Crime and deviance in the "Black Belt": African American youth in rural and nonrural developmental contexts. In *The Many Colors of Crime: Inequalities of Race, Ethnicity, and Crime in America* (pp. 122–137). https://www.scopus.com/inward/record.uri?eid=2-s2.0-44649190103&partnerID=40&md5=c7628cd110afc22bf489494460a771eb

von Essen, E., Hansen, H., Nordström Källström, H., Peterson, M. N., & Peterson, T. R. (2016). Illegal hunting Between social and criminal justice. In J. F. Donnemeyer (Ed.), *The Routledge International Handbook of Rural Criminology* (pp. 318–326). Routledge.

von Essen, E., Hansen, H., Peterson, M. N., & Peterson, T. R. (2017). Discourses on illegal hunting in Sweden: the meaning of silence and resistance. *Environmental Sociology, 4*(3), 10.

von Essen, E., Hansen, P., Nordström Källström, H., Peterson, M. N., & Peterson, T. R. (2015). The radicalisation of rural resistance: How hunting counterpublics in the Nordic countries contribute to illegal hunting. *Journal of Rural Studies, 39*, 10.

Wagner, K., Owen, S., & Burke, T. W. (2019). Not Wild about Wildlife Protection the Perceived Harmfulness, Wrongfulness, and Seriousness of Wildlife Crimes. *Society and Animals, 27*(4), 383-402. https://doi.org/10.1163/15685306-12341589

Watkins, A. M., & Taylor, T. J. (2016). The prevalence, predictors, and criminogenic effect of joining a gang among urban, suburban, and rural youth. *Journal of Criminal Justice, 47*, 133-142. https://doi.org/10.1016/j.jcrimjus.2016.09.001

Websdale, N. (1998). *Rural Woman Battering and the Justice System: An Ethnography*. Sage.

Webster, J. M., Dickson, M. F., Saman, D. M., Mateyoke-Scrivner, A., Oser, C. B., & Leukefeld, C. (2010). Substance use, criminal activity, and mental health among violent and nonviolent rural probationers. *Journal of Addictions and Offender Counseling, 30*(2), 99-111. https://doi.org/10.1002/j.2161-1874.2010.tb00060.x

References

Webster, J. M., Mateyoke-Scrivner, A., Staton, M., & Leukefeld, C. (2007). Rurality and criminal history as predictors of HIV risk among drug-involved offenders. *Substance Use and Misuse, 42*(1), 153-160. https://doi.org/10.1080/10826080601177291

Weisheit, R., Edward, L., & Falcone, D. N. (1995). *Crime and Policing in Rural and Small-Town America*. Waveland Pr Inc.

Weisheit, R. A., & Brownstein, H. (2016). Drug production in the rural context. In J. F. Donnermeyer (Ed.), *The Routledge International Handbook Of Rural Criminology* (pp. 235–241). Routledge.

Weisheit, R. A., Edward, L., & Falcone, D. N. (1993). Studying Drugs in Rural Areas: Notes from the Field. *Journal of Research in Crime and Delinquency, 30*, 19. https://doi.org/10.1177/0022427893030002005

Wells, L. E., & Weisheit, R. A. (2004). Patterns of rural and urban crime: A county-level comparison. *Criminal Justice Review, 29*(1), 1-22. https://doi.org/10.1177/073401680402900103

Wendt, S. (2016). Intimate violence and abuse in australian rural contexts. In J. F. Donnermeyer (Ed.), *The Routledge International Handbook of Rural Criminology* (pp. 191-198). Routledge.

White, R. (2016). Re-conceptualising folk crime in rural contexts. In J. F. Donnermeyer (Ed.), *The Routledge International Handbook of Rural Criminology* (pp. 299-306). Routledge.

Wike, T., Bouchard, L., Kemmerer, A., & Yabar, M. (2021). Victimization and Resilience: Experiences of Rural LGBTQ+ Youth Across Multiple Contexts. *Journal of Interpersonal Violence*, 1–28. https://doi.org/10.1177/08862605211043574

Wilhelmsson, M., & Ceccato, V. (2015, 2015/06/01/). Does burglary affect property prices in a non-metropolitan municipality? *Journal of Rural Studies, 39*, 210–218. https://doi.org/10.1016/j.jrurstud.2015.03.014

Wisniewski, K. D., Pringle, J. K., Allen, D., & Wilson, G. E. (2019, 2019/01/01/). Wildlife crime: The application of forensic geoscience to assist with criminal investigations. *Forensic Science International, 294*, e11–e18. https://doi.org/10.1016/j.forsciint.2018.10.026

Xi, Z. (2018). 'Cake Uncles' Formation of a Criminal Town in Rural China. In B. Bakken (Ed.), *Crime and the Chinese Dream* (1st ed., pp. 40–72). Hong Kong University Press. https://doi.org/10.2307/j.ctt22p7jc6.7

Yarwood, R., & Gardner, G. (2000). Fear of crime, cultural threat and the countryside. *Area, 32*(4), 403-411. https://doi.org/10.1111/j.1475-4762.2000.tb00156.x

Open Access This chapter is licensed under the terms of the Creative Commons Attribution 4.0 International License (http://creativecommons.org/licenses/by/4.0/), which permits use, sharing, adaptation, distribution and reproduction in any medium or format, as long as you give appropriate credit to the original author(s) and the source, provide a link to the Creative Commons license and indicate if changes were made.

The images or other third party material in this chapter are included in the chapter's Creative Commons license, unless indicated otherwise in a credit line to the material. If material is not included in the chapter's Creative Commons license and your intended use is not permitted by statutory regulation or exceeds the permitted use, you will need to obtain permission directly from the copyright holder.

Chapter 5
Safety Perceptions in Rural Areas

Rural areas are often associated with idyllic environments, and safety is an assumed part of these romanticized landscapes. Research around the world has long contested these simplistic views by showing evidence of the complexity of safety perceptions declared by those living on the rural-urban continuum. Anecdotal evidence indicates that people in rural areas with relatively little crime may express high levels of fear because of occasional crimes. To what degree does fear in rural areas reflect daily experiences, and which experiences are generating fear?

To start, we need to reflect upon the concepts of fear and fear of crime. According to Warr (2000, p. 453) fear is "an emotion, a feeling of alarm or dread caused by awareness of expectation of danger" while according to Ferraro (1995, p. 8), fear of crime is "an emotional reaction to dread or anxiety to crime or symbols that a person associates with crime." The risk of being victimized (or the perceived signs of increased risk of victimization) can at least hypothetically negatively affect one's perceived safety, although such a straightforward relationship is rarely found (Hale 1996), perhaps because this emotional reaction is situationally dependent. In other words, the reaction is determined by the particular setting at a specific point in time and space and may also be driven by memories and associations brought to the surface, which are, in turn, also influenced by individual and sociocultural contexts.

We adopt here the overarching concept of "safety" to bring together the meaning of fear (of crime) and the overall anxieties, as documented in the international literature, expressed by those living in areas on the rural-urban continuum. Thus, safety can be high when an individual feels safe or low when an individual declare feeling unsafe, that is, in fear or feeling worried. Safety is driven by overlapping factors: some are local, such as the experiences of the *rural environment*; others are *global contextual* such as those experienced through media; but both are mediated by *the individual characteristics* (or a combination of the individual characteristics) of those who express such feelings. How these factors take shape and interact in different rural contexts has been debated in criminology and other related disciplines over the past decades. Although victimization is influenced by gender and other individual characteristics, research has shown that it is the intersection of individual

© The Author(s) 2022
V. Ceccato, J. Abraham, *Crime and Safety in the Rural*, SpringerBriefs in Criminology, https://doi.org/10.1007/978-3-030-98290-4_5

characteristics that determines an individual's vulnerability to crime and fear of crime. This intersectionality, as a theory, is often used to assess how social and cultural categories interact (Crenshaw, 1989) and to interpret varied levels of safety perceptions (Gainey & Seyfrit, 2001).

The Rural Environment

Several studies have shown that rural areas generally seem to be linked to higher perceptions of safety among their residents compared to urban areas (Avery et al., 2019; Ball, 2001; Bankston et al., 1987; Belyea & Zingraff, 1988; Karakus et al., 2010; Menard, 1987; Rotarou, 2018). However, rural residents have in some cases reported greater worry of being alone at night and becoming victims of burglary compared to their urban counterparts (Mawby, 2007).

Rural-to-urban migrating residents have been declared feeling less safe when moving to urban areas than urban-to-urban migrants (Kennedy & Krahn, 1984). The safety perceptions of rural college and university students have also been observed in different contexts (De Angelis et al., 2017; Pritchard et al., 2015), and this included also the analysis of rural business perceptions of quietness and order (Mawby, 2004).

Overall, research on situational conditions of fear of crime crime in rural areas have not been paid as much attention as individual and social factors. Rural attributes such as remoteness and geographical isolation may have a positive impact on perceptions of safety (e.g., less accessibility for potential offenders), but open and less dense areas may increase worry as well (Panelli et al., 2005). So, while clearly defined, private space is necessary to improve perceptions of safety and barriers, and fortress-like structures can generate fear and suspicion also in rural areas. For example, on the former Australian frontier, historical, defensive architecture was considered as "physical manifestations of settler fear and aboriginal resistance" (Grguric, 2009).

Contextual Factors Affecting Safety

Poor safety perceptions can reflect "a condensation of broader concerns about crime, stability and social change" (Gray et al., 2008, p. 377). They have also been associated with structural and situational factors typical of rural environments, such as long-term unemployment or perceptions of exclusion from the local economy, combined with structural racism (Chakraborti & Garland, 2011; Crompton, 2008; Palmer, 1996).

There is growing evidence that people who do not fit into idealized constructions of rurality feel excluded from rural places (for several examples, see Yarwood (2010). Fear in this case, as suggested by Pain and Smith (2008), is central to the terrain of daily lived experience, rather than a straightforward relationship between the individual and a variety of societal structures; that is, fear is embedded in a network of moral and political geographies. The international literature confirms that this process goes hand in hand with long-term social and economic exclusion and discrimination related to gender, ethnicity, and length of residence (Babacan, 2012; Chakraborti & Garland, 2011; Garland & Chakraborti, 2004; Jensen, 2012; Scott et al., 2012).

Rural crime has often been perceived as the result of an intrusion by urban influence and/or other groups of individuals that "do not belong", for example, seasonal workers or local youth (Ceccato, 2015b, 2017; Little et al., 2005; Yarwood, 2010). This is also expressed in the case of "boomtowns," that is, smaller towns experiencing rapid economic and population growth. Krannich et al. (1985) showed that while actual victimization experiences in boomtowns did not differ from non-boomtowns, perceived fear was significantly higher.

Moreover, there is the "outsider's" perception of safety. Related research addressed topics of the victimization of domestic tourists in New Zealand (Buttle & Rodgers, 2014) and minority fears of genocide (Farrell et al., 1983). Chakraborti and Garland (2003) assessed attitudes toward crime and fear among migrants and minority groups in British rural areas, showing extensive victimization and fear, as well as mistrust of the criminal justice system because perceived lack of support.

Poor communication, lack of police response, and low conviction rates (Donnermeyer & Barclay, 2005; Smith, 2020) can leave individuals feeling like second-class citizens and neglected (Smith, 2020). One reason for the (feeling of) neglect is that the police, as well as those who devote their time to crime prevention, often work reactively, which requires an offense to be committed before any action can be taken. Unlike crime, safety is not typically considered a conventional policing matter and seems to be even less of an issue for those living in rural areas as in the public does not think it is important.

Farmers may develop activities that make them more exposed as crime target, not only in fairs but also via internet and various digital platforms. More recently, the publicness of certain activities (such as e-commerce for agri-foods) (Cristobal-Fransi et al., 2020; Mora-Rivera & García-Mora, 2021) has exacerbated differences between groups and fueled latent conflicts that then become a source of fear among those threatened on digital platforms – a problem that also challenges the capacity of local police forces.

Media consumption has also been shown to explain some fear of crime in rural areas, although the relationship was not significant in accounting for perceptions of disorder (Lytle et al., 2020). Norris and Reeves (2013) found that the link between fear of crime and rural residents who subscribe to authoritarian ideals is stronger when the "threat" is framed as "outsider" criminals compared to when it is framed as a local issue. Further studies have emphasized the social and cultural constructions of rural fear of crime, "cultural threat," and fear of the "other" (Ceccato, 2015a; Scott et al., 2012; Scott & Hogg, 2015; Yarwood, 2001; Yarwood & Gardner, 2000).

Intersectionality of Safety

There are individual modifiers of safety perceptions. Among the various sociodemographic characteristics, gender and age seem to significantly influence fear. Other individual characteristics interact with gender and sexual orientation and affect both feelings of safety and the statistical probability of victimization. Victimization is influenced by the intersection of gender and other individual characteristics; research has shown that it is the intersection (Crenshaw, 1989) of individual characteristics that determines an individual's vulnerability to crime and fear of crime (Gainey & Seyfrit, 2001).

Among the individual factors, prior victimization (or awareness of others' victimization) is often considered one determinant of a person's perceived safety. Although one's previous victimization is often associated with poor safety perceptions, research has shown ambiguous links between victimization and fear of crime (Cates et al., 2003; Garofalo & Laub, 1979). One possible explanation is that it is unclear if (and how) fear varies by types of crime or by its seriousness (Jackson & Gouseti, 2012). However, witnessing someone else's victimization, in particular a friend or family member, can affect ones' perceived safety (for a review, see, e.g., Skogan, 1987). Knowledge of someone else's victimization, especially someone geographically close, has also been linked with poor safety perceptions. Fear of "near repeat victimization" (Anderson & Pease, 1993) is associated with precautionary measures. For example, thefts of livestock from farms may mobilize neighboring farmers to be proactive out of the fear that something will also happen to their own livestock.

It has been found that both urban and rural women express greater fear than men, due to their higher vulnerability to sexual assault in conjunction with other victimization (Little et al., 2005; Pleggenkuhle & Schafer, 2018). The lack of perceived safety can have numerous inhibiting effects on the quality of life, especially in terms of women's mobility and physical activity (Timperio et al., 2015). Research on women's fear of crime have been dominated by accounts of urban women (Panelli et al., 2004), but although urban women may fear crime to a greater extent than rural women do (Timperio et al., 2015), it has also been found that rural areas have their own unique structures for triggering feelings of unsafety. Little et al. (2005) showed a study on New Zealand and the United Kingdom, in which the notion of rural space being safer than its urban counterpart was common even among rural women. In this case, it seems that fear may primarily be fear of strangers, which in turn may come at the cost of overlooking crime committed by local community members (Panelli et al., 2004).

It is perhaps even more important to reflect on the impact these feelings have on individuals living in rural areas, and how they can lead individuals to a "sense that they must always be on guard, vigilant and alert" (Gordon & Riger, 1989, p. 2). Such feelings have the power to modify behavior and affect daily activities (Jackson & Gray, 2010), including engaging in safety protection measures, particularly when local police stations have shut down or the act of reporting crime feels like "a waste of time" as the reported crime is not taken seriously (Ceccato, 2015c). A lack of satisfaction with the police has also been associated with higher levels of fear (Lytle & Randa, 2015).

Fear can also be revealed by silence. Low rates of reported violence against women have been associated with a "code of silence" imposed by patriarchal community values and a fear of ostracism if the violence becomes public (DeKeseredy et al., 2012). Reported rates of violence against women have differed from region to region in Sweden, which has been interpreted as a sign of differences in gender contracts across the country (Ceccato, 2016; Ceccato, 2018). Similarly, Ceccato et al. (2021) showed that crimes against farmers are underreported because they think the police cannot help them or their victimization has been normalized by society.

References

Anderson, D., & Pease, K. (1993). Biting Back: Preventing Repeat Burglary and Car Crime in Huddersfield. In R. V. Clarke (Ed.), *Situational Crime Prevention - Successful Case Studies*. (pp. 200–208)Lynne Rienner Publishers.

Avery, E. E., Baumer, M. D., Hermsen, J. M., Leap, B. T., Lucht, J. R., Rikoon, J. S., & Wilhelm Stanis, S. A. (2019). Measuring place of residence across urban and rural spaces: An application to fears associated with outdoor recreation. *Social Science Journal*. https://doi.org/10.1016/j.soscij.2019.08.007

Babacan, H. (2012). Racism Denial in Australia: The power of silence. *Australian Mosaic, 32*, 1–3. http://researchonline.jcu.edu.au/22526/

Ball, C. (2001). Rural Perceptions of Crime. *Journal of Contemporary Criminal Justice, 17*(1), 37–48. https://doi.org/10.1177/1043986201017001004

Bankston, W. B., Jenkins, Q. A. L., Thayer-Doyle, C. L., & Thompson, C. Y. (1987). Fear of criminal victimization and residential location: the influence of perceived risk (Louisiana). *Rural Sociology, 52*(1), 98–107. https://www.scopus.com/inward/record.uri?eid=2-s2.0-0023469009&partnerID=40&md5=5e7c2b6c8b09d74112015955be302775

Belyea, M. J., & Zingraff, M. T. (1988). Fear of crime and residential location. *Rural Sociology, 53*(4), 473–486. https://www.scopus.com/inward/record.uri?eid=2-s2.0-0024160425&partnerID=40&md5=1f20620ac46ea53cccf76831c607eee3

Buttle, J., & Rodgers, J. (2014). Panic about crime in New Zealand's rural paradise. *New Zealand Sociology, 29*(2), 31–4. https://www.scopus.com/inward/record.uri?eid=2-s2.0-84921712220&partnerID=40&md5=f96157f1d4913b4c84d8d8706e23b7fd

Cates, J. A., Dian, D. A., & Schnepf, G. W. (2003, 2003/09/01). Use of Protection Motivation Theory to Assess Fear of Crime in Rural Areas. *Psychology, Crime & Law, 9*(3), 225–236. https://doi.org/10.1080/1068316021000072184

Ceccato, V. (2015a). The natue of perceived safety in rural areas. In *Rural Crime and Community Safety* (pp. 121–133). Routledge.

Ceccato, V. (2015b). Perceived safety in Swedish rural areas. In *Rural Crime and Community Safety* (pp. 137–160). Routledge.

Ceccato, V. (2015c). Prevention of farm crimes and crimes against nature In V. Ceccato (Ed.), *Rural crime and community safety* (pp. 226–255). Routledge.

Ceccato, V. (2016). *Rural crime and community safety*. Routledge.

Ceccato, V. (2017). Fear of crime and overall anxieties in rural areas: The case of Sweden. In *The Routledge International Handbook on Fear of Crime* (pp. 354–367). https://doi.org/10.4324/9781315651781

Ceccato, V. (2018). Fear of crime and overall anxieties in rural areas : The case of Sweden. In G. M. Murray Lee (Ed.), *The Routledge International Handbook on Fear of Crime* (1st ed.). Routledge. http://urn.kb.se/resolve?urn=urn:nbn:se:kth:diva-233897

Ceccato, V., Abraham, J., Lundqvist, P. (2021). Crimes against animal production: Exploring the use of media archives. *International Criminal Justice Review, 31*(4): 384–404. https://doi.org/10.1177/10575677211041915

Chakraborti, N., & Garland, J. (2003). Under-researched and overlooked: An exploration of the attitudes of rural minority ethnic communities towards crime, community safety and the criminal justice system. *Journal of Ethnic and Migration Studies, 29*(3), 563–572. https://doi.org/10.1080/13691830305613

Chakraborti, N., & Garland, J. (2011). *Rural racism*. Routledge.

Cristobal-Fransi, E., Montegut-Salla, Y., Ferrer-Rosell, B., & Daries, N. (2020, 2020/02/01/). Rural cooperatives in the digital age: An analysis of the Internet presence and degree of maturity of agri-food cooperatives' e-commerce. *Journal of Rural Studies, 74*, 55–66. https://doi.org/10.1016/j.jrurstud.2019.11.011

Crenshaw, K. (1989). Demarginalizing the Intersection of Race and Sex: A Black Feminist Critique of Antidiscrimination Doctrine. *Feminist Theory and Antiracist Politics*, 139–167.

Crompton, J. L. (2008). Empirical evidence of the contributions of leisure services to alleviating social problems: A key to repositioning the leisure services field. *World Leisure Journal, 50*(4), 243–258. https://doi.org/10.1080/04419057.2008.9674564

De Angelis, J., Benz, T. A., & Gillham, P. (2017). Collective Security, Fear of Crime, and Support for Concealed Firearms on a University Campus in the Western United States. *Criminal Justice Review, 42*(1), 77–94. https://doi.org/10.1177/0734016816686660

DeKeseredy, W. S., Dragiewicz, M., & Rennisson, C. M. (2012). Racial/Ethnic Variations in Violence Against Women: Urban, Suburban, and Rural Differences. *International Journal of Rural Criminology, 1*(2).

Donnermeyer, J. F., & Barclay, E. (2005). The policing farm crime. *Practices and research, 6*(1), 3–17.

Farrell, W. C., Dawkins, M. P., & Oliver, J. (1983). Genocide Fears in a Rural Black Community: An Empirical Examination. *Journal of Black Studies, 14*(1), 49–67. http://www.jstor.org/stable/2784030

Ferraro, K. F. (1995). *Fear of crime: interpreting victimization risk*. SUNY Press.

Gainey, R. R., & Seyfrit, C. L. (2001). Fear of crime among rural youth: testing the generality of urban models to rural areas. *Sociological Focus, 34*(3), 269–286. http://www.jstor.org/stable/20832124

Garland, J., & Chakraborti, N. (2004). Another country? Community, belonging and exclusion in rural England. In *Rural Racism*. Willan.

Garofalo, J., & Laub, J. (1979). Fear of crime - broadening our perspective. *Victomology,, 3*, 242–253.

Gordon, M., & Riger, S. (1989). *The female fear*. The Free Press.

Gray, E., Jackson, J., & Farrall, S. (2008, July 1, 2008). Reassessing the Fear of Crime. *European Journal of Criminology, 5*(3), 363–380. https://doi.org/10.1177/1477370808090834

Grguric, N. K. (2009). Fortified homesteads: The architecture of fear in frontier South Australia and the Northern territory, CA. 1847–1885. In *Bastions and Barbed Wire: Studies in the Archaeology of Conflict* (pp. 59–85). https://doi.org/10.1163/157407808X382764

Hale, C. (1996). Fear of crime: A review of the literature. *International Review of Victimology, 4*, 79–150.

Jackson, & Gouseti, I. (Eds.). (2012). *Fear of Crime: An Entry to the Encyclopedia of Theoretical Criminology*. Wiley-Blackwell. http://ssrn.com/abstract=2118663.

Jackson, & Gray. (2010, January 1, 2010). Functional fear and public insecurities about crime. *British Journal of Criminology, 50*(1), 1–22. https://doi.org/10.1093/bjc/azp059

Jensen, M. (2012). *Rasism, missnöje och "Fertile Grounds" Östergötland Sverige jämförs med Birkaland Finland: Sverigedemokraterna vs Sannfinländarna* Linköping University]. Linköping. http://www.diva-portal.org/smash/record.jsf?pid=diva2:479299

Karakus, O., McGarrell, E. F., & Basibuyuk, O. (2010, 2010/03/01/). Fear of crime among citizens of Turkey. *Journal of Criminal Justice, 38*(2), 174–184. https://doi.org/10.1016/j.jcrimjus.2010.02.006

Kennedy, L. W., & Krahn, H. (1984). Rural-urban origin and fear of crime: the case for 'rural baggage' (Canada). *Rural Sociology, 49*(2), 247–260. https://www.scopus.com/inward/record.uri?eid=2-s2.0-0021578679&partnerID=40&md5=576500121c482355dcad54a53fff0125

Krannich, R. S., Greider, T., & Little, R. L. (1985). Rapid growth and fear of crime: a four-community comparison (USA). *Rural Sociology, 50*(2), 193–209. https://www.scopus.com/inward/record.uri?eid=2-s2.0-0022195257&partnerID=40&md5=ddcdac4da28b1a5e605a93d40310eee0

Little, J., Panelli, R., & Kraack, A. (2005, 2005/04/01/). Women's fear of crime: A rural perspective. *Journal of Rural Studies, 21*(2), 151–163. https://doi.org/10.1016/j.jrurstud.2005.02.001

Lytle, D., Intravia, J., & Randa, R. (2020). An understudied population? Exploring the factors associated with fear of crime in a semi-rural environment. *Deviant Behavior*, 1–17. https://doi.org/10.1080/01639625.2020.1793544

Lytle, D. J., & Randa, R. (2015). The Effects of Police Satisfaction on Fear of Crime in a Semirural Setting. *International Criminal Justice Review, 25*(4), 301–317. https://doi.org/10.1177/1057567715596048

Mawby, R. I. (2004). Crime and disorder: Perceptions of business people in cornwall, England. *International Review of Victimology, 11*(3), 313–332. https://doi.org/10.1177/026975800401100207

Mawby, R. I. (2007). Alternative measures of 'fear of crime': Results from crime audits in a rural county of England. *International Review of Victimology, 14*(3), 299–320. https://doi.org/10.1177/026975800701400302

Menard, S. (1987). Patterns of victimization fear of crime, and crime precautions in nonmetropolitan new mexico. *Journal of Crime and Justice, 10*(1), 71–100. https://doi.org/10.1080/0735648X.1987.9721335

Mora-Rivera, J., & García-Mora, F. (2021, 2021/03/01/). Internet access and poverty reduction: Evidence from rural and urban Mexico. *Telecommunications Policy, 45*(2), 102076. https://doi.org/10.1016/j.telpol.2020.102076

Norris, G., & Reeves, H. (2013). Fear of crime and authoritarianism: A comparison of rural and urban attitudes. *Crime Prevention and Community Safety, 15*(2), 134–150. https://doi.org/10.1057/cpcs.2013.2

Pain, R., & Smith, S. J. (2008). Fear: critical geopolitics and everyday life. In R. Pain & S. J. Smith (Eds.), *Fear: critical geopolitics and everyday life* (pp. 1–24). Ashgate.

Palmer, D. L. (1996). Determinants of Canadian attitudes toward immigration: More than just racism? *Canadian Journal of Behavioural Science/Revue canadienne des sciences du comportement, 28*(3), 180–192. https://doi.org/10.1037/0008-400X.28.3.180

Panelli, R., Kraack, A., & Little, J. (2005). Claiming space and community: Rural women's strategies for living with, and beyond, fear. *Geoforum, 36*(4), 495–508. https://doi.org/10.1016/j.geoforum.2004.08.002

Panelli, R., Little, J., & Kraack, A. (2004). A community issue? Rural women's feelings of safety and fear in New Zealand. *Gender, Place and Culture, 11*(3), 445–467. https://doi.org/10.1080/0966369042000258730

Pleggenkuhle, B., & Schafer, J. A. (2018). Fear of crime among residents of rural counties: an analysis by gender. *Journal of Crime and Justice, 41*(4), 382–397. https://doi.org/10.1080/0735648X.2017.1391109

Pritchard, A. J., Jordan, C. E., & Wilcox, P. (2015). Safety concerns, fear and precautionary behavior among college women: An exploratory examination of two measures of residency. *Security Journal, 28*(1), 16–38. https://doi.org/10.1057/sj.2012.39

Rotarou, E. S. (2018). Does Municipal Socioeconomic Development Affect Public Perceptions of Crime? A Multilevel Logistic Regression Analysis. *Social Indicators Research, 138*(2), 705–724. https://doi.org/10.1007/s11205-017-1669-2

Scott, J., Carrington, K., & McIntosh, A. (2012). Established-Outsider Relations and Fear of Crime in Mining Towns. *Sociologia Ruralis, 52*(2), 147–169. https://doi.org/10.1111/j.1467-9523.2011.00557.x

Scott, J., & Hogg, R. (2015, 2015/06/01/). Strange and stranger ruralities: Social constructions of rural crime in Australia. *Journal of Rural Studies, 39*, 171–179. https://doi.org/10.1016/j.jrurstud.2014.11.010

Skogan, W. G. (1987, January 1, 1987). The Impact of Victimization on Fear. *Crime & Delinquency, 33*(1), 135–154. https://doi.org/10.1177/0011128787033001008

Smith, K. (2020, 2020/12/01/). Desolation in the countryside: How agricultural crime impacts the mental health of British farmers. *Journal of Rural Studies, 80*, 522–531. https://doi.org/10.1016/j.jrurstud.2020.10.037

Timperio, A., Veitch, J., & Carver, A. (2015, 2015/05/01/). Safety in numbers: Does perceived safety mediate associations between the neighborhood social environment and physical activity among women living in disadvantaged neighborhoods? *Preventive Medicine, 74*, 49–54. https://doi.org/10.1016/j.ypmed.2015.02.012

Warr, M. (2000). Fear of crime in the United States: Avenues for research and policy. *Criminal Justice and Behavior, 4*, 451–489.

Yarwood, R. (2001). Crime and policing in the British countryside: Some agendas for contemporary geographical research. *Sociologia Ruralis, 41*(2), 201–219. https://doi.org/10.1111/1467-9523.00178

Yarwood, R. (2010, 2010/03/01). An exclusive countryside? Crime concern, social exclusion and community policing in two English villages. *Policing and Society, 20*(1), 61–78. https://doi.org/10.1080/10439461003611500

Yarwood, R., & Gardner, G. (2000). Fear of crime, cultural threat and the countryside. *Area, 32*(4), 403–411. https://doi.org/10.1111/j.1475-4762.2000.tb00156.x

Open Access This chapter is licensed under the terms of the Creative Commons Attribution 4.0 International License (http://creativecommons.org/licenses/by/4.0/), which permits use, sharing, adaptation, distribution and reproduction in any medium or format, as long as you give appropriate credit to the original author(s) and the source, provide a link to the Creative Commons license and indicate if changes were made.

The images or other third party material in this chapter are included in the chapter's Creative Commons license, unless indicated otherwise in a credit line to the material. If material is not included in the chapter's Creative Commons license and your intended use is not permitted by statutory regulation or exceeds the permitted use, you will need to obtain permission directly from the copyright holder.

Chapter 6
Police and Criminal Justice

The police as an organization can be defined as a state-empowered, civil force meant to enforce the law, and detect and prevent crime and public disorder (Ceccato, 2015b). The police are challenged by the geographical features of many rural regions, as they need to cover large areas that facilitate the offender's capability to escape and avoid detection. In general, formal rural policing has long been characterized by the isolated and lonesome nature of rural areas and a higher dependency on neighbors and the community in which the police live (Cain, 1973). Traditionally, in many countries there has been a tendency to rely on alternatives to formal policing (Mawby, 2011). In a broader sense, policing can in fact be described as "how the police, the public and other agencies regulate themselves and each other according to the dominant ideals of society" (Mawby & Yarwood, 2011, p. 1). As such, it is not necessarily the police themselves that are doing police work in practice, but other actors, including voluntary organizations and civil society who embrace the work of ensuring community safety.

The police's work and organization are and always have been different in urban and rural areas (Furuhagen, 2009). Yet, research on policing has largely focused on urban areas and been driven by a "metropolitan criminology," especially in the Global North (Carrington et al., 2015). Additionally, other parts of the criminal justice system also have their own unique relationship with the countryside, such as the largely rural prison industry in the United States and different effects of legislation. In this section, we report on the experience of rural police as "enforcers of the law" and through policing as the "softer approach to upholding public order".

The Organization of Rural Police

Ceccato (2015b) describes two accepted schools of policing: the Anglo-Saxon tradition, which involves community-based and civil forms of policing, often by unarmed guards and constables; and the continental tradition, which is more linked to armed forces and authoritarian forms of control. The Anglo-Saxon school has evolved in the United Kingdom and the United States, while the continental school originated in France and is also used in Germany, Italy, and other parts of southern Europe. Over time, the focus of police control has shifted, as in the rural provinces of Canada where, previously, the police acted more upon public disorder and controlling "dangerous classes" than on serious crime, but later this changed due to increases in violent crime (Lin, 2007).

In the past decades, police agencies have involved local citizens in policing: a practice sometimes referred to as "civilianization" (Crank, 1989; Weisheit et al., 1995). This model of policing has been controversial as some feel it undermines the police structure, but in rural areas the practice is believed to strengthen the close-knit bond between the community and the police (Crank, 1989). Lately, the concept of cooperation and building relationships between local agents and the police to tackle crime and fear of crime (i.e., community policing) has increased in popularity after being established in several countries (e.g., Ceccato, 2015b; Takahashi, 2016).

The geographical locations of police stations are still of central importance for today's police work, which involves online access to services, face-to-face community engagement, and coordination with third-party actors, such as voluntary organizations and civil society. Stassen and Ceccato (2021) investigated the access to and role of police stations in Sweden to find that traditional police stations play a key role, particularly in the most sparsely populated areas of the country. They also found that as the number of stations decreases, it becomes even more important for the remaining service points to be strategically located, so as to be able to carry out the needed support.

Rural Policing

Rural policing is expected to be different from urban policing because, for example, "officers in these agencies typically know the citizens personally, have frequent face-to-face contact with them, and engage in a variety of problem-solving activities that fall outside of law enforcement" (Weisheit et al., 1994, p. 549). This can harness the social control efforts of the partnered organizations and groups, thus aligning them with the efforts of the official crime control agencies (Yarwood, 2014). Examining rural policing is therefore an important endeavor as it can reveal more about rural society (Mawby & Yarwood, 2011), as exemplified below.

Payne et al. (2005), for instance, summarized research on rural law enforcement in the United States, and came to three major findings regarding policing styles in small towns. First, crime prevention and service activities tend to be prioritized by rural police, while urban police focus more on arrests and enforcement of the law. Rural policing has generally been less about life and death decisions and more about "balancing the challenges of remoteness, isolation and a lack of nearby back-up with community expectation and problem solving" (Wooff, 2015). Second, rural police are expected to carry out other tasks compared to urban police, due to the remoteness or lack of social services in rural areas. Third, rural policing includes more informal work (such as counselling families, helping file for welfare, and driving elderly persons to buy groceries) and providing non-compensated services to the community (Weisheit et al., 1995). However, according to Kaylen and Pridemore (2015), one in four rural residents also fail to report more serious events like violent victimization to the police, despite the injury being so serious that the victim needed medical attention. Reasons for underreporting have been discussed in chapter 2.

Differences in social media practices between urban and rural police have been investigated by, for example, Ceccato et al. (2021) who assessed the content of Tweets from official and personal accounts in urban and rural contexts in Sweden to identify potential urban-rural differences. Overall, official rural accounts generated less engagement than the personal rural accounts, which Tweeted less frequently but generated more engagement. Rural personal account holders tend to be "enthusiasts" (eldsjälar) who attract followers and reactions, such as likes and Retweets. These active officers are the ones dominating the local discourse and feeding the "crime talk," and are possibly the key faces of community policing.

Challenges for Policing in Rural Areas

One challenge lies in the fact that rural police districts often cover large areas, which makes it harder to police efficiently (Barclay & Donnermeyer, 2002; Ceccato, 2015a). Furthermore, over time, police presence has lessened in rural areas of, for example, the United Kingdom and Sweden, and it has increasingly become more centralized (Ceccato, 2016; Lindström, 2015). This, coupled with budget constraints and public pressure for more visible policing, may explain the increase in rural community policing and alternative policing (Yarwood, 2015; Yarwood & Edwards, 1995).

Community policing may take the form of neighborhood watch schemes (Shernock, 1986; Yarwood & Edwards, 1995), safety audits or night patrols. However, Yarwood (2015) discusses how such community initiatives can create problems, as it is often the local elite of rural communities that engage in policing and the exclusion of unwanted groups, criminal or not. Here we must differentiate between "demands to reduce crime and demands to exclude activities or people that are threatening to the elite rural ideal" (Mawby & Yarwood, 2011).

Given the emerging drug problems in rural Sweden, the police organizations in some remote rural areas are under-dimensioned. According to Stenbacka (2021), the police may fail to structure their work in a fruitful way, which in turn affects the working context and conditions of several other professions involved in related work, affecting indirectly vulnerable groups.

The policing of marginalized groups is also reported in different rural contexts. For example, influxes of Latin American immigrants into rural areas of the United States have entailed policing challenges, as language barriers and preconceived notions inhibit communication with and trust in the police (Culver, 2004). Taylor et al. (2015) showed that the perceptions of police fairness and police efficiency depend partially on racial and spatial factors. In the United States, white residents in rural counties perceived significantly higher police fairness than non-white residents in both urban and non-urban areas. The policing of indigenous peoples living in rural areas has historically involved oppression and subjugation (Behrendt et al., 2016; Cunneen, 2016; Cunneen, 2020; Griffiths, 2019; Jones et al., 2016; Yarwood, 2007), especially in Australia, Canada, New Zealand, and the United States, which has led to continued distrust and tension between law enforcement and residents. For example, Ruddell et al. (2014) found that remote and inaccessible aboriginal villages in Canada had several times higher crime rates and per capita costs of policing than the country's average.

The Rural Criminal Justice System

Rural experiences of the criminal justice system vary greatly: from, for example, the rates of prosecution and sentencing, to the spatial distribution of police institutions, courts, and correctional facilities. This subject has been examined within a range of different contexts (see, e.g., Austin, 1981; Bond-Maupin & Maupin, 1998; Campbell et al., 2014; Ferrazzi & Krupa, 2018; Romero, 2020; Steiner, 2005; Zaller et al., 2016). For example, the effects of legislation on the policing of rural youth have been found to be of limited success due to the situational contexts of rural regions, including geography, underdeveloped infrastructure, and restricted resources (Ricciardelli et al., 2017; Wright, 1997). Certain types of legislation also exacerbate the disproportionate targeting of minorities living in rural areas, such as Latin American immigrants in the rural United States (Gómez Cervantes et al., 2018). Legislation has also been devised to defend traditional, rural notions of culture and space, targeting "travelers" and environmental and animal rights activists (Parker, 1999).

The prison industry is a topic of research that has largely been studied in the United States, although exceptions include Meek (2006) who focused on British, incarcerated, rural youth and their experiences, and the study by Baloch (2013) on female prisoners in Pakistan, where rural inmates were found to be more vulnerable within the justice system. However, with over two million incarcerated people, the United States has the largest prison population in the world, both in absolute numbers and per capita, and it disproportionately consists of marginalized groups:

people of color, the poor, and the mentally ill (Perdue, 2018). Previously prisoners were largely held in urban areas, but during the 1990s, prisons were rapidly built outside of cities. Governing authorities in rural areas have introduced rural prison as financially beneficial, but rural county constituents have also historically objected, due to fears of decreasing land values and increasing crime rates (Daniel, 1991). Evidence shows that while rural prison development may potentially boost economies through increased job opportunities and tax revenue for those local communities, they may also exacerbate poverty and exclusion of certain community members, such as marginalized ethnic groups (Bonds, 2009). Furthermore, recent research carried out by Perdue (2018) describes how prison counties have been found to have higher poverty rates and lower per capita income than non-prison counties.

References

Austin, T. L. (1981). Criminal Sentencing in Urban, Suburban, and Rural Counties. *Criminal Justice Review, 6*(2), 31–37. https://doi.org/10.1177/073401688100600205

Baloch, G. M. (2013, 2013/10/10/). From Arrest to Trial Court: The Story of Women Prisoners of Pakistan. *Procedia - Social and Behavioral Sciences, 91*, 158–170. https://doi.org/10.1016/j.sbspro.2013.08.413

Barclay, E., & Donnermeyer, J. F. (2002). Property crime and crime prevention on farms in Australia. *Crime Prevention and Community Safety, 4*(4), 47–61. https://doi.org/10.1057/palgrave.cpcs.8140169

Behrendt, L., Porter, A., & Vivian, A. (2016). Factors affecting crime rates in six rural Indigenous communities. In J. F. Donnermeyer (Ed.), *The Routledge International Handbook of Rural Criminology* (pp. 33–44). Routledge.

Bond-Maupin, L., & Maupin, J. (1998, 1998/09/01/). Juvenile justice decision making in a rural hispanic community. *Journal of Criminal Justice, 26*(5), 373–384. https://doi.org/10.1016/S0047-2352(98)00017-8

Bonds, A. (2009). Discipline and devolution: Constructions of poverty, race, and criminality in the politics of rural prison development. *Antipode, 41*(3), 416–438. https://doi.org/10.1111/j.1467-8330.2009.00681.x

Cain, M. (1973). *Society and the policeman's role*. London: Routledge & Kegan Paul

Campbell, R., Bybee, D., Townsend, S. M., Shaw, J., Karim, N., & Markowitz, J. (2014). The impact of sexual Assault Nurse Examiner programs on criminal justice case outcomes: A multisite replication study. *Violence against women, 20*(5), 607–625. https://doi.org/10.1177/1077801214536286

Carrington, K., Hogg, R., & Sozzo, M. E. (2015). Southern Criminology. *British Journal of Criminology, 56*, 1–20.

Ceccato, V. (2015a). Farm crimes and environmental wildlife offenses. In *Rural Crime and Community Safety* (pp. 165–193). Routledge.

Ceccato, V. (2015b). Police, rural policing, and community safety. In *Rural Crime and Community Safety* (pp. 259–290). Routledge.

Ceccato, V. (2016). Crime and policing in Swedish rural areas. In J. F. Donnermeyer (Ed.), *The Routledge International Handbook of Rural Criminology* (pp. 387–396). Routledge.

Ceccato, V., Solymosi, R., & Müller, O. (2021). The Use of Twitter by Police Officers in Urban and Rural Contexts in Sweden. *International Criminal Justice Review*, 10575677211041926. https://doi.org/10.1177/10575677211041926

Crank, J. P. (1989, 1989/01/01/). Civilianization in small and medium police departments in Illinois, 1973–1986. *Journal of Criminal Justice, 17*(3), 167–177. https://doi.org/10.1016/0047-2352(89)90017-2

Culver, L. (2004, 2004/07/01/). The impact of new immigration patterns on the provision of police services in midwestern communities. *Journal of Criminal Justice, 32*(4), 329–344. https://doi.org/10.1016/j.jcrimjus.2004.04.004

Cunneen, C. (2016). Indigenous people and rural criminology. In J. F. Donnemeyer (Ed.), *The Routledge International Handbook of Rural Criminology* (pp. 365–372). Routledge.

Cunneen, C. (2020). *Conflict, politics and crime: Aboriginal communities and the police* [Book]. https://doi.org/10.4324/9781003115243

Daniel, W. R. (1991). Prisons and Crime Rates in Rural Areas: The Case of Lassen County. *Humboldt Journal of Social Relations, 17*(1/2), 129–170. http://www.jstor.org/stable/23262576

Ferrazzi, P., & Krupa, T. (2018). Remoteness and its impact on the potential for mental health initiatives in criminal courts in Nunavut, Canada. *International Journal of Circumpolar Health, 77*(1), Article 1541700. https://doi.org/10.1080/22423982.2018.1541700

Furuhagen, B. (2009). *Från fjärdingsman till närpolis - en kortfattad svensk polishistoria* (V. Polisutbildningen, Ed.). Växjö Polisutbildningen.

Gómez Cervantes, A., Alvord, D., & Menjívar, C. (2018). 'Bad Hombres': The effects of criminalizing latino immigrants through law and media in the rural midwest. *Migration Letters, 15*(2), 182–196. 10.33182/ml.v15i2.368

Griffiths, C. T. (2019). Policing and community safety in northern Canadian communities: challenges and opportunities for crime prevention. *Crime Prevention and Community Safety, 21*(3), 246–266. https://doi.org/10.1057/s41300-019-00069-3

Jones, N. A., Lithopoulos, S., & Rudell, R. (2016). Policing rural indigenous communities. In J. F. Donnermeyer (Ed.), *The Routledge International Handbook of Rural Criminology* (pp. 355–363). Routledge.

Kaylen, M. T., & Pridemore, W. A. (2015, 2015/06/01/). Measuring violent victimization: Rural, suburban, and urban police notification and emergency room treatment. *Journal of Rural Studies, 39*, 239–246. https://doi.org/10.1016/j.jrurstud.2014.11.013

Lin, Z. (2007). The Shift in The Objects of Police Control in the Prairie Provinces. In *Policing the Wild North-West* (pp. 67–84). University of Calgary Press. https://doi.org/10.2307/j.ctv6gqscx.7

Lindström, P. (2015, 2015/06/01/). Police and crime in rural and small Swedish municipalities. *Journal of Rural Studies, 39*, 271–277. https://doi.org/10.1016/j.jrurstud.2014.12.004

Mawby, R., & Yarwood, R. (2011). *Rural policing and policing the rural: a constable countryside?* Ashgate. https://doi.org/10.4324/9781315607191

Mawby, R. I. (2011). Plural policing in rural Britain. . In R. M. R. Yarwood (Ed.), *Rural policing and policing the rural: A constable countryside?* (pp. 57–67).

Meek, R. (2006). Social deprivation and rural youth crime: Young men in prison and their experiences of the "rural idyll". *Crime Prevention and Community Safety, 8*(2), 90–103. https://doi.org/10.1057/palgrave.cpcs.8150006

Parker, G. (1999). Rights, the environment and Part V of the Criminal Justice and Public Order Act 1994. *Area, 31*(1), 75–80. https://doi.org/10.1111/j.1475-4762.1999.tb00173.x

Payne, B. K., Berg, B. L., & Sun, I. Y. (2005, 2005/01/01/). Policing in small town America: Dogs, drunks, disorder, and dysfunction. *Journal of Criminal Justice, 33*(1), 31–41. https://doi.org/10.1016/j.jcrimjus.2004.10.006

Perdue, R. T. (2018). Linking environmental and criminal injustice: The mining to prison pipeline in central Appalachia. *Environmental Justice, 11*(5), 177–182. https://doi.org/10.1089/env.2017.0027

Ricciardelli, R., Crichton, H., Swiss, L., Spencer, D. C., & Adorjan, M. (2017). From knowledge to action? The Youth Criminal Justice Act and use of extrajudicial measures in youth policing. *Police Practice and Research, 18*(6), 599–611. https://doi.org/10.1080/15614263.2017.1363971

References

Romero, M. (2020). Rural Spaces, Communities of Color, and the Progressive Prosecutor. *The Journal of Criminal Law and Criminology (1973-), 110*(4), 803–822. https://doi.org/10.2307/48595415

Ruddell, R., Lithopoulos, S., & Jones, N. A. (2014). Crime, costs, and well being: Policing canadian aboriginal communities. *Policing, 37*(4). https://doi.org/10.1108/PIJPSM-01-2014-0013

Shernock, S. K. (1986, 1986/01/01/). A profile of the citizen crime prevention activist. *Journal of Criminal Justice, 14*(3), 211–228. https://doi.org/10.1016/0047-2352(86)90002-4

Stassen, R., & Ceccato, V. (2021). Police accessibility in Sweden: An analysis of the spatial arrangement of police services. *Policing: A Journal of Policy and Practice, 15*(2), 896–911.

Steiner, B. (2005). Predicting sentencing outcomes and time served for juveniles transferred to criminal court in a rural northwestern state. *Journal of Criminal Justice, 33*(6), 601–610. https://doi.org/10.1016/j.jcrimjus.2005.08.008

Stenbacka, S. (2021). Local policing in a global countryside – combating drugs in rural areas. *The Professional Geographer*.

Takahashi, Y. (2016). Crime and response in rural Japan. In J. F. Donnermeyer (Ed.), *The Routledge International Handbook of Rural Criminology* (pp. 10). Routledge

Taylor, R. B., Wyant, B. R., & Lockwood, B. (2015, 2015/01/01/). Variable links within perceived police legitimacy?: Fairness and effectiveness across races and places. *Social Science Research, 49*, 234–248. https://doi.org/10.1016/j.ssresearch.2014.08.004

Weisheit, R., Edward, L., & Falcone, D. N. (1995). *Crime and Policing in Rural and Small-Town America*. Waveland Pr Inc.

Weisheit, R. A., Wells, L. E., & Falcone, D. N. (1994, October 1, 1994). Community Policing in Small Town and Rural America. *Crime & Delinquency, 40*(4), 549–567. https://doi.org/10.1177/0011128794040004005

Wooff, A. (2015, 2015/06/01/). Relationships and responses: Policing anti-social behaviour in rural Scotland. *Journal of Rural Studies, 39*, 287–295. https://doi.org/10.1016/j.jrurstud.2014.11.003

Wright, L. E. (1997). Juvenile Crime in Rural Areas. *The Justice System Journal, 19*(3), 355–364. http://www.jstor.org/stable/27976954

Yarwood, R. (2007, 2007/03/01/). Getting just deserts? Policing, governance and rurality in Western Australia. *Geoforum, 38*(2), 339–352. https://doi.org/10.1016/j.geoforum.2006.08.005

Yarwood, R. (2014). Lost and found:The hybridnetworks of rural policing, missing people and dogs. *Journal of Rural Studies, (Submitted)*.

Yarwood, R. (2015, 2015/06/01/). Lost and hound: The more-than-human networks of rural policing. *Journal of Rural Studies, 39*, 278–286. https://doi.org/10.1016/j.jrurstud.2014.11.005

Yarwood, R., & Edwards, B. (1995, 1995/10/01/). Voluntary action in rural areas: the case of neighbourhood watch. *Journal of Rural Studies, 11*(4), 447–459. https://doi.org/10.1016/0743-0167(95)00030-5

Zaller, N., Cheney, A. M., Curran, G. M., Booth, B. M., & Borders, T. F. (2016). The Criminal Justice Experience of African American Cocaine Users in Arkansas. *Substance Use and Misuse, 51*(12), 1566–1576. https://doi.org/10.1080/10826084.2016.1188954

Open Access This chapter is licensed under the terms of the Creative Commons Attribution 4.0 International License (http://creativecommons.org/licenses/by/4.0/), which permits use, sharing, adaptation, distribution and reproduction in any medium or format, as long as you give appropriate credit to the original author(s) and the source, provide a link to the Creative Commons license and indicate if changes were made.

The images or other third party material in this chapter are included in the chapter's Creative Commons license, unless indicated otherwise in a credit line to the material. If material is not included in the chapter's Creative Commons license and your intended use is not permitted by statutory regulation or exceeds the permitted use, you will need to obtain permission directly from the copyright holder.

Chapter 7
Crime Prevention and Safety Interventions

Underlying many efforts to understand crime commission is attempting to find ways to prevent it. Crime prevention can be defined as "an activity, by an individual or a group, public or private, that precludes the incidence of one or more criminal acts" (Brantingham and Faust 1976, p. 284). Prevention may also include measures to improve the safety perceptions of those who may feel unsafe due to particular situational conditions in both rural and urban areas.

Rural and urban experiences of crime prevention policy implementation can be contrasting. In the late 1990s in countries like the United Kingdom and Sweden, crime legislation and national policy programs came into force that moved the responsibility for policing and crime prevention from national to local authorities (Justitiedepartementet 1996; Pierpoint et al. 1998). This trend has also been observed in Australia with policies that emphasize residents' personal responsibility regarding crime control (Lupton 1999). Pierpoint et al. (1998) argues that these types of policy shifts may have complex implications for crime prevention in rural communities. This is because rural areas may have a greater need for authorities with different political agendas to cooperate, impeding the formation of local crime prevention initiatives. Moreover, the economic strain caused by the needed implementations is likely to be felt in particular by rural authorities, whose resources often already are spread quite thin.

In general, crime prevention initiatives and safety intervention models have long been urban-centric, ignoring unique rural problems and challenges, patterns of crime, as well as the heterogeneity of different rural areas (Ceccato and Dolmen 2013; Smith and Huff 1982). The rural-urban interlinkages are continuously transforming the situational conditions in which crime occurs, but such dynamic conditions are rarely reflected in the way crime prevention is put into practice in rural areas. With globalization and following the, for example, expansion of ICT-networks (Ceccato and Dolmen 2013), crime opportunities are becoming less dependent on physical space, which demands a diverse understanding of rural areas to tackle rural crime (Bell and Hall 2007) and people's safety perceptions. We now present examples of knowledge about crime prevention and interventions that aim at improving safety perceptions in rural areas.

Community Policing in Action

Crime prevention in rural areas is largely characterized by forms of community policing and local partnerships, for example, neighborhood watch schemes and farm watch and patrols (Ceccato and Dolmen 2013). Such activity types have often been first utilized in and later imported from urban areas to rural areas despite the fact that formal policing has often been more prioritized and better funded in urban than in rural areas (Buck et al. 1983).

There exists a body of research on the role of community participation in crime prevention in rural areas. In the United Kingdom, for instance, interventions such as neighborhood watch schemes have been shown to contribute to improving safety perceptions and improving relationships with the police (Yarwood and Edwards 1995). In rural Sweden, there exist broader crime prevention initiatives focused on creating local partnerships, although participants often have an institutionalized role in these local partnerships as their participation is linked to their regular jobs within police organizations, social services or other, related organizations (Ceccato 2015d). Other international cases reported in the criminological literature indicate that these participatory schemes are not problem free, as they may suffer from considerable social bias (Lab and Stanich 1994; Shernock 1986; Smith and Lab 1991; Yarwood and Edwards 1995), and as they are said to be controlled by the local, rural elite that focuses more on the exclusion of marginalized groups than on preventing crime (Mawby and Yarwood 2011; Yarwood 2015).

Evidence from the Global South shows that community participation plays a central role in crime prevention, such as in Nigeria (Arisukwu et al. 2020), or efforts of ethnic vigilante groups like the Sungsungu people in Tanzania (Bukurura 1995; Jakobsen 2016; Kudo 2020; Mkutu 2010).

Technological Crime Prevention Measures

The application of technology to prevent crime in rural areas has been largely under-researched. Studies that exist have examined, for example, technological approaches to prevent farm theft (Harkness and Larkins 2020); housing design to prevent residential burglaries (Hamid and Yusof 2013); and effects of lighting on reducing violent crime (Arvate et al. 2018). Aransiola and Ceccato (2020) reviewed applications of modern technologies in situational crime prevention and found that traditional measures (locking doors, guard dogs, raising fences, etc.) were still the most common in rural areas, while modern measures (CCTV, security lights, alarms, drones, etc.) were generally more supplemental. CCTV and alarms have been shown to have little to no effect on preventing crime, especially on farms, but they have proven better at detecting and monitoring wildlife crime (Aransiola and Ceccato 2020; Liedka et al. 2019). There is evidence that lighting plays a positive role in deterring crime, such as security lights for farm crime (Aransiola and Ceccato 2020) and regular street lights for violent crime (Arvate et al. 2018).

Prevention of Some Typical Rural Issues

Issues of youth crime and delinquency are of central importance to crime prevention initiatives in rural areas due to the common perception of young people being disorderly, the association with drug and alcohol addiction, and the risk of the development of early career criminals (Ceccato 2015b). The international literature make reference to efforts to combat substance abuse among youths in Slovenia and have included stricter regulations on the sale of alcohol and presenting anti-drug propaganda in schools (Petrovskiy 2020). Crime prevention groups in, for example, Sweden have usually taken two approaches to youth problems in rural areas: the first targeting individuals already causing concern, and utilizing interventions involving the school, family, police, and social services; the second focusing on all young people with initiatives aiming to keep young people "busy" (Ceccato and Dolmen 2013).

The policing and prevention of drug crime in rural areas can be a controversial issue. The so-called war on drugs in the United States has been criticized for unfairly targeting the poor and people of certain ethnicities, which holds true for rural areas as well (see, e.g., Abadie et al. 2018; Shukla et al. 2019; Zaller et al. 2016). Police in Scotland have noted the difficulty in disrupting drug markets in certain rural areas as drug organizations from elsewhere can maintain "markets by proxy" in these areas (Clark et al. 2020). A number of strategies have been reported to reduce substance abuse among rural youth, including warding off the "boredom of the countryside" (Ceccato 2015b). In general, measures that include interactive elements and community-based efforts have had shown better outcomes (Milano et al. 2017; Stallwitz 2016).

As for farm crime, opportunity models have been found to be effective for prevention. Barclay and Donnermeyer (2011) applied routine activity theory, situational crime prevention, and crime pattern theory to study farm security in Australia. Results showed that, for example, better visibility of farm sheds and other buildings from the residence was linked to lower crime (of most types), while being located closer to highways increased the risk of being victimized by malicious damage, illegal hunting, and trespassing. Similarly, accessible rural areas in Sweden experienced the highest rates of theft of tractors, diesel and other fuels, and drug production, compared to remote rural and urban areas (Ceccato 2015c). Applications of CPTED (Crime Prevention Through Environmental Design) have also proven to be useful for farm crime prevention, such as when analyzing the relation between housing architectural design and farm burglaries (Molaei and Hashempour 2020)

Further challenges can be identified regarding the prevention of farm crime. The difficulty of policing and preventing farm crime has been emphasized repeatedly in the research, and it is partly due to the lack of available and detailed data from official sources which fail to distinguish between farm crime and other types of crime (Ceccato and Dolmen 2013; Mears et al. 2007a). This is further perpetuated by the poor crime reporting practices of farmers to the police (Barclay et al. 2004; Ceccato 2015e; Mears et al. 2007b), which may be due to low levels of trust in the police and/or public authorities (considering reporting as a "waste of time"); fear of being excluded by the community; but also traditionally having a higher tolerance for, or even expectation of certain crimes, such as crop theft for subsistence (Bunei et al. 2016; Ceccato 2015e; Donnermeyer 2017). Farmers also tend to be lax with farm security, perhaps due to perceptions of low crime risk (Barclay and Donnermeyer 2002; Smith 2019).

Domestic violence is a central topic when discussing rural crime and crime prevention. Similar to farm crime, violence against women is highly underreported (although this is more likely due to societal norms and shame), and accessibility to services such as women's shelters are very limited in rural areas (Ceccato 2015a). DeKeseredy (2020) described points that can help prevent rural violence against women, including education and creating awareness of the problem as important initial steps (although an overly critical tone may backfire). Placemaking has been considered as a way to create trust and shared history in the community through festivals, music, and art, which can be used to confront expressions of rural patriarchy (see also DeKeseredy et al. (2009) for a similar application of second-generation CPTED principles to prevent violence against women). Men's mindsets and understanding of violence against women must be changed to rework detrimental, trained behaviors. This issue has been attempted to be solved through, for example, men's forums and providing places for men to talk, including those with a background of domestic abuse (Ceccato 2015a).

As for preventing EWC, deterrence and opportunity-reducing measures are some common approaches, but due to the complex and ambiguous nature of these crimes, they may be hard to police. Fines are among the most common punishments for EWC, but as previously noted, larger corporations may simply incorporate these as 'the price of doing business'. The difficulty in ascertaining if a crime has occurred, coupled with low detection rates, makes it harder to enforce any measures. Also, relying too heavily on deterrence measures may disregard the various motivations for EWC, for example, non-compliance in the case of illegal hunting (von Essen et al. 2016). Reward and opportunity-reducing measures must be implemented together with efforts to increase awareness of and engagement in the problem in order to combat EWC (Ceccato 2015e). Furthermore, technology can be utilized to increase detection rates, thus improving the potential of preventative work. For example, CCTV can be used to monitor wildlife and offenders where guardianship is low. Gargiulo et al. (2016) found that remote sensing is a very reliable method to detect pollution from cattle farms, with a detection capability of 90%.

Crime prevention is a well-researched area within criminology in general, but, thus far, not enough emphasis has been given to rural problems and rural contexts, although research in this topic is steadily increasing in the last decades. International evidence shows that rural crime prevention relies highly on the community themselves to deter crime and tackle problems of poor perceived safety. Unfortunately, the perception of the "rural idyll" may have both diminished the perceived need for specific care for rural crime prevention and even made residents complacent about their personal security. Geographical obstacles, trust in police, unequal access to services, and rural norms and notions of who belongs to the community are just a few aspects that must be considered before developing and implementing crime prevention initiatives intended for areas on the rural-urban continuum.

References

Abadie, R., Gelpi-Acosta, C., Davila, C., Rivera, A., Welch-Lazoritz, M., & Dombrowski, K. (2018, 2018/01/01/). "It Ruined My Life": The effects of the War on Drugs on people who inject drugs (PWID) in rural Puerto Rico. *International Journal of Drug Policy, 51*, 121–127. https://doi.org/10.1016/j.drugpo.2017.06.011

Aransiola, T. J., & Ceccato, V. (2020). The role of modern technology in rural situational crime prevention. A review of the literature. In *Rural Crime Prevention* (1st ed., pp. 58–72). Routledge. https://doi.org/10.4324/9780429460135-6

Arisukwu, O., Igbolekwu, C., Oye, J., Oyeyipo, E., Asamu, F., Rasak, B., & Oyekola, I. (2020, 2020/09/01/). Community participation in crime prevention and control in rural Nigeria. *Heliyon, 6*(9), e05015. https://doi.org/10.1016/j.heliyon.2020.e05015

Arvate, P., Falsete, F. O., Ribeiro, F. G., & Souza, A. P. (2018). Lighting and Homicides: Evaluating the Effect of an Electrification Policy in Rural Brazil on Violent Crime Reduction. *Journal of Quantitative Criminology, 34*(4), 1047-1078. https://doi.org/10.1007/s10940-017-9365-6

Barclay, E., & Donnermeyer, J. F. (2002). Property crime and crime prevention on farms in Australia. *Crime Prevention and Community Safety, 4*(4), 47-61. https://doi.org/10.1057/palgrave.cpcs.8140169

Barclay, E., & Donnermeyer, J. F. (2011). Crime and security on agricultural operations. *Security Journal, 24*(1), 1-18. https://doi.org/10.1057/sj.2008.23

Barclay, E., Donnermeyer, J. F., & Jobes, P. C. (2004). The Dark Side of Gemeinschaft: Criminality within Rural Communities. *Crime Prevention and Community Safety, 6*(3), 7-22. https://doi.org/10.1057/palgrave.cpcs.8140191

Bell, E., & Hall, R. (2007). "dead in the water": Is rural violent crime prevention floating face-down because criminology can't handle context?. *Crime Prevention and Community Safety, 9*(4), 252-274. https://doi.org/10.1057/palgrave.cpcs.8150051

Brantingham, P. J., & Faust, F. L. (1976). A Conceptual Model of Crime Prevention. *Crime and Delinquency, 22*(3), 284-296.

Buck, A. J., Gross, M., Hakim, S., & Weinblatt, J. (1983, 1983/11/01/). The deterrence hypothesis revisited. *Regional Science and Urban Economics, 13*(4), 471-486. https://doi.org/10.1016/0166-0462(83)90029-7

Bukurura, S. H. (1995). Combating crime among the Sukuma and Nyamwezi of West-Central Tanzania. *Crime, Law and Social Change, 24*(3), 257-266. https://doi.org/10.1007/BF01312209

Bunei, E. K., Auya, S., & Rono, J. K. (2016). Agricultural crime in Africa. In J. F. Donnermeyer (Ed.), *The Routledge International Handbook of Rural Criminology* (pp. 117-123). Routledge.

Ceccato, V. (2015a). Challenges to preventing women abuse in rural communities. In *Rural Crime and Community Safety* (pp. 346–372). Routledge.

Ceccato, V. (2015b). Crime prevention in rural areas: Youth-related challenges. In *Rural Crime and Community Safety* (pp. 323–343). Routledge.

Ceccato, V. (2015c). Farm crimes and environmental wildlife offenses. In *Rural Crime and Community Safety* (pp. 165–193). Routledge.

Ceccato, V. (2015d). Police, rural policing, and community safety. In *Rural Crime and Community Safety* (pp. 259–290). Routledge.

Ceccato, V. (2015e). Prevention of farm crimes and crimes against nature. In *Rural Crime and Community Safety* (pp. 293–320). Routledge.

Ceccato, V., & Dolmen, L. (2013). Crime prevention in rural Sweden. *European Journal of Criminology, 10*(1), 89-112. https://doi.org/10.1177/1477370812457763

Clark, A., Fraser, A., & Hamilton-Smith, N. (2020). Networked territorialism: the routes and roots of organised crime. *Trends in Organized Crime*. https://doi.org/10.1007/s12117-020-09393-9

DeKeseredy, W. S. (2020). Preventing violence against women in the heartland. In A. Harkness (Ed.), *Rural Crime Prevention: Theory, Tactics and Techniques* (pp. 12). Routledge.

DeKeseredy, W. S., Donnermeyer, J. F., & Schwartz, M. D. (2009). Toward a gendered Second Generation CPTED for preventing woman abuse in rural communities. *Security Journal, 22*(3), 11.

Donnermeyer, J. F. (2017). The place of rural in a southern criminology. *International Journal for Crime, Justice and Social Democracy, 6*(1), 118-132. https://doi.org/10.5204/ijcjsd.v6i1.384

Gargiulo, F., Angelino, C. V., Cicala, L., Persechino, G., & Lega, M. (2016). Remote sensing in the fight against environmental crimes: The case study of the cattle-breeding facilities in southern Italy. *International Journal of Sustainable Development and Planning, 11*(5), 663-671. https://doi.org/10.2495/SDP-V11-N5-663-671

Hamid, L. A., & Yusof, W. Z. M. (2013, 2013/12/11/). Experiential Approach as a Design Innovation Solution to Prevent House Breaking Crime. *Procedia – Social and Behavioral Sciences, 107*, 145–152. https://doi.org/10.1016/j.sbspro.2014.02.293

Harkness, A., & Larkins, J. (2020). Technological approaches to preventing property theft from farms. In A. Harkness (Ed.), *Rural Crime Prevention: Theory, Tactics and Techniques* (pp. 226-244). Routledge.

Jakobsen, H. (2016). Community law enforcement in rural Tanzania. In J. F. Donnermeyer (Ed.), *The Routledge International Handbook of Rural Criminology* (pp. 409-415). Routledge.

Justitiedepartementet (Swedish Ministry of Justice) (1996). *Allas vårt ansvar. Ett nationellt brottsförebyggande program.* A. förlaget.

Kudo, Y. (2020, 2020/10/01/). Maintaining law and order: Welfare implications from village vigilante groups in northern Tanzania. *Journal of Economic Behavior & Organization, 178*, 607–628. https://doi.org/10.1016/j.jebo.2020.08.007

Lab, S. P., & Stanich, T. J. (1994). Crime prevention participation:An exploratory analysis. *American Journal of Criminal Justice, 18*(1), 1-23. https://doi.org/10.1007/BF02887636

Liedka, R. V., Meehan, A. J., & Lauer, T. W. (2019). CCTV and Campus Crime: Challenging a Technological "Fix". *Criminal Justice Policy Review, 30*(2), 316-338. https://doi.org/10.1177/0887403416664947

Lupton, D. (1999). Crime control, citizenship and the state: Lay understandings of crime, its causes and solutions. *Journal of Sociology, 35*(3), 297-311. https://doi.org/10.1177/144078339903500303

Mawby, R., & Yarwood, R. (2011). *Rural policing and policing the rural: a constable countryside?* Ashgate. https://doi.org/10.4324/9781315607191

Mears, D. P., Scott, M. L., & Bhati, A. S. (2007a). Opportunity theory and agricultural crime victimization. *Rural Sociology, 72*(2), 151-184. https://doi.org/10.1526/003601107781170044

Mears, D. P., Scott, M. L., & Bhati, A. S. (2007b). A process and outcome evaluation of an agricultural crime prevention initiative. *Criminal Justice Policy Review, 18*(1), 51-80. https://doi.org/10.1177/0887403406294586

Milano, G., Saenz, E., Clark, N., Busse, A., Gale, J., Campello, G., Mattfeld, E., Maalouf, W., Heikkila, H., Martelli, A., Morales, B., & Gerra, G. (2017). Report on the International Workshop on Drug Prevention and Treatment in Rural Settings Organized by United Nation Office on Drugs and Crime (UNODC) and World Health Organization (WHO) [Note]. *Substance Use and Misuse, 52*(13), 1801-1807. https://doi.org/10.1080/10826084.2017.1306564

Mkutu, K. A. (2010). Mitigation of armed criminality through an African indigenous approach: The case of the Sungusungu in Kenya. *Crime, Law and Social Change, 53*(2), 183-204. https://doi.org/10.1007/s10611-009-9217-x

Molaei, P., & Hashempour, P. (2020, 2020/09/01/). Evaluation of CPTED principles in the housing architecture of rural areas in the North of Iran (Case studies: Sedaposhte and Ormamalal). *International Journal of Law, Crime and Justice, 62*, 100405. https://doi.org/10.1016/j.ijlcj.2020.100405

Petrovskiy, A. (2020). Safety, Security, and Crime Prevention in Rural Areas of Krasnodarskyi Krai and the Republic of Adygea. *Journal of Criminal Justice and Security, 22*(3), 16.

Pierpoint, H., Gilling, D., & Francis, P. (1998). Crime prevention in rural areas [Note]. *Criminal Justice Matters, 33*(1), 25-28. https://doi.org/10.1080/09627259808552822

Shernock, S. K. (1986, 1986/01/01/). A profile of the citizen crime prevention activist. *Journal of Criminal Justice, 14*(3), 211–228. https://doi.org/10.1016/0047-2352(86)90002-4

Shukla, R. K., Stoneberg, D., Lockwood, K., Copple, P., Dorman, A., & Jones, F. M. (2019). The interaction of crime & place: an exploratory study of crime & policing in non-metropolitan

References

areas. *Crime Prevention and Community Safety, 21*(3), 200–214. https://doi.org/10.1057/s41300-019-00072-8

Smith, B. L., & Huff, C. R. (1982, 1982/01/01/). Crime in the country: The vulnerability and victimization of rural citizens. *Journal of Criminal Justice, 10*(4), 271-282. https://doi.org/10.1016/0047-2352(82)90099-X

Smith, G., & Lab, S. P. (1991). Urban and Rural Attitudes toward Participating in an Auxiliary Policing Crime Prevention Program. *Criminal Justice and Behavior, 18*(2), 202-216. https://doi.org/10.1177/0093854891018002008

Smith, R. (2019). The 'Fortress Farm': articulating a new approach to redesigning 'Defensible Space' in a rural context. *Crime Prevention and Community Safety, 21*, 15.

Stallwitz, A. (2016). Approaching rural drug issues from the perspective of community psychology. In J. F. Donnermeyer (Ed.), *The Routledge International Handbook of Rural Criminology* (pp. 265-272). Routledge.

von Essen, E., Hansen, H., Nordström Källström, H., Peterson, M. N., & Peterson, T. R. (2016). Illegal hunting Between social and criminal justice. In J. F. Donnemeyer (Ed.), *The Routledge International Handbook of Rural Criminology* (pp. 318-326). Routledge.

Yarwood, R. (2015, 2015/06/01/). Lost and hound: The more-than-human networks of rural policing. *Journal of Rural Studies, 39*, 278–286. https://doi.org/10.1016/j.jrurstud.2014.11.005

Yarwood, R., & Edwards, B. (1995, 1995/10/01/). Voluntary action in rural areas: the case of neighbourhood watch. *Journal of Rural Studies, 11*(4), 447-459. https://doi.org/10.1016/0743-0167(95)00030-5

Zaller, N., Cheney, A. M., Curran, G. M., Booth, B. M., & Borders, T. F. (2016). The Criminal Justice Experience of African American Cocaine Users in Arkansas. *Substance Use and Misuse, 51*(12), 1566-1576. https://doi.org/10.1080/10826084.2016.1188954

Open Access This chapter is licensed under the terms of the Creative Commons Attribution 4.0 International License (http://creativecommons.org/licenses/by/4.0/), which permits use, sharing, adaptation, distribution and reproduction in any medium or format, as long as you give appropriate credit to the original author(s) and the source, provide a link to the Creative Commons license and indicate if changes were made.

The images or other third party material in this chapter are included in the chapter's Creative Commons license, unless indicated otherwise in a credit line to the material. If material is not included in the chapter's Creative Commons license and your intended use is not permitted by statutory regulation or exceeds the permitted use, you will need to obtain permission directly from the copyright holder.

Chapter 8
Emergent Topics in Research in Rural Areas

Throughout this book, we motivate why crime and safety perceptions in rural areas are important issues worthy of attention. We also provide evidence from a rich body of criminology literature extending over four decades, a scholarship that has engaged researchers and practitioners across the globe. However, despite an increase in the research, most aspects of crime and safety perceptions in rural contexts have been overlooked until recently. There exist several avenues of research that remain open for further investigation in general, and from a sustainability perspective in particular. In this chapter, we propose a research agenda based on a selected most pressing research areas.

Concept and Theories

Crucial questions are not yet answered regarding whether a new set of concepts and definitions, theories, and methods is necessary or even desirable to capture the reality of crime and safety in rural contexts. There is an emergent call for theoretical frameworks that can provide a better understanding of crime and safety in rural conditions, and that recognize the hybrid, globalized nature of these spaces, their contextual differences, and the safety needs of their residents. Despite some clear efforts in the past decade, the process of establishing specific concepts and definitions, theoretical frameworks, and methods tailored for rural contexts is still a work in progress, as the urban-centric theories and models continue to dominate criminology research. The legacy of the rural-urban dichotomy is still very much present in rural crime research. Future research could explore new conceptualizations of "the rural" that capture the complexities of areas exposed to various degrees of rural-urban interlinkages in order to better explain these areas' crime and safety conditions. For example, as a starting point, we suggest the term *rural-urban continuum* as a focus area of analysis. The rural-urban continuum encompasses heterogenous and interlinked areas from remote and desolated spaces to accessible connected environments of the urban fringe; often globalised and not self contained.

© The Author(s) 2022
V. Ceccato, J. Abraham, *Crime and Safety in the Rural*, SpringerBriefs in Criminology, https://doi.org/10.1007/978-3-030-98290-4_8

Interdisciplinary approaches might be more appropriate to conceptualize and understand problems of, for example, organized crime and the impact of climate change on crime that can take different shapes in areas on the rural-urban continuum.

Data and Methods

Future studies should further develop the very fundamentals of rural crime research. In order to be able to compare areas on the rural-urban continuum, methods should be tested which better characterize these areas, and which avoid sharp demarcations in the degree or quantity of rural/urban differences. Methods also need to be able to capture the flows of people, activities, and goods in space in areas on the rural-urban continuum. Steps forward have already being taken in this direction; see, for instance, the work by Shimada and Suzuki (2021).

There also exist related issues of data scarcity and methodological adequacy in rural contexts which should be discussed. It is not always easy to identify patterns of human activities in rural areas that are criminologically relevant because these patterns are fewer, sparser, than those found in urban areas. The scarcity and sparsity are not only spatial but also temporal, which means that current environmental criminological theories and analytical tools that typically fit urban environments may not be adequate to the study of crime in remote, sparsely populated rural environments. Crime goes under-detected in rural areas, and this is also problematic. Some types of crimes may never be discovered or revealed (Ceccato and Uittenbogaard 2013). When crime is detected, it may not be reported to the police for any number of reasons. Long distances to a police station (or lack of access to the internet) make crime reporting practices more difficult in rural areas (Stassen and Ceccato 2019). In particular rural areas, the lack of nearby structures (such as a house, farm, roads, forests) makes it particularly difficult to register the exact location of a crime. The problem of denominator when representing rates of crime is also a recurrent problem. The scarcity and sparsity of events is also a limiting factor when modelling a phenomenon in rural areas. Standard statistical methods of analyzing crime rates are inappropriate for such data, because the population sizes are small relative to the rates. This problem can be resolved with specialized statistical techniques such as negative binomial regression models that take into account the contribution of population size (see, e.g., Kaylen and Pridemore 2013; Osgood and Chambers 2003). In summary, the way official data are recorded and manipulated – as the urban dictates the norm for data collection – leads to potential inaccuracy issues and biases; therefore, more research should be devoted to the topic.

Research on Teaching Rural Criminology Skills

Not many studies focus on teaching the skills needed to study rural criminology. An exception is the work by Barclay et al. (2016), who suggest among other things the importance of connecting and contextualizing specific cases of rural crime to general criminological theories and concepts. Further research is needed on the applicability of fieldwork inspection with protocols (Ceccato 2019), safety surveys, and use of apps to collect data as teaching techniques in rural criminology, as well as their usefulness to engage students. There is a vast number of subjects in rural criminology that demand special attention from researchers interested in improving teaching the skills.

Endemic Offending and Criminal Motilities

An "eternally" under-researched topic in rural criminology is to what extent offenders are outsiders versus endemic to the community. Local criminals may be accepted as "part of the community" and their crimes not reported because their actions have become normalized. Studying criminal motilities is important for crime prevention but requires access to data that are currently either incomplete, scarce, confidential, or unavailable due to geoprivacy regulations. In addition, there do exist a few studies on women as rural offenders, including a few historical studies, but otherwise the gendered nature of breaking the law has been relatively neglected in rural crime studies.

The "Illicit Spaces" of Organized Crime in Rural Areas

Several researchers have called for more research on the "illicit spaces" of organized crime (e.g., Hall 2012; Yarwood 2021). The expectation is that the study of organized crime groups could not only reveal much about the spatiality and regulation of global crime, but also inform about the processes, flows, and impacts of globalization in areas on the rural-urban continuum. Illicit spaces for drug-related crimes and endangered species, or prostitution, are already found in rural areas across the globe and deserve more attention as research topics.

Situational Conditions of Crime and Fear

The situational-based perspective can be applied to prevent crime and other events, such as injuries, in rural areas. Although most situational crime perspectives are poorly tested in rural contexts, a few examples are emerging in the international literature (Hodgkinson and Harkness 2020; Stassen and Ceccato 2020). Also, little is known about the use of CPTED (Crime Prevention Through Environment Design) in its original form (Crowe 2013; Jeffery 1977) in small towns and villages. CPTED is about using design and planning principles to prevent crime and promote safety by positively influencing human behavior through natural surveillance, territoriality, access control, target hardening, activity support, and maintenance. The second generation of CPTED applies design-appropriate, community-based prevention strategies to improve the security of women living in rural areas and help protect them from abuse by spouses and partners (see, for instance, DeKeseredy et al. (2009).

Three new developments within CPTED show potential for areas on the rural-urban continuum. The first is CPTEM (Crime Prevention Through Environmental Management by Ward et al. (2019)), which involves the maintenance of existing CPTED measures but also longer-term planning and adjusting for new uses of space. The second is HPTE (Health Promotion Through Environmental Design by Kent and Wheeler (2016)) and, finally, the third is IPTE (Injury Prevention Through Environmental Design by Thodelius (2018)).

Safety in Privately Owned, Public Places

More knowledge is needed about the nature of crime and safety in privately owned, public places in rural areas, such as bus and train stations, outlets, bars, and restaurants. Issues of public conduct and surveillance but also of integrity are also relevant to be further insvestigated from a criminological perspective. Key questions include who is accountable or responsible when "something happens" and when police forces cannot be present. The impact of an increasing share of voluntaries as well as private security services in rural policing deserves further research. Such matters are of particular importance for municipalities that receive large inflows of tourists and have strong, nightlife-based economies.

Risky Homes, Risky Paths

Previous research has long shown that women and individuals with special needs are victimized more often and feel less safe than the rest of the population. Violence may be common in domestic environments in rural areas (see the vast body of research by for instance, DeKeseredy et al., 2008; DeKeseredy, 2021) but also tolerated in public spaces or over the internet. Older adults may be overrepresented in some rural areas; therefore, it is crucial to investigate the interplay of local norms and actions of local actors in supporting the more vulnerable groups, both in their homes and/or in public spaces. These different, yet interrelated topics, lack in the most recent criminological research. Regardless of where one lives, in big cities or rural villages, people must feel safe in their daily activities and trips, from door-to-door. For people living in areas on the rural-urban continuum "the whole journey approach" to safety should also be considered given the United Nations 2030 Agenda and its goals for sustainable development.

Another topic needing further research in rural contexts is the relationship between safety perceptions and the use of various spaces by different users. As illustrated in Chap. 5, safety perceptions in rural areas are dependent on multiscale factors and are often not well matched with patterns of victimization or individual characteristics. More research into contextual factors is recommended as they might prove better at explaining people's overall anxieties in rural environments (Ceccato 2018), for example, job loss, poor health, as well as more structural factors such as population inflows.

Gendering and Queering the Rural

LGBTQ+ safety needs and the othering process they experience is an emerging field of research that has gained more attention in the past few years. The imposition of binary gender norms in rural environments is not well researched in terms of both those who transgress those norms in their daily lives and those whose lives are lived within such constraints. Yet, the rural "other" has been presented in a number of studies on sexuality and safety, but remains an area of interest in criminology. Bell (2000), for instance, which is a seminal study on cultural constructions of rural gay masculinity in the United States, showed a blurred rural-urban divide. More recently, Conner and Okamura (2021) illustrated the advantages of living in rural areas for LGBTQ+ rights advocates, while DeKeseredy et al. (2014) showed that the way the media has portrayed the sexuality of rural inhabitants in the United States (no matter their gender or sexual orientation) is distorted and serves the interests of particular rationalities of abuse. Missing in the current criminological research is a better understanding of why certain rural places impact positively on LGBTQ+ safety, while others, negatively.

Technology, Offending, and Crime Prevention

New information technologies have implications for offending but also for crime prevention and delivery of emergency services in rural areas. On the one hand, the police's use of social media to communicate with the public has passed the "public information channel" stage (Dai et al. 2017) as it affects the public's perception of the police as well. Research should delve deeper into the evolution and nature of information sharing via social media by police officers in both rural and urban areas, and whether such practices improve police legitimacy. On the other hand, it is also unclear which (new) types of crimes are facilitated by these information technologies. For example, the county lines drug trafficking in the UK, overdose cases linked to apps used for drug delivery to one's door via traditional mail in northern Sweden (Stenbacka 2021), or drones used to support emergency services (Schierbeck and Claesson 2021).

Police, Policing, and Digitalization

Future research should focus on investigating how ICT and digitalization in general are affecting the ways in which people interact with the police, as it is unclear how to best adapt current methods of policing to changing technological conditions. These issues are especially important for those living in sparsely populated areas that are becoming more reliant on digital access to police services, from recording crime to issuing passports. Traditional police work remains a current challenge in the rural, much due to geographical restrictions but also limitations of police resources and preparedness (Helsloot and Ruitenberg 2004). Issues of police accountability and legitimacy, and of the relative institutional importance of the police, are also important considerations that should be further investigated.

Weisheit et al. (1993) suggested long ago that rural areas still miss the tools and resources necessary to combat drug-related crime, and the latest ICT and digital technologies can certainly be added to that list. Parochial community policing practices may not be enough to tackle problems faced by the police with regard to drug trafficking (see, e.g., Yarwood (2021) and other organized crime problems that also manifest in the most remote areas; see, for example, Stenbacka (2021).

Even though there has occurred a pluralization of police functions in many Western democracies, as well as increased cooperation between public, private, and civil society in policing activities, there remains a fundamental question about the role of the police as the "main" security providers. Because rurally located police and police stations still have a role to play, as they positively contribute to public reassurance among other things (Stassen and Ceccato 2021), it becomes increasingly important to reassess the role of police given the increasing participation of, for instance, private-sector and voluntary organizations in police work.

Sex Trafficking and Prostitution in the Rural

Prostitution, despite being a prominent social problem, is rarely considered in rural contexts. Scott (2016), for instance, noted that the high informal control in rural areas may have minimized street prostitution but had not reduced such activities in private homes or brothels. The author also suggests that a closer examination of rural prostitution could improve the understanding of how social control is practiced in rural areas. In general, research is needed to understand the contexts which simultaneously encourage and/or criminalize prostitution. Possible links between arranged marriage and violence against women (Ceccato 2015), human trafficking (in particular, sex trafficking), and prostitution in areas on the rural-urban continuum should also be investigated further.

Corruption and Financial Crimes

Corruption in rural contexts was the focus of several criminological studies in the past decade. An example was the study by Cheng and Urpelainen (2019) who provided a look into criminal politicians and their effects on communities in rural India, where politicians with criminal charges were linked to exacerbating household poverty. Similarly, Banerjee et al. (2014) assessed criminal politicians in India, but from the perspective of rural voters and whether they were unconcerned or ignorant of the corruption. Meng (2016) studied corruption related to land use expropriation led to protests and violence in rural China, while Nasrin (2011) contributed with a study of rural dowry practices in Bangladesh. Further research is needed on the relationship between corruption, poverty, environmental crimes, and quality of democratic institutions in rural areas across the globe.

Animal (Ab)Use and Farmers' Victimization

Further research is needed to explore the interplay between animal rights, animal rights activists, and farmers, including criminalization and victimization. As this has strong ties to the rural, studying it is essential to a gaining a comprehensive understanding of crime in rural areas (Lovell submitted). Previous research suggests that techniques of neutralization (Sykes and Matza, 1957) can be successfully applied in a range of different contexts, such as "wildlife crime connected to agriculture, rationalizations are culturally complex and do not simply rely on economic motivations" (Ceccato et al. 2021, submitted; Enticott 2011). More research is needed to provide a better understanding of how individuals rationalize the offence, namely, whether and how they defend the act is necessary, deny there are victims, and appeal to the value of preserving values.

Increased integration of human-animal relationships (Philo and Wilbert 2000) and rural criminology may be valuable. Research has previously shown links between violence against animals and violence between humans, for example, domestic violence (Cleary et al. 2021; McPhedran 2009), and further investigations of the implications of rural contexts of this are encouraged. Additionally, a less anthropogenic perspective on rural crime, such as viewing animal abuse a worthy area of study on its own, may provide additional opportunities for empirical investigations, development of new theories, and practical applications (Flynn 2011).

Impact of Increased Energy Demand on Rural Crime

We face an imminent global energy crisis, much due to an escalation in energy demand, a dependency on fossil fuels, and an increase in the global population (Coyle and Simmons 2014). The demand for natural gas is projected to steadily increase, and while the increase in the demand for oil is slowing, oil production is expected to continue to expand over the coming decades (IEA 2021). This development is expected not only to impact the climate, but also may have considerable social impacts, not the least in rural areas. One reason is that, at least in the United States in the 2010s, much of the expansion in fossil energy extraction took place in the rural (Opsal and O'Connor Shelley 2014). Such expansions are often welcomed by local authorities, as they may lead to "boomtowns," that is, rapid economic and population growth in small towns (see, e.g., Ruddell 2017). Boomtowns often enjoy low unemployment and increased business, although these benefits are often only short term (Jacquet 2014). Additionally, while the impacts of the growth differ from area to area, boomtowns can experience increased rates of violence and other crime compared to non-boomtowns (see, e.g., Archbold 2015; Ruddell et al. 2014). Ruddell (2017) noted that besides crime, additional negative impacts on quality of life can also be observed, such as environmental pollution of air, water, and land, and increased rates of traffic accidents. The author points out that it is often the most vulnerable and marginalized (such as women, indigenous peoples, and youth) who are impacted the most by these negative effects. In general, concerns have been expressed that rural areas lack the basic infrastructure, access to services, and ability to police and govern the sudden increase in population (Heitkamp and Mayzer 2018; Jacquet 2014). Further research is needed to understand how future energy developments will affect rural crime in the long term. While there needs to exist parallel efforts to find solutions to the energy crisis, it is also important to assess how to maximize rural community preparedness and minimize the negative effects of rapid booms (and potential busts) in rural areas.

Environmental and Wildlife Crime and Green Criminology

An area of research that is bound to grow is the study of environmental and wildlife crime (EWC). Such crimes are a global issue, not only because they often have a transnational dimension, but also because environmental problems ultimately affect people's lives on a global scale. EWC is not often considered within rural criminology, even though such crimes often take place in the most remote areas of the globe. Despite an increasing global awareness of the scale of the problem, this topic of research is still in its infancy. To help investigate EWC, new data-related advances are being made; for example, GIS and remote sensing data are being used together with newer types of data, such as crowdsourced data (often involving different sensors, imagery, and complex spatial mapping) as well as with other spatial analytical tools, including network analysis and machine learning (for a review, see Ceccato, 2022).

The emergent field of green criminology (White, 2013; Nurse and Wyatt, 2020) has already recognised the impact of extensive extraction of natural resources in parts of the Global South. This includes deforestation, pollution of water, and loss of biodiversity, which have resulted in the illegal occupation of the land, the sexual exploitation of women and children, and the murder of indigenous and rural peoples (Böhm 2020; Global Witness 2020; Goyes 2021). There are examples of research on the effects of globalization and illicit spaces on rural environments that go beyond the common boundaries of traditional research disciplines, but further efforts are required. For more examples of research needed in this area, see Ceccato and Trujillo (in press).

Effect of Climate Change on Crime and Safety

Researchers and policy analysts have argued that climate change will increase social conflict, especially because of competition over scarce resources, including fresh water, food, fuel, and land. The impacts of global change have already been observed such as flooding, drought, and heat. As an emergent and ever more urgent topic with potential future effects on all levels of society, from individuals to governments, across the globe, it demands serious consideration in future research. For instance, crime in general has been positively linked to temperature levels (Anderson and Anderson 1998; Ranson 2014). Climate change will cause hotter weather increasing irritability, aggressiveness, and more violent crimes (Anderson et al. 2000). Rural areas of the Global South may be of special concern, as both relatively high temperatures and high rates of violence can already be found there.

Rural Safety as a Public Health Issue

The physical and mental health impacts of crime and fear of crime on rural residents is still an area that needs further attention. Although most rural areas are attractive places, where people's access to nature and sense of community are often associated with good health, this picture oversimplifies the complex conditions of those living in areas on the rural-urban continuum. As previous research indicated, the reduction of farmers' mental health reflects increasing stressors due to environmental, structural and economic changes in agriculture and society in general. In other parts of the world, rural areas are contested spaces where violence may be part of the part of daily life. Therefore, we expect that research into this topic can inform researchers, practitioners, and policy makers and help them make rural places more safe, inclusive, and sustainable.

References

Anderson, C. A., & Anderson, K. B. (1998). Temperature and aggression: Paradox, controversy, and a (fairly) clear picture. In *Human aggression: Theories, research, and implications for social policy.* (pp. 247-298). Academic Press. https://doi.org/10.1016/B978-012278805-5/50011-0

Anderson, C. A., Anderson, K. B., Dorr, N., DeNeve, K. M., & Flanagan, M. (2000). Temperature and aggression. In *Advances in experimental social psychology* (Vol. 32, pp. 63-133). Elsevier.

Archbold, C. A. (2015). Established-outside relations, crime problems, and policing in oil boomtowns in western North Dakota. *Criminology, Criminal Justice, Law and Society, 16*(3), 19-40. https://www.scopus.com/inward/record.uri?eid=2-s2.0-85025120416&partnerID=40&md5=998ea22a6913cbb876f72d1c2c8669fc

Banerjee, A., Green, D. P., McManus, J., & Pande, R. (2014). Are poor voters indifferent to whether elected leaders are criminal or corrupt? A vignette experiment in rural India. *Political Communication, 31*(3), 391-407. https://doi.org/10.1080/10584609.2014.914615

Barclay, E., Meisel, J., DeKeseredy, W. S., & Nolan, J. (2016). Teaching rural criminology. In J. F. Donnermeyer (Ed.), *The Routledge International Handbook of Rural Criminology* (pp. 431-436). Routledge.

Bell, D. (2000). Farm Boys and Wild Men: Rurality, Masculinity, and Homosexuality*. *Rural Sociology, 65*(4), 547-561. https://doi.org/10.1111/j.1549-0831.2000.tb00043.x

Böhm, M. L. (2020). *Empresas transnacionales, recursos naturales y conflicto en América Latina. Para una visibilización de la violencia invisible.* .

Ceccato, V. (2015). Violence against women in rural communities. In *Rural Crime and Community Safety* (pp. 226–252). Routledge.

Ceccato, V. (2018). Fear of crime and overall anxieties in rural areas: The case of Sweden. In G. M. Murray Lee (Ed.), *The Routledge International Handbook on Fear of Crime* (1 ed.). Routledge. http://urn.kb.se/resolve?urn=urn:nbn:se:kth:diva-233897

Ceccato, V. (2019, 2019/04/03). Fieldwork protocol as a safety inventory tool in public places. *Criminal Justice Studies, 32*(2), 165–188. https://doi.org/10.1080/09589236.2019.1601367

Ceccato, V. (2022) Geographical information and GIS in rural criminology. In: R. A.Weisheit, J.R. Peterson, & A. Pytlarz (Eds.), Research Methods for Rural Criminologists. Routledge, 127–142.

Ceccato, V.; Trujillo, M. Rural criminology in South America. In: Encyclopedia of Rural Crime. Harkness, J. Peterson, M. Bowden, C. Pedersen and J. F. Donnermeyer. (in press)

Ceccato, V., Lundqvist, P., Abraham, J., Göransson, E., & Svennefelt, C. A. (2021, 2021/07/31). The Nature of Fear Among Farmers Working with Animal Production. *International Criminology*. https://doi.org/10.1007/s43576-021-00024-z

Ceccato, V., Lundqvist, P., Abraham, J., Göransson, E., & Svennefelt, C. A. (submitted). Crimes against animal production in Sweden: An assessment of 2009-2019s media archives *International Criminal Justice Review*.

Ceccato, V., & Monica, P. (submitted). *Rural criminology in South America*. Bristol University Press.

Ceccato, V., & Uittenbogaard, A. C. (2013). Environmental and Wildlife Crime in Sweden. *International Journal of Rural Criminology, 2*(1), 23-50. http://kb.osu.edu/dspace/handle/1811/51122.

Cheng, C. Y., & Urpelainen, J. (2019). Criminal Politicians and Socioeconomic Development: Evidence from Rural India. *Studies in Comparative International Development, 54*(4), 501-527. https://doi.org/10.1007/s12116-019-09290-5

Cleary, M., Thapa, D. K., West, S., Westman, M., & Kornhaber, R. (2021). Animal abuse in the context of adult intimate partner violence: A systematic review. *Aggression and Violent Behavior*, 101676.

Conner, C. T., & Okamura, D. (2021). Queer expectations: An empirical critique of rural LGBT+ narratives. *Sexualities*, 13634607211013280. https://doi.org/10.1177/13634607211013280

Coyle, E. D., & Simmons, R. A. (2014). *Understanding the global energy crisis*. Purdue University Press.

Crowe, T. (2013). *Crime prevention through environmental design* (Vol. null).

Dai, M., He, W., Tian, X., Giraldi, A., & Gu, F. (2017). Working with communities on social media. *Online Information Review, 41*(6), 782-796. https://doi.org/10.1108/OIR-01-2016-0002

DeKeseredy, W. S. (2021) Woman abuse in rural places. Routledge.

DeKeseredy, W. S., Donnermeyer, J. F., & Schwartz, M. D. (2009). Toward a gendered second generation CPTED for preventing woman abuse in rural communities. *Security journal, 22*, 178-189.

DeKeseredy, W. S., Schwartz, M. D., & Alvi, S. (2008). Which women are more likely to be abused? Public housing, cohabitation, and separated/divorced women. *Criminal Justice Studies, 21*(4), 283-293.

DeKeseredy, W. S., Muzzatti, S. L., & Donnermeyer, J. F. (2014, 2014/05/01). Mad Men in Bib Overalls: Media's Horrification and Pornification of Rural Culture. *Critical Criminology, 22*(2), 179–197. /https://doi.org/10.1007/s10612-013-9190-7

References

Enticott, G. (2011, 2011/04/01/). Techniques of neutralising wildlife crime in rural England and Wales. *Journal of Rural Studies, 27*(2), 200-208. https://doi.org/10.1016/j.jrurstud.2011.01.005

Flynn, C. P. (2011). Examining the links between animal abuse and human violence. *Crime, Law and Social Change, 55*(5), 453-468.

Global Witness. (2020). *Defending tomorrow: The climate crisis and threats against land and environmental defenders.* https://www.globalwitness.org/en/campaigns/environmental-activists/defending-tomorrow/

Goyes, D. R. (2021). Environmental Crime in Latin America and Southern Green Criminology. In *Oxford Research Encyclopedia of Criminology and Criminal Justice.*

Hall, T. (2012, 2013/06/01). Geographies of the illicit: Globalization and organized crime. *Progress in Human Geography, 37*(3), 366–385. https://doi.org/10.1177/0309132512460906

Heitkamp, T., & Mayzer, R. (2018). Implications for practice: risks to youth in boomtowns. *Child Welfare, 96*(4), 47-71.

Helsloot, I., & Ruitenberg, A. (2004, 2004/09/01). Citizen Response to Disasters: a Survey of Literature and Some Practical Implications. *Journal of Contingencies and Crisis Management, 12*(3), 98–111. https://doi.org/10.1111/j.0966-0879.2004.00440.x

Hodgkinson, T., & Harkness, A. (2020). Introduction: Rural crime prevention in theory and context. In *Rural Crime Prevention* (pp. 1-16). Routledge.

IEA - International Energy Agency. (2021). *World Energy Outlook 2021.* https://iea.blob.core.windows.net/assets/888004cf-1a38-4716-9e0c-3b0e3fdbf609/WorldEnergyOutlook2021.pdf

Jacquet, J. B. (2014). Review of risks to communities from shale energy development. *Environmental science & technology, 48*(15), 8321-8333.

Jeffery, C. R. (1977). *Crime Prevention through Environmental Design.* (2nd ed.) Sage.

Kaylen, M. T., & Pridemore, W. A. (2013, , February 13 2013). The Association Between Social Disorganization and Rural Violence Is Sensitive to the Measurement of the Dependent Variable. *Criminal Justice Review.* https://doi.org/10.1177/0734016813476715

Kent, J., & Wheeler, A. (2016, 2016/01/02). What can Built Environment and Health Professionals Learn from Crime Prevention in Planning? Introducing 'HPTED'. *Urban Policy and Research, 34*(1), 39–54. https://doi.org/10.1080/08111146.2015.1034852

Lovell, J. S. (submitted). Animal rights and activism. In A. Harkness (Ed.), *Encyclopedia.*

McPhedran, S. (2009). Animal abuse, family violence, and child wellbeing: A review. *Journal of Family Violence, 24*(1), 41-52.

Meng, Q. (2016). Corruption and land use expropriation in rural China. In J. F. Donnermeyer (Ed.), *The Routledge International Handbook of Criminology* (pp. 223-230). Routledge.

Nasrin, S. (2011). Crime or custom?: Motivations behind dowry practice in rural Bangladesh. *Indian Journal of Gender Studies, 18*(1), 27–50. https://doi.org/10.1177/097152151001800102

Nurse, A., & Wyatt, T. (2020). Wildlife criminology. Bristol University Press.

Opsal, T., & O'Connor Shelley, T. (2014). Energy Crime, Harm, and Problematic State Response in Colorado: A Case of the Fox Guarding the Hen House?. *Critical Criminology, 22*(4), 561-577. https://doi.org/10.1007/s10612-014-9255-2

Osgood, D. W., & Chambers, J. M. (2003). Community Correlates of Rural Youth Violence. *Juvenile Delinquency Bulletin*(may), 12.

Philo, C., & Wilbert, C. (2000). Animal Spaces, Beastly Places: An introduction. In C. Philo & C. Wilbert (Eds.), *Animals Spaces, Beastly Places* (pp. 1-36). Routledge.

Ranson, M. (2014, 2014/05/01/). Crime, weather, and climate change. *Journal of Environmental Economics and Management, 67*(3), 274-302. https://doi.org/10.1016/j.jeem.2013.11.008

Ruddell, R. (2017). *Oil, gas, and crime: The dark side of the boomtown* [Book]. https://doi.org/10.1057/9781137587145

Ruddell, R., Jayasundara, D. S., Mayzer, R., & Heitkamp, T. (2014). Drilling down: An examination of the boom-crime relationship in resource-based boom counties. *Western Criminology Review, 15*(1), 3-17. https://www.scopus.com/inward/record.uri?eid=2-s2.0-84901422952&partnerID=40&md5=dde7fddb8f0f7f62415533c6a52e3944

Schierbeck, S., & Claesson, A. (2021). Drönare användes för att flyga ut hjärtstartare vid misstänkt hjärtstopp. *Läkartidningen* https://lakartidningen.se/klinik-och-vetenskap-1/nya-ron/2021/08/dronare-anvandes-for-att-flyga-ut-hjartstartare-vid-misstankt-hjartstopp/

Scott, J. (2016). Rural prostitution. In J. F. Donnermeyer (Ed.), *The Routledge International Handbook of Rural Criminology* (pp. 75-82). Routledge.

Shimada, T., & Suzuki, A. (2021). Using a Rural Index to Assess Crime Risk and Crime Prevention Behavior Across the Urban–Rural Continuum: A Japanese Case Study. *International Criminal Justice Review*, 10575677211039998. https://doi.org/10.1177/10575677211039998

Stassen, R., & Ceccato, V. (2019). Police Accessibility in Sweden: An Analysis of the Spatial Arrangement of Police Services. *Policing: A Journal of Policy and Practice.* https://doi.org/10.1093/police/paz068

Stassen, R., & Ceccato, V. (2020). Environmental and Wildlife Crime in Sweden from 2000 to 2017. *Journal of Contemporary Criminal Justice, 36*(3), 403-427. /https://doi.org/10.1177/1043986220927123

Stassen, R., & Ceccato, V. (2021). Police accessibility in Sweden: An analysis of the spatial arrangement of police services. *Policing: A Journal of Policy and Practice, 15*(2), 896-911.

Stenbacka, S. (2021). Local policing in a global countryside – combating drugs in rural areas. *The Professional Geographer.*

Sykes, G. M., & Matza, D. (1957). Techniques of neutralization: A theory of delinquency. *American sociological review, 22*(6), 664-670.

Thodelius, C. (2018). *Rethinking Injury Events. Exploration in Spatial Aspects and Situational Prevention Strategies* Chalmers tekniska högskola]. Göteborg.

Ward, A., McCord, E. S., & Felson, M. (2019). How to ruin CPTED: Rebuilding Crime Prevention Through Environmental Design. In R. Armitage & P. Ekblom (Eds.), *Rebuilding Crime Prevention Through Environmental Design: Strengthening the Links with Crime Science.* Routledge.

Weisheit, R. A., Edward, L., & Falcone, D. N. (1993). Studying Drugs in Rural Areas: Notes from the Field. *Journal of Research in Crime and Delinquency, 30*, 19. https://doi.org/10.1177/0022427893030002005

White, R. (2013). The conceptual contours of green criminology. In *Emerging issues in green criminology* (pp. 17-33). Palgrave Macmillan, London.

Yarwood, R. (2021). The Geographies of Crime and Policing in the Global Countryside. *The Professional Geographer.*

Open Access This chapter is licensed under the terms of the Creative Commons Attribution 4.0 International License (http://creativecommons.org/licenses/by/4.0/), which permits use, sharing, adaptation, distribution and reproduction in any medium or format, as long as you give appropriate credit to the original author(s) and the source, provide a link to the Creative Commons license and indicate if changes were made.

The images or other third party material in this chapter are included in the chapter's Creative Commons license, unless indicated otherwise in a credit line to the material. If material is not included in the chapter's Creative Commons license and your intended use is not permitted by statutory regulation or exceeds the permitted use, you will need to obtain permission directly from the copyright holder.

Chapter 9
Implications for Practice

> *Make cities and human settlements inclusive, safe, resilient and sustainable. From the United Nations 2030 Agenda for Sustainable Development (UN 2015).*

Safety and security are an important part of social sustainability as a safe environment enables the fulfillment of the most basic human needs. This is made clear in the objectives of the United Nations 2030 Agenda for Sustainable Development, which was adopted by all United Nations Member States in 2015. Using these principles as a background, we draw from previous chapters to propose recommendations on how to respond to issues of crime and safety in areas on the rural-urban continuum. The recommendations are based on the assumption that there is no silver bullet that can solve all types of crime and safety problems in rural environments. Thus, we offer reflections on several issues that may fit some contexts better than others.

Previous research has evidenced overarching trends that are place invariant. First, rural areas are composed of hybrid, heterogonous spaces, the criminogenic conditions of which reflect their positions on the rural-urban continuum scale. Second, rural crime rates are as a rule lower than urban, but greater increases in rural compared to urban rates have been observed in several countries (with some evidence of convergence). Third, globalization is shaping crime in rural areas, which is imposing new challenges on the police and criminal justice, and demanding new modes of crime prevention and policing. Fourth, while victimization and safety perceptions are gendered, an intersectional perspective is required to understand and meet people's safety needs. Worldwide, sexual crimes against women in all areas on the rural-urban continuum represent a somewhat invisible problem and demand more attention. Finally, the scale and nature of rural problems in the Global South open unique opportunities for cross-country and multisectoral research cooperation in order to deal with globally relevant problems central to sustainability.

National and Regional Contexts

In an attempt to guide actions toward achieve the United Nations 2030 Sustainable Development Goals, the implementation of a system of ongoing, self-evaluating safety guidelines is fundamental at both national and regional levels and tailored to specific environments on the rural-urban continuum. As suggested by Ceccato and Assiago (2020), there is a risk that if a safety guideline is merely voluntary, as it is now in many countries around the world, safety as an integral part of sustainability is unlikely to be incorporated into daily practice. Therefore, in order to ensure that safety guidelines are put into practice, a mandate for municipalities and regional bodies must exist to support county administrative boards or similar authorities. Existing interfaces between academia, governmental authorities, municipalities, police, public and private enterprises, data production agencies, non-governmental organizations, etc., can also be beneficial for such processes. It is also important to create educational opportunities tailored to those working in rural contexts, in which learning about crime and safety guidelines is offered to experts working on crime prevention and safety-enabling measures at the municipal and regional levels. This way, safety through inclusive policies and practices can be fostered by prioritizing the voices of the most marginalized to articulate their own needs, by supporting their own efforts to create safe and secure places, and by placing these at the core of a roadmap toward fostering safety for all across the rural-urban continuum. Note that decades of research discussed in previous chapters of this book show that areas of the rural-urban continuum are special from a criminological perspective and deserve more attention. In the next sessions, we offer suggestions for professionals to better delineate crime prevention measures and/or safety interventions. These suggestions can also be suitable for students, more as 'a critical guide for reflection', than as a normative list of 'what to do'.

Local Contexts

We propose a set of suggestions on how to respond to issues of crime and safety in areas on the rural-urban continuum. First, it is important to start by identifying the problem (e.g., farm crime, domestic violence, environmental crime). Regardless of its size or urgency, the key is to first obtain good knowledge of the phenomenon in question. A detailed analysis of the problem is important, both to get as accurate a picture of it, but also to find the most suitable solutions. This demands systematic work (i.e., crime-specific, site-specific, time-specific, context-specific, and group-specific), but also working critically with previously existing knowledge. Gain knowledge about criminal dynamics and their connection to major societal problems in the countryside. Previous research in rural areas shows that it is important to avoid directly importing models based on other contexts, but instead consider observing national guidelines and adapting them to the rural context in question. Before interventions are put into place, measure the baseline conditions; after interventions have been executed, it is also essential to evaluate if they had the desired effect.

If the identified problem is related to safety perceptions (not crime), note that previous research has shown that overall anxieties in rural areas may be affected by many factors other than crime itself. Therefore, it is important to adapt safety initiatives to the distinct needs of communities as well as groups of individuals. In many rural areas, different groups have different safety needs as they run different risks of becoming a victim of crime, that is, some feel unsafe although their risk of victimization is low. Public participation frameworks and action research can be useful ways of implementing these evaluations. Individual factors play an important role in defining perceptions of the risk of crime and safety. Although gender and age are perhaps the most significant factors affecting individual's safety perceptions, previous victimization, socioeconomic status and ethnic background are also important. In rural settings, external factors such as effects of globalization but also local ones, such as population in/outflow have been linked to changes in declared safety levels. Investigating the specific causes of poor safety perceptions in rural areas is therefore crucial for criminological research and for improving safety conditions.

Second, consider who should be involved in the work as well as their roles and responsibilities. Promoting sustainable and safe rural environments requires well-coordinated action by interdisciplinary working groups as well as joint efforts from civil society. Previous research has shown that many problems which occur in the most remote areas may go under-detected (e.g., environmental and wildlife crime, domestic violence) by police authorities and local safety experts, often because of poor reporting practices. Other problems may be normalised as 'acceptable behavior' and are not recognised as 'issues worth of attention' by safety professionals and local community. Tailored courses and programs directed to professionals in particular can be advisable to raise the team's awareness of common crime and safety problems, their implications and possible interventions that promote support to the victims and long term solutions.

Third, challenges in rural crime prevention may include residents' apathy to crime victimization as well as low trust and confidence in the police and other authorities. Therefore, educating residents of the importance of minimizing crime victimization and how to implement measures and practices to deter crime is only one part of the solution. Authorities must also learn to know their community, identify what reason there is behind an indifference to crime problems, or a lack of trust in the police and/criminal justice. It is also important to know which kind of knowledge is currently missing to be able to meet the expectations of the residents. This is especially important when concern is related to marginalized community members, where lack of knowledge may cause certain forms of victimization (such as hate crime) to be unrecognized.

In conclusion, what bears repeating is that approaches for ensuring rural safety must be carefully tailored to the existing conditions of the specific area in question. Any observations made must be positioned in a greater context, whether in terms of physical, social, cultural, geographical, and/or temporal aspects. One must recognize that the full impact of crime may go beyond a sole victim, and perceptions of safety are not created in a vacuum. Finally, it is also important to consider that crime and safety are unequally distributed in society and, as such, interventions must be tailored to the needs of different groups.

References

Ceccato, V., & Assiago, J. (2020). 23 Responding to crime and fear in public places. *Crime and Fear in Public Places*, 433.

UN – United Nations. (2015). *Transforming our World: The 2030 Agenda for Sustainable Development*. https://www.unfpa.org/resources/transforming-our-world-2030-agenda-sustainable-development

Open Access This chapter is licensed under the terms of the Creative Commons Attribution 4.0 International License (http://creativecommons.org/licenses/by/4.0/), which permits use, sharing, adaptation, distribution and reproduction in any medium or format, as long as you give appropriate credit to the original author(s) and the source, provide a link to the Creative Commons license and indicate if changes were made.

The images or other third party material in this chapter are included in the chapter's Creative Commons license, unless indicated otherwise in a credit line to the material. If material is not included in the chapter's Creative Commons license and your intended use is not permitted by statutory regulation or exceeds the permitted use, you will need to obtain permission directly from the copyright holder.

Chapter 10
Conclusions and Recommendations

Expanding our knowledge on rural crime and safety is not only an important step for the future of criminology, but a prerequisite for ever obtaining a truly sustainable society. Rural criminology is becoming a dynamic field of research and quite diverse in terms of research topics, including violence and property crime, but also environmental crime, organized crime, domestic violence, drug production and distribution, as well as responses to crime with policing, crime prevention, and fear of crime. Most publications reviewed for this book are from Anglo-Saxon countries: mainly the United States followed by the United Kingdom, Australia, and Canada. More recently, articles and book chapters have also been published by authors and on study areas in the Global South.

The reviewed literature is quite definitive about the complexity of rural areas and how their nature affects what crime occurs there. The research reveals critical perspectives of the rural, particularly in relation to the globalization process of the countryside, the impact of organized crime on peoples and communities, new facets of social exclusion in rural contexts, and violence against women and gender relationships. The studies also provide examples of how new ideological trends and ICT are influencing criminogenic conditions in the countryside (e.g., computer-based fraud, illegal animal rights activism, animal abuse, drugs, wage theft, slavery, racism). In addition, studies include perspectives from a range of different societal groups such as women, ethnic minorities and indigenous peoples, youth, and farmers, to name a few.

Rural criminologists have continued to combat the persistent notion of the "rural idyll," as well as emphasizing that the stereotypical "tight-knit communities" have downsides to them as well. Rural dwellers may overall experience less victimization and fear of crime than urbanites, but note that this trend can vary disproportionately between different countries and within different socioeconomic groups and perhaps offer therefore a limited basis for safety interventions. Women, the LGBTQ + community, ethnic minorities, and low-income persons are rural victims whose experiences must not be neglected, as they additionally have less access to physical and social support systems. Communities may be exclusionary and even hostile to those that do not fit the norms or ideals of the community, for example, discouraging reporting victimization or harassment of "outsiders." While rural communities have seen success with community policing initiatives, this has too been observed to often be used to target the rural "other." The adoption of crime prevention measures has also been comparatively low among certain rural residents such as farmers, but increased attention surrounding technological measures may indicate a growing interest in improving rural safety.

For decades, criminology has relied on urban understandings of rural crime and rural offenders. Thus, researchers are calling for new or updated models that can better explain the mechanisms behind rural crime and its prevention. Therefore, new approaches to tackle crime and safety issues along the rural-urban continuum should be an area of future research. The emergent research topics in rural criminology include a discussion about the need for new concepts and theories that cover topics such as situational conditions of crime and fear, endemic offending and criminal motilities, offending and crime prevention, technology, climate change and crime, organized crime, LGBTQ+ gendered and intersectional perspectives on victimization and safety perceptions.

The paucity of knowledge on victimization, crime prevention, and safety perceptions in rural contexts can be at least partially associated with the inadequacy of reliable official data and/or the lack of methods capable of capturing the complexities of the rural-urban continuum. Certainly, issues of data scarcity and sparsity when it comes to rural areas are a limiting factor for many of the standard methods used in criminology, such as tools to detect spatial concentration, measures of risk, and modelling (for a further discussion, see Ceccato, 2022). The study of rural safety should welcome interdisciplinary approaches, including theories and methods from other disciplines. Lessons from psychology, geography, and computer science can provide guidance on how to deal with an ever-increasing amount of data from relatively new sources, for example, crowdsourced data, social media data, but also data from remote sensing including drones.

Ground-breaking methodologies are needed to support knowledge transfer from theory to practical action (Laub 2012) in rural areas. Simultaneously, practitioners need to support academics with lessons from on-the-ground experience. Addressing rural criminological issues requires an engaging and well-informed process of knowledge creation, exchange, and diffusion that activates a range of stakeholders including academics, safety experts, private sector actors, and practitioners from different fields that reflect different realities.

In summary, rural criminology is opening up to an ever more diverse set of perspectives and topics, well befitting the challenges that characterize both twenty-first century criminology and the demands of the 2030 sustainability agenda.

Rural Criminology and the 2030 SDGs

The world is facing a range of difficult challenges. Climate change is an ever-looming threat against our global civilization, potentially causing irreversible damage to ecosystems, global resource scarcity, and violent conflicts (Evans 2010). The COVID-19 pandemic has both laid bare and exacerbated the societal inequalities both between and within countries, and the crisis has affected (and is still affecting) the already most vulnerable across the globe (Berkhout et al. 2021).

In combatting these many challenges, rural areas are both areas of concern and key components in reaching the United Nations SDGs. Environmental and wildlife crimes, that is, events that are essentially rural phenomena, are threats to the protection, restoration, and promotion of both ecosystems and biodiversity (SDGs 14 and 15). Similarly, addressing the illegal dumping of waste and ensuring the good health of all people are more relevant today than ever (SDGs 3 and 6), especially as the wildlife trade contributes to the spread of zoonotic diseases (UNEP, 2020). Furthermore, the impacts of crime and fear of crime on rural residents' physical and mental health cannot be ignored (SDG 3).

Hate crimes, discrimination, and inequalities based on race, class, gender, and sexuality (SDGs 5 and 10) are issues of concern in rural areas, where they may in fact be of a more severe nature than in other places. Cases of rural domestic violence may remain hidden due to "cultures of silence," while rural members of the LGBTQ+ community face disproportionate victimization rates as well as difficulties in accessing support after hate-crime victimization. Economic inequality between urban and rural areas often results in fewer resources for both rural residents and rural governing and policing authorities. Additionally, in the battle to achieve peace, justice, and strong institutions (SDG 16), it is vital to not neglect the rural areas of the Global South, where some experience exceptionally high rates of violence, organized crime networks, and widespread corruption.

Areas on the rural-urban continuum can also be drivers of sustainable development. Agriculture plays an important role in ensuring food security, and it remains an important source of employment (in non-Western rural communities in particular) (SDGs 2 and 8). Much of the larger, remaining ecosystems, such as forests, are typically located in remote rural areas and are important mitigation tools in terms of CO_2 reduction (Malhi et al. 2002).

Unless deliberated and coordinated plans focusing on improving the safety of rural environments are put into action, no change will occur. This demands concerted efforts on local and national (even regional and global) levels involving both a broad range of stakeholders and the adoption of multi-pronged strategies tailored to specific types of problems (SDG 17). Only then, we will have a chance to ensure more inclusive, safe, and sustainable rural environments. If we aspire to create sustainable environments, rural criminology can contribute by tackling the most emergent safety challenges across the globe. The examples provided by this book illustrate how each of us can contribute by intently directing our research aims toward the 2030 Sustainable Development Goals and the most pressing rural safety challenges.

References

Berkhout, E., Galasso, N., Lawson, M., Morales, P. A. R., Taneja, A., & Pimentel, D. A. V. (2021). *The Inequality Virus*. https://www.oxfam.org/en/research/inequality-virus

Ceccato, V. (2022) Geographical information and GIS in rural criminology. In: R. A.Weisheit, J.R. Peterson, & A. Pytlarz (Eds.), Research Methods for Rural Criminologists. Routledge, 127–142.

Evans, A. (2010). *Resource Scarcity, Climate Change and the Risk of Violent Conflict* (World Development Report, Issue).

Laub, J. H. (2012, Dec 21). Translational Criminology: A Message from the Director [Video]. National Institute of Justice. YouTube. https://www.youtube.com/watch?v=nK8vIuoCLFA

Malhi, Y., Phillips, O. L., Lloyd, J., Baker, T., Wright, J., Almeida, S., Arroyo, L., Frederiksen, T., Grace, J., & Higuchi, N. (2002). An international network to monitor the structure, composition and dynamics of Amazonian forests (RAINFOR). *Journal of Vegetation Science, 13*(3), 439-450.

UNEP & ILRI - United Nations Environment Programme and International Livestock Research Institute (2020). Preventing the Next Pandemic: Zoonotic diseases and how to break the chain of transmission. Nairobi, Kenya. https://www.unep.org/resources/report/preventing-future-zoonotic-disease-outbreaks-protecting-environment-animals-and

Open Access This chapter is licensed under the terms of the Creative Commons Attribution 4.0 International License (http://creativecommons.org/licenses/by/4.0/), which permits use, sharing, adaptation, distribution and reproduction in any medium or format, as long as you give appropriate credit to the original author(s) and the source, provide a link to the Creative Commons license and indicate if changes were made.

The images or other third party material in this chapter are included in the chapter's Creative Commons license, unless indicated otherwise in a credit line to the material. If material is not included in the chapter's Creative Commons license and your intended use is not permitted by statutory regulation or exceeds the permitted use, you will need to obtain permission directly from the copyright holder.

Index

A
Agricultural crime, 50
Animal liberation movement, 20
Animal welfare movement, 20

C
Climate change, 109
Corruption, 106
COVID-19 pandemic, 119
Crime prevention
    CCTV and alarms, 94
    community participation, 94
    definition, 93
    EWC, 96
    initiatives and safety intervention models, 93
    policing, 95, 113
    policing and prevention, 95
    in rural areas, 94
    technology, 94
    United Kingdom and Sweden, 93
    youth crime and delinquency, 95
Crime trends
    between rural and urban areas, 42
    challenges, 46–47
    criminogenic conditions, 46
    public's perception of crime, 42
    Rural-Urban Continuum, 42–46
    self-reported victimization, 44
    violent crimes, 45
Criminal justice system, 30
Criminology, 101, 118

D
Discrimination
    LGBTQ+ persons, 57
Domestic violence, 96
Drug-related offenses
    environmental and wildlife crime (EWC), 59
    methamphetamine, 58
    substance abuse, 58

E
Economic inequality, 119
Environmental and Wildlife Crime (EWC), 31, 108

F
Food fraud, 63

G
Gay, Lesbian, Straight Education Network (GLSEN), 57
Globalization, 113
Green criminology, 108
Ground-breaking methodologies, 118

H
Hate crime, 55

L
LGBTQ+ community, 117

N
National and regional contexts
    criminal dynamics, 114
    fostering safety, 114
    gender and age, 115
    knowledge, 114
    residents, 115
    rural environments, 115
    rural safety, 115
    safety guidelines, 114
    safety initiatives, 115

O
Offenders
    Environmental and Wildlife Crime (EWC), 49
    farming and farmers, 48
    in rural, 47
Organized crime, 61
    drug trade, 61
    food fraud and theft, 63
    gang crime, 62
    human trafficking, 62

P
Placemaking, 96
Police and criminal justice
    civilianization, 86
    community policing, 87
    criminal justice system, 88
    face-to-face community engagement, 86
    marginalized groups, 88
    metropolitan criminology, 85
    rural policing, 86
Policing, 106, 117
Property crimes
    agricultural crime, 50
    chronic problem in rural areas, 51
    farmers, 51
    housebreaking crime, 50
    urban versus rural areas, 50
    victimization, 50
Prostitution, 106

R
Racist harassment, 56
Research, rural areas
    concepts and definitions, 101
    corruption, 106
    CPTED, 103, 104
    data scarcity, 102
    domestic environments, 104
    drug-related crimes, 103
    environmental pollution, 108
    EWC, 108
    fundamentals, 102
    global energy crisis, 107
    human-animal relationships, 107
    ICT and digitalization, 105
    knowledge, 104
    local authorities, 108
    local criminals, 103
    physical and mental health impacts, 109
    police functions, 106
    police legitimacy, 105
    and policy analysts, 109
    prostitution, 106
    rationalities, 105
    rural contexts, 104
    rural criminology, 102
    rural environments, 105
    rural-urban interlinkages, 101
    situational-based perspective, 103
    situational crime perspectives, 103
    skills, 103
    statistical techniques, 102
    technologies, 105
    traditional police work, 106
Rural attitudes toward immigration, 56
Rural communities, 118
Rural crime and community safety
    animal liberation movement, 20
    animal welfare movement, 20
    climate change, 19
    commodification, 14
    constant transformation, 11
    crime opportunities, 12
    crime underreporting, 17
    drug production, 14
    gendered approach, 18
    heterogeneous entities, 10
    honor killings, 13
    interdependent entities, 15
    intersectional perspectives, 18
    low crime rates, 12
    misconceptions, 11
    policing and crime prevention, 17
    public health issue, 16
    Queering the rural-urban continuum, 18

safety perceptions, 13
technology, 18
theoretical legacy, 15
UN-Sustainable Development Goals (SDG), 21
Rural crime prevention, 31, 115
Rural criminologists, 117
Rural criminology, 103
climate change, 119
critical perspectives, 37
domestic violence, 119
environmental criminology, 36
reviewed publications, 33, 36
SDGs, 119
theoretical traditions, 36
Rural-urban continuum, 1, 2, 114, 119
crime, 3
crime prevention, 4
farm crime, 3
fear of crime, 4
gender-based violence, 4
globalization, 4
policing, 4
rural crime, 3
security, 3
social sustainability, 5
sustainable development, 5
Sustainable Development Goals (SDGs), 5
urban fringe, 3
Rural-urban continuum scale, 113

S
Safety perceptions
contextual factors, 78–79
individual characteristics, 77
intersectionality, 80–81
rural environment, 78
Sexual crimes, 113
Social disorganization theory, 36
Social values, 56
Sustainable rural environments, 119

U
United Nations 2030 Agenda for Sustainable Development, 113
United Nations 2030 Sustainable Development Goals, 114

V
Victimization, 49–63
property crime, 49, 51
Victims, 117
Violence, 30, 52
gendered violence, 54–55
general violence, 52–53

GPSR Compliance

The European Union's (EU) General Product Safety Regulation (GPSR) is a set of rules that requires consumer products to be safe and our obligations to ensure this.

If you have any concerns about our products, you can contact us on

ProductSafety@springernature.com

In case Publisher is established outside the EU, the EU authorized representative is:

Springer Nature Customer Service Center GmbH
Europaplatz 3
69115 Heidelberg, Germany

www.ingramcontent.com/pod-product-compliance
Ingram Content Group UK Ltd.
Pitfield, Milton Keynes, MK11 3LW, UK
UKHW020240040925
462575UK00004B/173